Reprints of Economic Classics

Observations on the Subjects Treated of
In Dr Smith's Inquiry

OBSERVATIONS

ON THE

SUBJECTS TREATED OF

IN

DR SMITH'S INQUIRY

INTO THE

NATURE AND CAUSES OF

THE WEALTH OF NATIONS

BY

DAVID BUCHANAN

[1817]

WITH APPENDICES:

SIR ISAAC NEWTON'S *Memorial on the Gold and Silver Coins 1717*
AND OTHER DOCUMENTS

THE ADAM SMITH LIBRARY

REPRINTS OF ECONOMIC CLASSICS

AUGUSTUS M. KELLEY · PUBLISHERS
NEW YORK · 1966

LIBRARY OF CONGRESS CATALOGUE CARD NUMBER
65 - 26360

PRINTED IN THE UNITED STATES OF AMERICA
by SENTRY PRESS, NEW YORK, N. Y. 10019

OBSERVATIONS

ON THE

SUBJECTS TREATED OF

IN

DR SMITH'S INQUIRY

INTO THE

NATURE AND CAUSES OF

THE WEALTH OF NATIONS;

BY DAVID BUCHANAN.

SECOND EDITION.

VOL. IV.

EDINBURGH:
PRINTED FOR OLIPHANT, WAUGH & INNES, EDINBURGH;
AND OGLES, DUNCAN & COCHRAN, 37, PATER-
NOSTER ROW, AND 295, HOLBORN,
LONDON.

1817.

LIBRARY
FLORIDA STATE UNIVERSITY
TALLAHASSEE, FLORIDA

CONTENTS.

INTRODUCTION.

ON THE PRINCIPLES OF METALLIC CURRENCY.

Different metals employed in the currency of a country in different periods of improvement. The functions of those different metals pointed out. Distinction between the currency used in the great payments, and the inferior or subsidiary currencies used for the smaller payments. In all the currencies of Europe, copper coin a subsidiary currency. Silver coin a subsidiary currency in Britain, though not in any other country. This great change effected in the reign of King William III. Account of the state of the currency at that period. Proposed remedy of Sir Isaac Newton for the scarcity of silver coin. Present state of the silver coin considered. Plan for its reformation. Account of the measures lately pursued in regard to the copper coin..Page 1

ON THE PRICE OF SUCH COMMODITIES AS YIELD A RENT.

The price of such commodities as are produced by labour and yield no rent, determined by their original cost. The price of such commodities as afford a rent has no connection with the original cost. Principles on which the price of such commodities is regulated............................ 33

CONTENTS.

ON THE WAGES OF LABOUR.

Principles of Mr Malthus regarding population and labour. Effect of increasing wealth on the wages of labour. Wages of labour not regulated by the price of corn. Principle upon which its wages are regulated. Plans for improving the condition of the labourer considered. English system of poor laws.. 42

ON STOCK.

No evil arising from an excess of capital. Its increase causes a diminution of profit. Ratio in which profit diminishes as capital increases.. 75

ON THE PRICE OF GOLD AND SILVER SINCE THE YEAR 1773.. 80

ON PAPER CURRENCY.

Its value regulated by the common principle, namely, the proportion between the supply and the demand. Its convertibility into specie necessary for the due restriction of the supply. Necessary tendency to supplant the precious metals. Its progress in this country. System of money dealing connected with it. Facilities thence arising for cash transactions. Favourable to the extension of credit. Dangers to which it is exposed. Interruption of credit in 1792, in 1797, in 1810. Subsequent state of the paper currency of this country. Connection of its value with the market price of bullion, and state of the exchange. Propriety of suspending the cash payments of the bank of England considered.. 87

ON PRODUCTIVE AND UNPRODUCTIVE LABOUR.

Dr Smith's distinction between productive and unproductive labour well founded. Misapprehended by later writers. Theory of the Economists examined............... 131

ON THE PROGRESS OF NATIONAL OPULENCE.

Connection between the industry of the country and the industry of the town. Alternate progress of trade and ag-

CONTENTS.

riculture. Dr Smith's theory respecting the progress of Europe considered. Cause of the rapid growth of America. State of property and manners determined by the equivalent received for the surplus produce of the soil. Warlike manners of Greece and Rome connected with the state of property.. 137

ON THE LAWS FOR REGULATING THE EXPORTATION AND IMPORTATION OF CORN.. 147

ON COMMERCIAL TREATIES.

Commercial propositions made by Great Britain to Ireland in 1785. Commercial arrangements connected with the Legislative Union between the two countries. Mr Pitt's Commercial Treaty with France........................ 161

ON NATIONAL DEFENCE.

System of defence for an invaded country attacked by a regular army and defended by an irregular army. System of warfare between two regular armies engaged in the attack and defence of a country defended by fortified towns. Those principles illustrated by a reference to history. Invasion of Greece by the Persians. Contests of the Greeks with each other. Invasion of Persia by Alexander. Rise and decline of the Roman power. Contests of the middle ages. Invasion of Holland by Louis XIV. Wars of King William—of Marlborough—of Frederick the Great—American war. View of the modern system of tactics. Campaign of 1795 in Germany by the Archduke Charles, and in Italy by Bonaparte. Campaign of 1805, &c. Concluding remarks... 173

OF THE AFFAIRS OF THE EAST INDIA COMPANY.

1. Of the constitution and transactions of the Company in Europe.

2. Of the transactions of the Company in India.

Nature of its trade before acquiring sovereignty. Its subsequent effects on the internal trade of India. Its administration of the land revenues considered. Nature of

CONTENTS.

these revenues. State of property and manners under the Mogul government. State of the country immediately before the acquisition of the Dewannee by the Company. Mode of regulating the revenues. Reformations adopted by Marquis Cornwallis. Their effects. Company considered in its mercantile capacity. Growth of debt. Present state of its concerns.......................... 208

OF TAXATION.

Of the British property tax. Mode of assessing commercial incomes considered. Mode of assessing the income arising from land, whether belonging to the proprietor or farmer. Mr Pitt's plan for the redemption of the land tax considered. Of taxes on consumable commodities. Account of the taxes on spirits. Policy of prohibiting distilleries considered................................ 263

OF PUBLIC DEBTS.

Policy of the funding system considered. View of the British finances since 1786. Present state. Concluding remarks... 296

INTRODUCTION.

THE great change effected by Dr Smith's work, in the state of political science, affords the most decisive evidence of its originality and value. Before its publication, no work had appeared in this country, to command the conviction of mankind, on the subjects to which it relates; and, with the exception of Sir James Steuart's treatise on political economy, which, though not devoid of merit, abounds too much in confused and erroneous statements to attract much attention, no attempt was even made to explain the relations of society with a view to legislation and government. All the knowledge which existed of these matters was either too obvious and familiar to merit the praise of originality, or it was comprehended in detached maxims, occasionally thrown out by speculative writers, but neither strictly demonstrated, nor followed out to solid practical conclusions. The consequence was, that the science was either left open to prejudice, or to opposite theories, all equally uninteresting, and equally remote from the truth.

In France, the subject was more studied; and, on many important questions, the doctrines of the French writers are in the highest degree liberal and enlightened. They were undoubtedly the first to perceive that human laws, in order to be useful, must necessarily conform to those more general laws, on which society is founded; and that the true object of the legislator, is to uphold the social system as it is already constituted, in place of interfering to regulate or to alter the natural course of things, according to his own limited notions of expediency. In pursuance of these views, they are clear and consistent in disapproving of all commercial restraints. Commerce they maintain to be placed wholly without the sphere of legislative control; and even the trade in corn, which has been sometimes stated as an exception to the general doctrine, they hold to be equally entitled to the common privilege of entire toleration. The laws for regulating the interest of money, and, generally, all the exclusive preferences held out for the encouragement of domestic industry, they also condemn, on the clear principle, that every man has a right to dispose of what belongs to him, to the best advantage; that commercial transactions are so many voluntary contracts, with which third parties have no concern ; and that the purpose of the law is to protect, and not to disturb individuals, in their peaceable efforts for the improvement of their condition. But, with these just and enlightened doctrines, the French system connects various dogmas, of which the truth and utility are more questionable. The most remarkable of these is the notion, that agriculture is the original source of all income; that all taxes, out of whatever revenue they are paid in the first instance, fall ultimately on the rent of land ; and that, in place of raising the public revenue by the expensive and vexatious process of duties on consumable commodities, the simple expedient of a direct land tax should be at once resorted to. That this theory is founded on error, I have elsewhere endeavoured to shew*; while the arguments by which it is supported, turn frequently on points fitter for the metaphysician than for the statesman; and it is indeed the great defect of this class of writers, that though, by the boldness and originality of their speculations, they may be said to have pointed out the path of true science, they are continually led astray from their main object, by a propensity to subtlety and conceit. Hence it is that their reasonings, though frequently ingenious, are also obscure, desultory, and inconclusive; and it is seldom that they are pursued, with brevity and vigour, to any just or striking conclusion. This tendency to abstract and metaphysical discussion, which distinguishes the productions of the economical school, has

* See observations on Productive and Unproductive Labour.

considerably detracted from their popularity and value; and it will accordingly be found, that the theories of those writers, though they have excited some speculative controversy, have never been much felt in the affairs of the world; while in other respects they have been injurious, by giving the character of verbal disputation, to a science replete with practical truth.

It may be also remarked of the French authors, that however consistently they maintain the doctrine of the freedom of trade, they seem to deduce it from the principles rather of abstract right, than of general expediency. In this strain, Turgot remarks, in a letter to Dr Price*, in which he blames the newly established government of America for regulating trade, for authorising exclusive corporations, and for prohibiting

* Œuvres de Turgot, tom. ix. p. 383.

the exportation of certain commodities, " que la loi de la liberté entière de tout " commerce est un corrollaire du droit " de proprieté*." It was to justice, rather than to policy, that they looked for the perfection of civil society: and they generally reason in reference to this principle; not reflecting, how much more powerfully men feel the operation of self interest than of justice, and how useless it is, therefore, to build schemes of practical improvement on the vain chimeras of moral perfectibility. In proving their doctrines to be just, rather than expedient, the French writers are also excluded from all those instructive and practical views of society and of manners, which render science so much more certain and interesting, by bringing it home to the business of life.

* That the law of complete commercial freedom follows as a corrollary from the right of property.

The Inquiry into the Nature and Causes of the Wealth of Nations stands in decided contrast to all abstract theory. It is a great display of reason on the business of the world; touching society in all its essential relations, containing lessons for government as well as for common life, and embracing subjects formerly placed without the limits of philosophy. It has been followed by suitable effects; having laid the foundation of a new science, and effected a permanent change in the opinions of mankind, and the policy of states.

But, with all the high qualities of commanding reason, Dr Smith has not published a perfect work. In fixing on the wealth of nations as the object and limit of his inquiries, he has adopted a narrow view of his subject; since the science of which he treats is evidently a higher branch of legislation, and must, therefore, embrace many interesting questions wholly unconnected with wealth. Human society is a great scheme of policy and justice; and as buying and selling must, under every form of it, make a great part of the business of mankind, it is highly important so far to explain the nature of trade, as to secure it against unjust and impolitic restraints. Political economy will therefore embrace the consideration of trade as part of its subject; and the effect of good government will also be to protect trade, and to enable the people to acquire wealth. But wealth is not the direct object of government, nor is it of political economy, which is a speculation founded on the principles of justice and policy, of which government is the practical result, and of which the object is to explain those fundamental laws of society to which all human regulations must necessarily be subordinate; that legislation may be confined within its proper province, and that the statesman, knowing the limits of his power, may no longer rashly interfere with the natural course of things, nor seek to introduce, on his own partial views of expediency, schemes of improvement which are at variance with the general good. In this view of the science, it must comprehend many interesting questions, which, as they have no relation to wealth, Dr Smith is precluded from considering by the terms of his plan; and, though he deviates, in the course of his inquiries, from his own rule, the subject is, in consequence of the restraint which he has imposed on himself, occasionally presented to the reader in rather an aukward and uninteresting form. In examining, for instance, in what manner a state can be best defended, he converts the question of policy into one of economy; considering, not what is the best, but what is the cheapest, system of defence. It is in this way that he finds it necessary to reconcile the discussion of his subject with the plan of his inquiry; although, in the course of his remarks, he throws off this restraint, and discusses the question on views, not of economy, but of policy. Dr Smith has also erred occasionally from too great a fondness for system. On some subjects his views are hasty, partial, and inaccurate; while on others, the truth and value of his doctrines seem to justify, and even to require farther explanation.

Since the publication of Dr Smith's work, Mr Malthus is the only author, who can be said to have extended the boundaries of political science. In his original and instructive essay, he has traced, with discrimination and accuracy, the great law by which population and subsistence respectively increase; and his views are demonstrated with such variety of illustration, that they are no longer questioned. Some imperfect anticipations occur in former works, of the same doctrine. Sir James Steuart, in particular, expresses himself very clearly on this subject, when he compares the progress of population to the movements of a spring loaded with a variable weight. The want of subsistence he considers as the weight which depresses the elastic principle of population; and, in proportion as it is withdrawn, mankind, according to his notion, increase until they advance beyond the limits of their food, within which they are again quickly brought back by poverty and want: and in this alternate course of discouragement and increase, varying with the supply of subsistence, Sir James Steuart describes the human race as gradually multiplying. There are some original remarks on the same subject by the author of L'Ami des Hommes, who pointedly states, that while agriculture keeps its ground, neither disease nor war will cause any permanent decrease of people. He has a chapter entitled, 'Subsistence the Measure of Population;' and the commonly supposed causes of depopulation, such as the celibacy of monks, war, navigation, emigration to the New World, he considers as roots from which new branches of population gradually spring. The world he compares to a garden, planted in all its parts; and without an increase of subsistence, he observes, not a single new plant can grow up but by displacing some other. By war and disease the void spaces are made, which the power of population fills up; and, if the agriculture of a country is not injured, its inhabitants, he finally insists, can neither be permanently diminished by disease nor by war*. But these remarks, however striking or just, are incidentally introduced; and, far from pursuing this train of reasoning to its fair results, the ingenious author turns aside to details comparatively frivolous and inconclusive. The great merit of Mr Malthus consists in clearly discerning the value of the principle thus carelessly cast aside by former writers, and in tracing it to all its legitimate conclusions; demonstrating, in the clearest manner, that the want of subsistence is the great obstacle to the population of the world; that the tendency of mankind to multiply faster than food can be provided for their support, is the root of many of the evils which afflict society; and that without a previous increase of subsistence, laws for the encourage-

* L'Ami des Hommes, vol. i. chap. ii. p. 15, 16. 23.

ment of marriage are not only useless, but pernicious, as they necessarily lead to an excess of population, and to misery and want among the labouring classes, which all the artificial devices of legislation will neither relieve nor palliate. On those various points the reasonings of Mr Malthus are interesting and original; and though former writers may have incidentally suggested similar doctrines, to him unquestionably belongs the merit, of having improved scattered hints into a solid system of science, and of having made a valuable addition to the stock of practical truth.

The object of the present work is, to rectify what is amiss in Dr Smith; to supply omissions; to give his reasonings an application to modern times; and to exhibit, as far as the author is qualified, a complete system of political economy. In considering the subsequent history of the world, it is obvious that additions have now become necessary to Dr Smith's work; and the subjects of Paper Currency, Finance, Taxation, the East India Company, have only to be mentioned, to suggest the materials of important discussion. There is another subject which he has considered, namely, the military policy of states, and the power of armies; and here it is scarcely necessary to remark, what a fruitful theme modern history affords for new and interesting speculation.

The three volumes of Dr Smith's original work contain incidental remarks on the text, with notes of reference; while dissertations of a general nature are reserved for this additional volume, to which the notes of the preceding volumes of course refer.

EDINBURGH,
Sept. 14. 1814.

OBSERVATIONS

ON THE SUBJECTS TREATED OF

IN

DR SMITH'S WORK.

ON THE PRINCIPLES OF METALLIC CURRENCY.

THE reasons that have induced mankind to convert metals into coin, in preference to every other commodity, have been already explained by Dr Smith; and it is indeed sufficiently obvious, from a consideration of their qualities, that no other substance would answer the purpose equally well. In different periods of improvement, however, different metals have been fixed upon for this purpose; and the same metals have also, at different times, prevailed more or less in the currency of every country. The use of money being to facilitate exchanges, it will naturally consist of the metal most suited to the nature of the exchanges, and of course to the payments which it is designed to effect. Where the payments are large, it will be most convenient to use a metal containing a great value in little bulk; as in that case the same sum can be counted and weighed in much less time. But, for trifling payments, a coarser metal will answer better; as a precious metal could not be conveniently divided into sufficiently small portions for the purpose required. The smallest payments occur in the retail trade; and it is for this trade, accordingly, that coins of a very low denomination are found necessary. By enabling the retail dealer to fix a just price upon the smallest portion of his goods, he can suit his trade to the demand of his customers, however trifling. Farthings, for example, which have been long disused in the general payments of the country, have been sometimes required about London for the retail trade of beer, which being sold in small quantities, a coin proportionally small is wanted, to measure the value of what is thus purchased. With a large coin there could be no accurate measurement of value; and no business could therefore be done, unless under some different and less convenient arrangement. Grocers, also, and other retail dealers, occasionally require farthings for the management of their business.

In an early stage of society, when nations are poor, and their payments trifling, copper has frequently been known to answer all the purposes of currency*; and it is coined into pieces of very low denominations, in order to facilitate the inconsiderable exchanges which then take place. In the early ages of the Roman republic, a copper coinage effected all the necessary payments; and it was not till conquest had introduced luxury and wealth, that the Romans found it necessary to employ silver coins. Their copper coins were also of very low denominations. In Scotland, there appears to have been formerly no less than four denominations of copper coin below a halfpenny. According to Lord Liverpool, there was formerly no copper coin in England. The fourth part of the silver penny, equal in value to three farthings of the money of the present times, was the lowest denomination of coin in the reign of William the Conqueror. Yet it is not easy to believe that all the inconsiderable exchanges of those times could have been car-

---

* Lord Liverpool on the Coin, p. 146.

ried on with a currency of which the lowest coin was equal in value to three farthings.

The general wealth of a country is very accurately measured by the nature of its payments and the state of its coin; and the decided prevalence of a coarse metal in its currency, joined to the use of coins of very low denominations, marks a rude state of society. In the progress of improvement, accordingly, those coins fall into disuse. Being chiefly used for the petty retail of consumable articles, they are gradually thrown out of employment, as the retail transactions grow more considerable, in consequence of the increasing wealth of the country. Silver is also, at the same time, introduced into the more important transactions of commerce in place of copper; and, as wealth continues to increase, and to be more equally diffused, gold at last is the only metal in which the larger payments can be effected.

The business of the currency thus naturally divides itself into two distinct departments; the duty of effecting the main payments being of course reserved for the more precious metal, while the inferior metals are still retained for more trivial exchanges, and are thus merely subservient to the main currency.

Between the first introduction, however, of a more precious metal into the currency of a country, and its exclusive use in the main payments, there is a wide interval; and the payments of the retail trade must, in the mean time, have grown so considerable, in consequence of the increase of wealth, that they can, in part at least, be conveniently managed by the new and more valuable coin; since no coin can be used for the main payments which is not suited, at the same time, to the transactions of the retail trade. It is from the consumer that every trade, whether it be a trade of production or manufacture, derives the ultimate return of its capital. The capital of the retail dealer is immediately replaced by the money of the consumer; the retail dealer transmits what he receives for the sale of his goods to the wholesale merchant, who, in like manner, pays it away to the manufacturer or to the farmer; so that, though the most precious metal might be most conveniently used in the main payments, the currency which carries on the retail business must still mix in all the great transactions of trade. It will be collected by the retail dealer in sufficient quantities for his wholesale payments, by whom it will accordingly be paid away in large sums; and thus it will circulate, and perform the functions of the main currency. Though all the larger payments might be more conveniently effected in gold, yet a country must still have a currency suited to the small scale of its retail transactions; since its consumable commodities could not otherwise be divided into sufficiently small portions for the wants of the community. That metal, therefore, whether silver or copper, which will both answer this purpose, and will also effect, though with less convenience, the main payments, must still form the prevailing coin of a country.

In all the metallic currencies of Europe, copper is a subsidiary currency; no payment being ever made in that metal, unless it be too inconsiderable for any of the silver coins. But, although gold has been long introduced into all the continental currencies, it has not supplanted silver in the main payments. The nature of payments on the continent does not, it seems, permit the use of silver as a subsidiary currency. Although gold would clearly answer better for the greater payments, yet silver must still be collected, in large sums, by the retail dealers. The disposal of their goods must still bring them a considerable proportion of silver currency, which they can employ in no other way than in paying the demands of the wholesale merchant. In Britain, it is evident that the quantity of silver in circulation does not exceed what is wanted for the smaller payments, as it is often difficult to procure change for a guinea; and silver coin has at times been sold for a premium. Silver is hardly ever seen in a larger sum than twenty shillings; and, in point of fact, few payments of that amount are ever made in silver.

Before the reign of William III. silver, we are told *, was brought in large bags to the treasury in payment of the national revenue. But at this period the great change took place, which for ever excluded it from the main payments; and the facts then disclosed deserve the more attention, as we have no exact knowledge of any such crisis in the currency of other countries. It would be interesting to trace, if we had materials for so curious an inquiry, the rise and decline of a particular metal in the currency of a country; but the want of facts is a complete bar to such an investigation. The period when silver was substituted for copper

* Lord Liverpool on the Coin.

in the currencies of Europe, is buried in obscurity; for such matters, unfortunately, seldom engage the notice of historians. It is to war and politics that their attention is chiefly directed; while, for those favourite topics, the precious details of domestic history are thrown into the shade. In most parts of Europe, in America, and throughout India, silver still continues to be used in the main payments; and we have no data to calculate when gold may take the lead in the currency of those countries. Such an era may not occur in the revolution of centuries; and in every view, therefore, it is worth while to attend to the state of the British currency at the period alluded to.

The exclusive introduction of gold into the main payments of England, was a clear proof that the returns of the retail trade were by this time chiefly made in that metal; which might have been the case, though no single payment had ever exceeded or even equalled any of the gold coins; because, in the general abundance of gold and scarcity of silver, gold coins would naturally be offered for small sums, and a balance of silver demanded in return; by which means gold, by thus assisting in the retail tráde, and economising the use of silver, even for the smaller payments, would prevent its accumulation by the retail dealer; and as it was formerly found necessary, when silver was used for the retail trade, to employ it also in the great payments, in like manner gold cannot now be exclusively employed in the main payments, without occasionally doing the duty of silver in the retail trade. If gold were not used for this purpose, more silver would be required, which would in that case be collected by the retail dealer in sufficient quantities for his wholesale payments, and would thus encroach on the functions of the higher currency.

The substitution of gold for silver in the main payments, must immediately occasion an excess of the latter currency, and consequently a fall in its value; the effect in this case being precisely the same as if an addition had been made to the currency in general, without any corresponding addition to the demands of trade. This fall in the value of silver coin will afford the necessary temptation to melt it down. The silver will be more valuable in the form of bullion than of coin; and this will continue until the quantity in circulation is no more than sufficient for the smaller payments. At the time the great change took place in the currency of Britain, the silver coin had been so much debased by clipping, that a guinea passed for 30s. To remedy this defect, a new silver coinage had been just issued, to the amount in tale of L. 6,882,908. 19s. 7d. But, silver being now excluded from the main payments, the quantity issued was far more than could be employed in the smaller payments. The excess accordingly encumbered the circulation, and the silver coin fell $4\frac{1}{2}$ per cent. under its intrinsic value. A guinea was rated by act of Parliament at 22s., which was about 1s. 4d. more than its real value. It fell to 21s. 6d., which was still 10d. more than its value in silver bullion, though it may be considered as its fair market price in silver coin. French louis-d'ors and Portugal moidores exchanged also for more than their worth in silver coin. The receivers of taxes were prohibited from receiving the latter coin at more than 27s. 6d., though it passed for 28s.; against which, several gentlemen in the west of England petitioned the treasury, alleging, that " when those " coins went at 28s. their country was full of " gold, *which they wanted very much.*" Silver was clearly worth more, therefore, in bullion than in coin; and the greater part of the excellent currency recently issued was, in consequence, converted into bullion and exported. Though government had spent about L.2,700,000 on this coinage of silver, yet in seventeen years it had almost wholly disappeared.

Alarmed by this unaccountable diminution of the silver coin, the ministers referred the matter to Sir Isaac Newton, who, in his report to the Lords of the Treasury *, shewed, from the relative value of gold and silver all over Europe, that silver was underrated in the British currency in proportion to gold; and, on this account, being more valuable in bullion than in coin, it was melted down and exported. By the regulations of the mint, which gave 22s. for a guinea, silver was no doubt greatly underrated in coin; but as the mint estimation was not followed in the market, where it appears that 21s. 6d. was only given for a guinea, it could not have occasioned the evil complained of. Even in the market, however, the silver coin was still underrated, and its low estimation was

* See Sir Isaac Newton's Report on the State of the Coin; which, as it contains some useful information on this subject, the reader will find in the Appendix, Note [A.]

no doubt the immediate cause of its being melted down and exported; but as this low estimation was its market price, the statement of Sir Isaac Newton left the main fact of its depreciation still unaccounted for. He mentions, however, a very important circumstance relative to Sweden, by which, if he had duly considered it, he might have discerned the true nature of the change then going on in England. In Sweden, the value of silver was higher in proportion to gold than in any other part of Europe; and Sweden, it appears, which had formerly been content with a copper currency, began now to abound in silver. The same change was going on both in England and Sweden. Their increasing wealth required a more valuable currency to transact their payments; and the high price of silver coin in Sweden, and its low price in England, were necessary to perfect the desired improvement.

By Sir Isaac Newton's advice, a royal proclamation was issued, reducing the guinea to 21s.; and the accuracy of this valuation may be inferred from the ready obedience paid to it, as it is only in that case that royal proclamations are attended to. Sir Isaac Newton remarks, that if silver coin continued so scarce it would be sold for a premium. The fall in its value had by this time cleared the currency of what was superfluous; and the quantity in circulation did not probably exceed what was wanted for the smaller payments. Silver coin had therefore begun to recover its value; and though at 21s. for a guinea, it was still underrated about 4d. in proportion to gold, this trifling error could hardly occasion the melting down of the coin.

To the accident of silver being underrated in proportion to gold, Lord Liverpool, in his valuable work on the British coin, ascribes in part its exclusion from the main payments. The same cause, however, had frequently before excluded silver from the circulation; but it was soon found that it could not be wanted; and it was therefore more accurately valued, for the purpose of being again introduced into the currency, and used as formerly in the main payments. It seems likely, however, that the decline of silver in the currency of a country must generally lead to some temporary scarcity of silver coin in particular transactions; and it is not until this inconvenience is counterbalanced by the superior utility of gold, that silver can be converted into a subsidiary currency.

It is evident that the coin used for the larger payments can only pass current at its intrinsic worth; and all attempts, accordingly, to alter its value, either by debasement or by raising its denomination, have uniformly produced a corresponding rise of prices. Men are alarmed when they see the fundamental principles of value thus shaken; and they plainly perceive, that the ruin and injustice of such arbitrary innovations must finally bring back the coin to the sure standard of intrinsic worth. They refuse, therefore, to transfer their property on the faith of this artificial and uncertain value stamped upon it; and in all their transactions, they are guided not by its nominal but by its real value. They do not chuse to give up the security of substantial property for the guarantee of tyranny and fraud.

But intrinsic worth does not appear necessary to a subsidiary currency, because its depreciation cannot be attended with such injurious effects. If we suppose copper, which, throughout the whole of Europe, is used solely for the smaller payments, to be depreciated 50 per cent.

so that twenty-four halfpence really contained copper equal only to the value of sixpence, how trifling is the risk of taking such a currency in payment, so long as it is confined to small sums? Though it should be even found necessary to make it pass for its intrinsic value, the loss of an individual must still be trifling. He might possibly have in his possession twenty-four of these halfpence; in that case he would lose exactly the half of that sum: but surely the apprehension of such a loss would never induce him to compare the value of copper in coin and its value in the market; still less would he refuse it in case he found any deficiency. When payments amount to L.1000 or L.2000, the case is different: it then becomes of importance to examine the currency in which the payment is made, both as to its weight and fineness, and to exact strict compensation for every deficiency. Without this necessary caution, trade would be a continual fraud, to which no man could submit without being speedily ruined. The coin, therefore, in which the greater payments are made, must in all cases be brought to the test of its intrinsic worth; while it is the peculiar distinction of a currency confined to the smaller payments, that it will circulate for an arbitrary value.

In Rome, while copper was the prevailing coin, it was current only for its intrinsic worth; and in the first Punic war it was, accordingly, by diminishing its weight, that the public and all other creditors were defrauded. Silver had been introduced about five years before the commencement of that war *; and it gradually superseded copper in the main payments, though we cannot fix the precise period of this change. The fact seems certain, however; and it is on this ground that Gibbon defends Justinian † for taking one-seventh from the weight of the copper coin. Copper was at this latter period confined to the smaller payments; and on this account, what was formerly a mischievous fraud was now an improvement. Gold was introduced into the Roman currency sixty-two years after silver ‡; but it never seems to have excluded silver from the main payments;

* Metrologie; ou Traité des Mesures, Poids, et Monnoies des anciens peuples et modernes; Par M. Paucton, p. 385.
† Decline and Fall of the Roman Empire, Vol. III p. 86.
‡ Metrologie, &c. p. 412.

for the same historian, in his account of the Roman taxation*, states, that it required a particular law to enforce the payment of the public revenue in gold. Pliny mentions, that the tribute of the conquered provinces was formerly exacted in silver; and he expresses his wonder that gold was not preferred. Gold, however, it appears, had afterwards become the more desirable currency, though silver had been still collected in sufficient quantities for the main payments, otherwise the order to receive gold alone in payment of taxes would have been useless.

In India, copper does not appear to be a subsidiary currency; and, accordingly, it will not pass current but for its intrinsic worth. The rupee, a silver coin of the value of about 2s. 3d., is the money of account; in relation to which, the mohour a gold coin, and the pice a copper coin, are allowed to find their value in the market; and it invariably happens, that the number of pice currently exchanged for a rupee varies with the weight and value of the coin; while in this country, on the contrary, twenty-four halfpence invariably exchange for a shilling without regard to their weight.

* Vol. III. p. 106.

In India, the retail dealer must still collect considerable quantities of copper in return for his goods; and he cannot afford to take it, therefore, but for its intrinsic worth *.

In the currencies of Europe, where copper is confined to the smaller payments, it passes for whatever value is fixed on it, without any examination either of its weight or fineness. Before the year 1798, the copper coin of Great Britain was in a very debased state: even the mint coins of England, when newly issued, were rated a good deal higher than their value in copper; a great proportion of them were besides much worn. The copper coin of Scotland was in a worse state; and the copper currencies of both countries were composed in a great measure of counterfeits. Although these counterfeits were occasionally refused, yet the mint halfpence, whether English or Scots, were always taken in payment, although their current value was probably double their real value; and even the counterfeits, after some little clamour, were current equally with the mint coins. Private copper coins also passed for the same value and with equal facility as other coins, until their circulation was finally stopped by the new issue of copper coins in 1798.

* See Sir George Barlow's able and accurate Report on the Trade, Mint, and Customs of Benares.

OF METALLIC CURRENCY. 19

In the currency of Britain, silver being a subsidiary currency circulates at an arbitrary value. Twenty-one shillings, though, according to Lord Liverpool, they have lost about 29 per cent. of their value, still exchange for a guinea, which is perfect in its weight. During the reign of King William, when the silver coin was in the same debased state, and when the gold coin was perfect in its weight, the case was different; 30 worn and debased shillings being at that time given for a guinea *. Silver was then used in the main payments; and it would not circulate but for its intrinsic worth. Since the great reformation of the currency in the reign of King William, silver coin has been confined to the smaller payments, and its current value has, in consequence, lost all connection with its intrinsic value. In the reign of Henry VIII. also, during the great debasement of the coin which then took place, silver, which was greatly overvalued in proportion to gold, would not circulate but for its intrinsic worth; and it is related by Stowe, that he had seen twenty-one

* The silver was debased one half; and a guinea ought, therefore, to have passed for 42s. But it was received in payment of taxes at its nominal value, which somewhat kept up its current value.

shillings given for an angel, a gold coin, the current value of which was only ten shillings *.

Dr Smith has entirely overlooked this peculiar property of a subsidiary currency; and he falls, in consequence, into some serious mistakes. In investigating the value of the precious metals at different periods, he takes corn as his measure for silver as well as gold. Corn, from the steadiness of its own value, he considers as a sure test of the value of other commodities; and he holds every rise in its price, therefore, to be merely nominal, and a proof only of the declining value of the precious metals; the same quantity of corn selling, in consequence, for a greater quantity of those metals, or in other words for a higher price †. But when gold is once substituted for silver, in great transactions, it is not for silver but for gold that commodities are exchanged; and it is clear, therefore, that their price, or the quantity of gold given for them, cannot indicate the value of silver. The market price of corn implies its worth in gold, in which its price is paid, and not in silver; and because

* Lord Liverpool on the Coin, p. 88—90.
† See vol. I. Digression concerning the variation in the value of silver during the course of the four last centuries.

its price is high or low, or in other words, because more or less gold is given for it, no inference can thence arise as to the value of silver. The market price of corn only shews the value of that for which it is exchanged. But when all the great transactions of the market are settled in gold, it is for gold that it is exchanged, and not for silver. When Dr Smith, therefore, infers the value of silver from the market price of corn, he is not aware, that owing to the decline of silver in the currency of this country, its value has long ceased to influence the price of that or of any other commodity.

Money being the foundation of all mercantile contracts, it is of great consequence that it should remain steady in its value. The value of coin is, however, exposed to vary; 1*st*, From the varying value of the metals of which it is made; and, 2*dly*, From the wear and tear of circulation; light and worn coins being inferior in value to those which remain perfect in their weight. When two metals are used in the main payments, this inconvenience is the more felt, as the coins of the respective metals are liable to vary, not only in relation to commodities, but in relation also to each other; a rise in the value of either metal destroying the established proportions of the currency, and rendering it profitable to convert coin into bullion. When silver coin, for example, is ordered by the regulations of the mint to be exchanged for gold coin at less than its intrinsic value, there is an obvious advantage in converting it into bullion, and selling it for what it may bring in the market. If either of the two metals, therefore, is undervalued in coin, it is generally melted down and restored to its true value in bullion. These inconveniences are inseparable from a metallic currency; as, however accurately gold and silver may be estimated in the currency, there is no guarding against the varying value of those metals in relation to each other; and in that case it becomes profitable to convert into bullion the coin that is current at an under value.

Both gold and silver have been alternately banished from the currency of England by an erroneous estimation of their value. They have occasionally, also, passed current at a value different from that set upon them by the regulations of the mint. After the discovery of the American mines silver fell in its value when compared with the gold; the gold coins were in consequence either melted down or exported; and James I. was under the necessity of raising their value nearly eleven per cent. when compared with the silver coins. It appeared, however, that this rise in the value of the gold coin was too great, as the silver coin, after this alteration, was almost wholly banished from circulation. The value of silver, however, when compared with gold continued very rapidly to fall; so that a new valuation of gold became very soon necessary; and the currency was exposed to continual disorder from the constantly declining value of silver, until at length it reached its lowest depression.

By charging something, however, for the workmanship of the coin, the temptation to melt it down will be in all cases diminished. Without some charge of this sort, it may always be converted into bullion without any loss; and in the event of a wrong estimation of its worth there will be a profit on the operation. But the price paid for workmanship being of course lost by the destruction of the coin, hence arises some security for its preservation. If twenty ounces of coined metal, for example, be equal, taking the workmanship into account, to twenty-one ounces of bullion, unless a rise of more than 5 per cent. take place in the price of bullion, there will be a loss, instead of a profit, in melting down the coin.

To remedy the defects in the British currency, Lord King proposes to make an accurate estimate of the value of gold and silver, and to review it occasionally, declaring at the same time, by public authority, for what value in silver coin the guinea shall pass current.

A writer in the Edinburgh Review, in the course of his remarks on Lord Liverpool's work, proposes to coin guineas and shillings of a known weight and fineness, and to allow their current rate to be adjusted in the market. Both these plans evidently proceed upon the same misconception, namely, the necessity of intrinsic worth for the circulation of the silver coin.

Lord Liverpool is of opinion that the intrinsic value of the silver coins in metal and workmanship, the average value of the metal being taken for a number of years back, should regulate their current value; while he proposes, with some inconsistency, that the charge of manufacturing the gold coins should be taken out of the silver coins; in which case the intrinsic value of the latter in metal and workmanship could not be equal to their current value. There can be no good reason, besides, for charging the expence of the gold coinage to the account of the silver coin.

Those who have had the charge of the British coin never seem to have thought of any suitable plan for the regulation of the inferior currencies; and the silver coin has accordingly, for more than a century, been left to its fate, though it might have been renewed with little trouble, and without any expence. Silver coin being at present underrated in proportion to gold, there is a profit on converting it into bullion; and, accordingly, all new coins vanish from circulation as soon as they are issued. In the present circumstances of the currency, therefore, no addition can be made to the stock of silver specie; which accordingly consists of old and worn coins without any remains of their former appearance; and which, though deficient about one-third in their weight, still circulate, in consequence of being confined to the smaller payments, for their original worth. The state of the silver currency thus presents every facility for forgery and fraud; while its high value in circulation is a standing inducement to attempts of this sort.

It has been already shown that intrinsic worth must always belong to the principal coin, while the inferior currencies will circulate with equal convenience at an arbitrary value. Were a new silver currency, therefore, to be issued, at one-third more than its intrinsic worth, it could hardly be affected by any change in the market price of silver, as the metal must rise more than 30 per cent. before it could be profitable to convert coin into bullion. The high value of the coin would undoubtedly afford a temptation to forgery; but to guard against this evil some dependence must be had on the excellence of the workmanship. Lord Liverpool remarks, that " They (the silver coins). " are not only made of a metal which takes " a fair and easy impression, but, being of a " greater number of denominations than those " of any other metal, their various sizes afford a " larger scope to the engravers and artists, for " the exercise of their respective talents, in " design and execution." Such pains might therefore be bestowed on the mint silver coins as to defy imitation.

We have no data to calculate the quantity

of silver coin in circulation. The result of some calculations by Lord Liverpool makes its amount L.3,960,435; though he is of opinion that this is an over-statement. The silver coin issued at the great recoinage in the reign of William III. amounted in nominal value to L. 8,076,092. But after silver was confined to smaller payments, the quantity in circulation would of course be greatly reduced. It is not likely that the nominal value of the silver coin is at present more than L.2,000,000; and by issuing a currency to that amount, its nominal value being one-third more than its real value, government might gain one-third of that sum, while the new currency would answer quite as well, though deficient in weight. To supply the want of silver coin, a currency of this sort has been accordingly issued by the Bank of England, under the title of Bank Tokens. Its real worth is not equal to its nominal value; and it is on this account not so liable to be melted down*.

* Since the issue of this currency the market price of silver bullion has been gradually rising, and though the bank dollars have been successively raised in price, they are now of more value in bullion than in coin, and are, in consequence, gradually disappearing. The cause of this rise in the market price of bullion I have endeavoured to explain when treating of paper currency.

With respect to the copper coins, they have been of late years regulated on the most mistaken views. Previous to the year 1798, when a new copper coinage was undertaken, the copper coins circulated without any inconvenience for more than their intrinsic worth. In 1798, we are informed by Lord Liverpool, that it was resolved to adopt intrinsic worth as the basis of the new copper coinage then to be issued; and according to this principle, acted upon for the first time, 1815 tons of copper were coined by Mr Boulton into twopenny pieces, penny pieces, halfpence and farthings, amounting in nominal value to L.282,075. 5s. 8½d*.

By this new plan of giving intrinsic worth to the copper coins, they were only made more heavy and cumbersome; while the value of the metal they contained, being exactly equal to their current value, it was clear that a rise in the market price of copper would turn the scale in its favour; in which case it would be profitable to convert the coin into bullion, as it would be worth more in that form than in currency. A rise in the market price of copper

* Twopenny pieces - L. 6,019. 15s. 8d.
  Penny pieces - - - - - 183,177. 18s. 6d.
  Halfpence - - - - - - - 88,506. 18s. 4d.
  Farthings - - - - - - - - 4,370. 13s. 2d.

accordingly took place, before the issue of the new coin was completed, and it was found necessary, therefore, to provide for its safety by a diminution of its weight; so that the halfpence and farthings last issued were not so heavy in proportion as the penny and twopenny pieces. The price of copper still rising, the new currency at last wholly disappeared; and in the more populous parts of the country a base currency was substituted in its place. By this plan, therefore, the community was put to a double charge; 1*st*, A very useless expence for metal was incurred by the great weight of these copper coins; and, 2*dly*, The loss of this excellent currency, in consequence of the quantity of metal it contained, occasioned the expence of a new coinage.

With respect to the particular sum for which the inferior currencies should be made a legal tender, it is clear that, as the use of copper is to aid, not to suspersede, silver, its station in the currency is thus fixed; and it should not therefore be made a legal tender for any sum above sixpence, the lowest silver coin; while silver, for a like reason, should not be made a legal tender for more than a guinea. In matters of this sort, however, laws are in general of little avail. In this country, for example, silver is at present a legal tender for L.25. But in the present state of the currency, when it is often difficult to procure change for a guinea, it is obvious that payments to that amount can never be generally made in silver. If silver, therefore, never exceeds what is wanted for the smaller payments, it cannot be collected in sufficient quantities for the larger payments; and though there were no law limiting its legal tender, it could not, in these circumstances, be generally offered in payment of large sums. If silver, on the other hand, exceed what is wanted for the smaller payments, no law restricting its legal tender will prevent its accumulation by the retail dealer; as he may soon collect a large quantity of silver, though none of his payments should ever exceed 20s., for which sum silver ought always to be a legal tender. It has been already shown that the use of gold in the main payments necessarily implies also its use in the retail trade; those who have guineas offering them for small purchases, and receiving, with the commodity purchased, a balance of silver in return; by which means the surplus of silver that would otherwise incumber the retail

OF METALLIC CURRENCY.

dealer, is drawn off and dispersed into general circulation. But if there is as much silver as will transact the small payments, independent of gold, the retail dealer must then receive silver for small purchases, and it must of necessity accumulate in his hands. In this country an excess of copper coin was issued during the year 1798, by private traders; and though copper is not a legal payment for more than sixpence, the surplus soon found its way into the coffers of the retail dealers, who naturally tried, by various expedients, to force it back into circulation; from which, however, it was sure to return, and finally to settle in their hands. It was accordingly found that, when this currency was stopped, copper had accumulated with the retail dealers, in sums of L. 20, L. 30, and even L.50, which they were finally obliged to dispose of for their intrinsic worth. The evil arose from the excessive issue of those coins by private traders, on whom all recourse was gradually lost; and the currency thus imposed on the public was a sure source of loss wherever it was accumulated. It was against an evil of this sort that Swift, without seeing its precise nature, wrote so powerfully in the Drapier's Letters. The halfpence then to be issued in Ireland were to be circulated at more than their intrinsic worth, for the benefit of an individual of the name of Wood, who had thus an interest in their excessive issue. This, and not the overvaluation of the coin, was the real evil, as it clearly led to an over-issue of copper, which would have gradually accumulated, and brought certain loss on all retail dealers.

Though no law restricting the legal tender of the inferior currencies can prevent their accumulation by the retail dealers, in the event of their excessive issue, some such regulation seems, nevertheless, necessary; as a degraded currency might otherwise be generally offered in payment of large sums, by which means, all who had money to receive would be exposed to serious injury.

ON THE PRICE OF SUCH COMMODITIES AS YIELD A RENT.

The price of those commodities which are produced by labour and capital, cannot for any length of time be either higher or lower than what is sufficient to pay the common rate of wages and profit. Where it is higher, capital will be attracted from other trades by the temptation of extraordinary profit, until the supply be increased and the price reduced; and where it is lower, capital will be withdrawn from the unprofitable trade until the price rise in consequence of the diminished supply. This result seems to be self-evident, because no commodity will be produced unless it can be sold for a price sufficient to repay the labour and the stock, with its ordinary profit, employed in producing it.

But this principle does not apply to the produce of land, which is generally sold for a price sufficient not only to repay the wages of labour and the profits of stock, but to yield a surplus or rent for the benefit of the proprietor. This high price is evidently not necessary to insure production, for although land yielded no rent it would still be cultivated. As long as its produce is sufficient to pay the wages of labour and the profits of stock, the labourer and the farmer will have all the inducement which they ever had to continue their industry. There will be no proprietor indeed to receive a return from their labour and capital; but that labour and capital will be still as well paid as before, and the same motives to exertion will consequently remain. The whole produce of a mine or of a coal pit is frequently no more than sufficient to pay wages and profit; in which case nothing remains for the landlord's rent; but we do not find that the mine is less diligently worked on this account.

The high price which leaves a surplus or rent to the landlord, after paying wages and profit, being no way necessary to production, must be accounted for on a different principle; and it seems accordingly to arise from the comparative scarcity in which articles that yield a rent are generally produced. It is clear that the quantity of a commodity consumed, can never for any length of time exceed the quantity produced; and it is by a rise of price that the consumption is confined within the limits of the supply; while, in the case of a more abundant supply, the consumption is accelerated by a fall of price. The price is, in this manner, the great regulator of consumption; and where a commodity is sold at such a price as to leave a surplus after paying all the necessary expences of its production, it will always be found that this high price is required to proportion the consumption to the supply. It is necessary, for example, that the yearly supply of corn should last until the produce of the succeeding season reach the market; and the price, by which the daily and weekly consumption is regulated, according to the supply of the year, is always such as to leave a rent or surplus above wages and profit. The price of every commodity which affords a rent is regulated in the same manner. A certain price is necessary to proportion the consumption to the supply; and rent is the consequence of this high price. " High or low " wages," Dr Smith justly observes, " are the " causes of high or low price; high or low rent

" is the effect of it. It is because high or low
" wages or profit must be paid, in order to
" bring a particular commodity to market, that
" its price is high or low. But it is because its
" price is high or low, a great deal more or
" very little more, or no more than what is suf-
" ficient to pay those wages and profit, that it
" affords a high rent, or a low rent, or no rent
" at all*."

The price of such commodities as yield a rent being fixed with a view to regulate consumption, is in this manner wholly independent of their original cost; and though it may cost more or less to bring them to market, they will not on this account be sold for a higher or a lower price; for while the price answers its great purpose of suiting the consumption to the supply, it will not be affected by other causes. The corn of improved and fertile districts; the corn of lands recently brought under tillage at a great expence; the corn brought from a distance subject to all the charges of conveyance; and the corn produced in the immediate vicinity of the market, are all sold for the same price. There is but one market price for corn of equal quality whatever may have been its original

* Vol. I. Book I. Chap. XI.—Of the Rent of Land.

cost; and indeed the very existence of rent, or of a surplus independent of the expences of production, is of itself a sufficient proof that those expences neither limit nor determine the price.

The price which exactly proportions the consumption of corn to the supply may be called its natural price. It is the centre point to which the market price continually tends; and while it may finally settle there, it is evident that it cannot long remain either above or below it; because a higher or a lower price implies an excess either of consumption or of supply, and it is for the express purpose of correcting such irregularities that the price is fixed.

The price of corn, which always affords a rent, being in no respect influenced by the expences of its production, those expences must be defrayed out of the rent; and when they rise or fall, therefore, the consequence is not a higher or a lower price, but a higher or a lower rent. In this view, all taxes on farm servants, horses, or the implements of agriculture, are in reality land taxes; the burden falling on the farmer during the currency of his lease, and on the landlord when the lease comes to be renewed. In like manner, all those improved implements of husbandry which save expence to the farmer, such as machines for threshing and reaping; whatever gives him easier access to the market, such as good roads, canals, and bridges, though they lessen the original cost of corn, do not lessen its market price. Whatever is saved by those improvements, therefore, belongs to the landlord as part of his rent.

A writer in the Edinburgh Review, in reasoning against a bounty on the exportation of corn, supposes, by way of illustration, a bounty granted on production, which he concludes would occasion a fall of price. " Its immediate effect," he observes, " would evidently be to lower both " the money price and the real price to all pur- " chasers in the home market. Part of the old " price, instead of being paid by the purchaser " himself, would now be paid for him by the " public, and while he paid so much less, the " farmer would receive altogether the same " sum as before. The farmer would no doubt " be willing enough to keep up the market " price to its original rate, that he might thus " increase his receipts by the whole of the " bounty; but the same power of competition " which had before adjusted his profits would

" continue to adjust them to the same rate,
" by reducing his receipts from the private pur-
" chaser, in proportion to his new receipts from
" the public. Notwithstanding this bounty,
" therefore, the profits of the farmer would, by
" the operation of the principle of competition,
" subside towards their former level*."

The writer here evidently mistakes the nature of rent, which is really a bounty on the production of corn. It is a surplus paid by the consumer over and above the profits of the farmer, and is in substance, therefore, the same as the bounty proposed to be paid by the public. Such a bounty, were it actually paid, would increase the rent. It would not reduce the price of corn, which depends on its plenty or scarcity; and a bounty on production, which would not increase the supply, would not therefore reduce the price.

Rent being a surplus above wages and profit, whatever yields this surplus may be said to pay a rent. The inventor of a machine for abridging labour, were he to keep his secret, might sell his goods for such a price as would yield a rent or surplus above wages and profit; but when the secret is known, and others come to abridge

* Edinburgh Review, Vol. V. p. 194.

labour in the same way, the competition reduces the price, and his advantage is lost. In this manner improvements in manufactures benefit society by a fall of price on the goods manufactured; but improvements in agriculture, which occasion no fall of price, benefit only the landlord by an increase of rent. Manufacturing industry increases its produce in proportion to the demand, and the price falls; but the produce of land cannot be so increased; and a high price is still necessary to prevent the consumption from exceeding the supply.

When Dr Smith considers the extraordinary profit derived from secrets in manufactures as the high price of the manufacturer's private labour *, he clearly mistakes the nature of this profit, which is in no respect different from the rent of land. It is a surplus above wages and profit, which the consumers are content to pay rather than want the commodity. And wherein does it then differ from the surplus paid for the produce of land? The produce of some fine vineyards can be sold, it appears, at a price which leaves even a greater surplus than the price of corn †. Now, supposing the quality for which this price is paid were derived, not from the soil or situation, but from some secret process of manufacture, in what respect would the gain in either case differ, unless that it would be called profit or rent according as it arose from the manufacture or from the land?

* See Vol. I. Chap. VII. † Ibid.

ON THE WAGES OF LABOUR.

THE price of labour, like that of every commodity which is bought and sold, rises or falls with the demand; a great or a small demand being invariably followed by high or low wages. But the demand itself is regulated by certain general causes, and particularly by the state of the national stock; which being the great fund for the employment and support of labour, the demand will vary in proportion as it increases or declines.

This has been sufficiently explained by Dr Smith; and Mr Malthus, pursuing the same views, has pointed out the process by which these effects are produced. The progress of population, as it is illustrated by that original writer, influences so immediately the condition of the labourer, that the subject seems to require a short abstract of his leading doctrines.

The tendency of mankind to increase beyond the means of their subsistence is the great principle on which the whole theory of population may be said to rest, and it is confirmed by the most decisive facts. Where there is plenty of provisions, the population of a country will double in fifteen years; and examples of this rapid progress have actually occurred in new colonies, with plenty of subsistence for their increasing inhabitants. The question is, why there is not everywhere the same rapid increase; and why the human race does not thus perpetually double in a geometrical series, until they fill the whole earth? If a population of ten thousand is doubled in fifteen years, why should not ten millions be doubled in a like period? The reason plainly is, that the food for ten millions cannot be so easily doubled as the food for ten thousand. In a new settled country it is the abundance of land and subsistence which allows the population freely to expand. But as inhabitants multiply, the demand for new land increases, while the supply gradually diminishes; and the country being at length wholly occupied and filled with inhabitants, new land can no longer be procured; so that while the population could still be doubled in fifteen years, their means of support can now only arise from the slow process of improved cultivation. It thus appears, that while the principle of population daily gathers new strength and new powers of increase, the facilities for supplying food are daily diminishing; and it seems quite certain, that if a country long settled and well peopled were to increase, for ever so short a period, with the rapidity of a new colony, it would be speedily brought back, by famine and disease, to the standard of its food. It farther appears, that when a country is wasted by disease new inhabitants quickly arise to repair the loss. The abundance of food and the scarcity of hands occasion both cheapness and high wages*. There is thus every encouragement to marriage; and accordingly we find, from the parish registers, that a period of great mortality is regularly followed by an unusual proportion of marriages. The births follow in due course; and thus the void occasioned by disease is speedily filled up.

* It is against this supposed evil that the 25th of Edward III. is directed. "Whereas," it commences, "late "against the malice of servants which were idle, and *not* "*willing to serve after the pestilence without taking excessive* "*wages;* it was ordained," &c.

A country wasted by disease is in the same condition as a new colony; there is a great supply of food and a limited supply of people; the principle of population is set free from its ordinary restraints; and inhabitants soon multiply, to consume the surplus subsistence of the country, and to fill up the measure of its population. The same principle is exemplified in some of the unhealthy villages of Holland, where, though the proportion of deaths is great, the inhabitants are not the fewer on this account. The loss is made up by a greater proportion of births; there is a quicker process both of renovation and of decay; and were the fact otherwise,—were the power of population insufficient to supply this waste, the human race would perish under the casualties to which it is exposed.

But if the population be thus kept up under a more than ordinary mortality, it is evident that a principle which acts so powerfully must be repressed where no such mortality prevails; where there is no such void to be filled up; and where, if the population increased at the same rate, it must be speedily reduced by famine and disease within its limited supply of food. In healthy and well peopled communities the want of subsistence is accordingly the great obstacle to any rapid increase of inhabitants, and it is by lowering the wages of labour that it operates on the great body of the community.

The wages of labour, though paid in money, really consist of the necessaries which money purchases. It is from this fund that labour is paid; and where there is no such fund there will be no great demand for labour, because there is no provision for its payment. In new colonies, the progress of cultivation is continually enlarging the funds for the support of labour. The necessaries of life are in abundance, the demand for labour is great, and there are ample funds for its payment. In such favourable circumstances population rapidly increases; the supply of labourers gains upon the demand, and wages decline. At length, however, the funds for the maintenance of labour become stationary; and as a limited supply of food can only support a limited number of people, it is clear that population must soon be checked and become stationary also. But population may be retarded either by calamities which occasion a positive loss of people, or by causes which prevent their increase; and the prevalence of the one or the other of these causes will determine the condition of the labourer. *First*, the inhabitants of a country may so increase in relation to subsistence, that numbers will be left unprovided for by the least failure of the ordinary supply. When this happens, famine and disease will bring the population within the limits of its food; and here of course wages will be low, and the labourer's condition miserable. *Secondly*, the natural dread of want, or the desire of comfort, may avert these consequences, by discouraging marriage, and thus preventing so great an increase of inhabitants. The effect of this principle, which regulates the proportion between population and subsistence, will of course depend on the general state of manners among the labourers themselves. Where the labourer is content, as in China, to propagate his race at the expence of every comfort, population will increase until poverty and wretchedness become the general condition of the labouring classes. But in a community of a different character, where the habits of the labourer are improved, he will not submit to marry and rear a supply of labour on such hard conditions; and in these circumstances population can never increase so far as to diminish the rate of wages below what is necessary to maintain him in comfort. The labourer may thus be said to have the fixing of his own wages, because when the supply of food is stationary, it will depend on himself at what point to stop the supply of people.

In a declining community where there is a continual decrease both of subsistence and of revenue, the labourer, whatever be his habits, will be in poverty, as the inhabitants will be rapidly reduced by famine and disease to the diminished supply of their food. Here his struggle will be vain even for bare necessaries; and his misery will continue, until the prevailing mortality has cleared the country of the population which it cannot support. But in a civilized community, such calamitous effects can be produced by nothing short of hostile violence or civil commotion.

Dr Smith observes, that the demand for labour necessarily increases with the revenue and stock of the society. " The increase of reve-
" nue and stock," he continues, " is the in-
" crease of national wealth. The demand for
" those who live by wages, therefore, naturally
" increases with the increase of national wealth,
" and cannot possibly increase without it."

Mr Malthus maintains that an increase of the national stock, unless where it partly consists of food, will not be followed by a rise of wages; because, while there is no increase of food, the labourer, though he may receive more money, will not by that means be enabled to procure more necessaries. The wealth of a society, he observes, may, according to Dr Smith's definition, increase, without having a proportional tendency to increase the comforts of the labouring part of it; and after adding, that the comforts of the poor must necessarily depend on the funds destined for their maintenance, he thus proceeds:—" The error " of Dr Smith lies in representing every in- " crease of the revenue or stock of a society, " as a proportional increase of these funds. " Such surplus stock or revenue will indeed " always be considered by the individual pos- " sessing it, as an additional fund from which " he may maintain more labour; but, with re- " gard to the whole country, it will not be an " effectual fund for the maintenance of an ad- " ditional number of labourers, unless part of " it be convertible into an additional quantity " of provisions; and it will not be so converti-

"ble where the increase has arisen merely
"from the produce of labour, and not from
"the produce of land. A distinction may in
"this case occur between the number of hands
"which the stock of the society could employ,
"and the number which its territory can main-
"tain.

"Dr Smith defines the wealth of a state to
"be the annual produce of its land and labour.
"This definition evidently includes manufac-
"tured produce as the produce of the land.
"Now, supposing a nation, for a course of
"years, to add what is saved from its yearly
"revenue to its manufacturing capital solely,
"and not to its capital employed upon land, it
"is evident that it might grow richer accord-
"ing to the above definition, without a power
"of supporting a greater number of labourers,
"and therefore without any increase in the real
"funds for the maintenance of labour. There
"would, notwithstanding, be a demand for la-
"bour, from the extension of manufacturing
"capital. This demand would of course raise
"the price of labour; but if the yearly stock
"of provisions in the country were not increas-
"ing, this rise would soon turn out to be merely

" nominal, as the price of provisions must neces-
" sarily rise with it *." Mr Malthus then states,
that by the improvements in manufacturing machinery which would take place, the annual
produce and the wealth of the country might,
according to the definition, be increasing, and
that not very slowly; and he farther adds,—
" The question is, How far wealth, increasing
" in this way, has a tendency to better the con-
" dition of the labouring poor? It is a self-
" evident proposition, that any general ad-
" vance in the price of labour, the stock of
" provisions remaining the same, can only be a
" nominal advance, as it may shortly be fol-
" lowed by a proportional rise in provisions.
" The increase in the price of labour, which we
" have supposed, would have no permanent ef-
" fect in giving to the labouring poor a greater
" command over the necessaries of life. In
" this respect they would be nearly in the same
" state as before †."

Mr Malthus here takes it for granted, that every addition to the labourer's wages will be employed in purchasing food. It is evident,

* Essay on Population, Vol. II. Book III. Chap. VII. p. 191.
† Ibid. p. 193.

however, that if his former wages were sufficient to supply him with abundance of food, the addition will be spent not in purchasing more, but in purchasing other necessaries and comforts. The demand for labour, occasioned by an increase of wealth, will therefore raise wages, not by giving the labourer more provisions which he does not want, but more money which will enable him to extend his enjoyments. An increase of food will indeed be required for the support of more people; but by means of higher wages the same number of people, with the same supply of food, will acquire a larger share of general comforts.

Reasoning upon the fallacy that every increase of wages will be spent in purchasing food, Mr Malthus assumes, that though a demand for labour, occasioned by an increase of trading capital, would raise its money price, the price of provisions would rise along with it; and that the additional money of the labourer would consequently bring him no real increase of enjoyments. But upon this principle, it is evident that wages might continue rising *ad infinitum*. It is not by money, but by what is purchased with money, that wages are really paid; and it is of no moment whether the money given to the labourer be denominated five, ten, or twenty shillings, provided these sums are all of the same value in the market. The labourer, therefore, when he found his increased wages attended with no real improvement of his condition, would demand a second rise on the same principle which enabled him to obtain the first; and thus the money price of labour would continue rising until stopped by a real rise of wages.

Every increase of capital, therefore, tends directly to raise wages, and indirectly to ameliorate the condition of the labourer by the general improvement of society. The progress of wealth gives rise to a more refined and luxurious consumption; and as the community advances in taste and opulence, the growing demand for luxuries naturally calls forth the exertions of skill and ingenuity in every branch of manufacture. A new class of workmen gradually arises, whose industry being more highly prized, is better rewarded than common labour; and thus, by employing the labourer in works of superior art and elegance, for which he receives higher wages, an increase of capital leads to a substantial improvement of his condition.

Mr Malthus proceeds to illustrate his doctrine by referring to the situation of China, as to which Dr Smith had remarked, that with different laws and institutions, and with greater attention to foreign commerce, the wealth of that country might be increased. " The ques-" tion is," as Mr Malthus suggests, " Would " such an increase of wealth be an increase of " the real funds for the maintenance of labour, " and consequently tend to place the lower " classes in China in a state of greater plenty?"

Upon this subject it is to be observed, that in China, owing to the redundant population, the market is always overstocked with common labourers, who are consequently reduced to bare necessaries; and to persons in their condition, it is evident that without an increase of food, no rise of wages will be attended with any benefit, nor in such circumstances, can any great demand for labour arise, because there are no funds for its payment. But with regard to the superior order of labourers who are employed in the finer manufactures, it is evident that their wages may be increased not by more food, which they do not want, but by comforts and luxuries, to which there is no limit.

" If trade and foreign commerce," Mr Malthus proceeds to observe, " were held in great

" honour in China, it is evident that, from the
" great number of labourers, and the cheapness
" of labour, she might work up manufactures
" for foreign sale to an immense amount. It is
" equally evident, that from the great bulk of
" provisions, and the amazing extent of her in-
" land territory, she could not, in return, import
" such a quantity as would be any sensible ad-
" dition to the annual stock of subsistence in
" the country. Her immense amount of manu-
" factures, therefore, she would exchange chief-
" ly for luxuries collected from all parts of the
" world. At present, it appears that no labour
" whatever is spared in the production of food.
" The country is rather overpeopled in propor-
" tion to what its stock can employ; and labour
" is therefore so abundant, that no pains are
" taken to abridge it. The consequence of this
" is, probably, the greatest production of food
" that the soil can possibly afford; for it will be
" generally observed, that processes for abridg-
" ing agricultural labour, though they may en-
" able a farmer to bring a certain quantity of
" grain cheaper to market*, tend rather to di-

---

* Mr Malthus has here fallen into the error of supposing, that because it costs less to produce corn, it will therefore be brought cheaper to market. In the observations On the

"minish than increase the whole produce. An
"immense capital could not be employed in
"China in preparing manufactures for foreign
"trade, without taking off so many labourers
"from agriculture as to alter this state of
"things, and in some degree to diminish the
"produce of the country. The demand for ma-
"nufacturing labourers would naturally raise
"the price of labour; but as the quantity of
"subsistence would not be increased, the price
"of provisions would keep pace with it, or even
"more than keep pace with it, if the quantity
"of provisions were daily decreasing. The
"country would, however, be evidently advan-
"cing in wealth; the exchangeable value of
"the annual produce of its land and labour
"would be annually augmented; yet the real
"funds for the maintenance of labour would
"be stationary, or even declining; and conse-
"quently the increasing wealth of the nation
"would tend rather to depress than to raise the
"condition of the poor. With regard to the
"command over the necessaries of life, they
"would be in the same, or rather worse state

Price of such Commodities as yield a Rent, I have endeavoured to shew, that though corn is produced cheaper, it will not therefore be sold cheaper.

" than before; and a great part of them would
" have exchanged the healthy labours of agri-
" culture for the unhealthy occupations of ma-
" nufacturing industry *."

Mr Malthus here supposes, for the sake of the argument which it affords, a case which can never happen, namely, a community improving in all the arts which minister to comfort and elegance, and neglecting agriculture, on which it must depend for subsistence. He supposes that, while a nation is rapidly accumulating commercial wealth, capital will be withdrawn from agriculture; whereas, it is obvious, that a proportion of the additional capital acquired by trade will be employed in the improvement of land; that an increase of produce will be the consequence; and that additional funds will thus be provided for the maintenance of labour. It is not easy to imagine, therefore, how, even in China, an increase of commercial wealth will tend to depress the condition of the poor?

Mr Malthus, whose general doctrine leads him to overrate agriculture at the expence of trade, observes, in comparing the progress of two countries, the one devoted to agriculture

* Essay on Population, Vol. II. Book III. Chap. VII. p. 203—205.

and the other to trade, that in the one " which
" had applied itself chiefly to agriculture, the
" poor would live in greater plenty, and popu-
" lation would rapidly increase; in that which
" had applied itself chiefly to commerce, the
" poor would be comparatively but little bene-
" fited, and consequently population would
" either be stationary or increase very slowly."
Take Poland for an example, whose surplus
subsistence does not support a native population, being exported for the manufactures of
richer countries. Labour is paid not merely
with food, but with lodging and clothing, a
supply of which is provided by trading capital.
An increase of food, therefore, without any increase of trading capital, is not of itself a fund for
the support of more labour; and Poland, without manufactures, is forced to export her surplus subsistence for the manufactures of other
countries. It is not food which is here wanting
for the maintenance of labour, but capital to
supply materials, and skill to set industry to
work; and were this want supplied, the surplus
subsistence of the country, which is now exported for the produce of other nations, would
be speedily absorbed by a rising generation of
its own industrious manufacturers. The ac-

count which Mr Malthus gives of an agricultural country, is thus contradicted by the fact; for we here find population with plenty of food kept back by the want of employment.

The wages of labour, it has already been remarked, consist not in money, but in what money purchases, namely, provisions and other necessaries; and the allowance of the labourer out of the common stock will always be in proportion to the supply. Where provisions are cheap and abundant, his share will be the larger; and where they are scarce and dear, it will be the less. His wages will always give him his just share, and they cannot give him more. It is an opinion indeed adopted by Dr Smith, and most other writers, that the money price of labour is regulated by the money price of provisions, and that when provisions rise in price, wages rise in proportion. But it is clear that the price of labour has no necessary connexion with the price of food, since it depends entirely on the supply of labourers compared with the demand. Besides, it is to be observed that the high price of provisions is a certain indication of a deficient supply, and arises in the natural course of things for the purpose of retarding the consumption. A smaller supply of food shared among the same number of consumers, will evidently leave a smaller portion to each, and the labourer must bear his share of the common want. To distribute this burden equally, and to prevent the labourer from consuming subsistence so freely as before, the price rises. But wages it seems must rise along with it, that he may still use the same quantity of a scarcer commodity; and thus nature is represented as counteracting her own purposes,—first raising the price of food to diminish the consumption, and afterwards raising wages to give the labourer the same supply as before.

The English poor laws have been justly found fault with, for giving money to the labourer in proportion to the price of corn. But do we not charge nature with a similar error, when we maintain that wages keep pace with the price of provisions; that when the price of provisions rises to curtail the consumption of the labourer, wages rise for the opposite purpose of still leaving him the same abundant supply? Every failure in the supply of food requires a diminished consumption; and consumption can only be diminished by a rise of price. It is the rise of price which measures out to the labourer his diminished allowance from a deficient crop; and a rise of wages could in that case only create an unavailing struggle for more provisions than the supply affords.

The great evil of the labourer's condition is poverty, arising either from a scarcity of food or of work; and in all countries, laws without number have been enacted for his relief. But there are miseries in the social state which legislation cannot relieve; and it is useful therefore to know its limits, that we may not, by aiming at what is impracticable, miss the good which is really in our power.

By the increase of population, without any increase of food, the same supply must be divided among a greater number of consumers, each of whom will of course have a smaller share; and the same effects must follow from a decrease of food without any decrease of people. In such cases the law has generally interfered, either to regulate wages, or to extort money from the rich to be divided among the poor. But the evil is a scarcity of food; and for this there is no sufficient remedy but an additional supply: Laws and donations of money are alike ineffectual, because it is not money, but food which is required. Though the wages of every labour-

er were doubled or tripled, this want would still remain, nor can any one class obtain relief from the general pressure except at the expence of another. Every society is, besides, chiefly composed of labourers, and as there is no other order of men to fill their place, it is by their privations alone that a deficient supply can be made to last as long as the produce of ordinary years. These views are illustrated by Mr Malthus with singular originality and clearness. " The price of labour," he observes, " when
" left to find its natural level, is a most impor-
" tant political barometer, expressing the rela-
" tion between the supply of provisions and
" the demand for them—between the quantity
" to be consumed and the number of consum-
" ers; and, taken on the average, independent-
" ly of accidental circumstances, it further ex-
" presses, clearly, the wants of the society re-
" specting population, that is, whatever may
" be the number of children to a marriage ne-
" cessary to maintain exactly the present po-
" pulation, the price of labour will be just suf-
" ficient to support this number, or be above
" it, or below it, according to the state of the
" real funds for the maintenance of labour,
" whether stationary, progressive, or retro-

" grade. Instead, however, of considering it
" in this light, we consider it as something
" which we may raise or depress at pleasure,
" something which depends principally on his
" Majesty's Justices of the Peace. When an
" advance in the price of provisions already
" expresses that the demand is too great for
" the supply, in order to put the labourer in
" the same condition as before, we raise the
" price of labour, that is, we increase the de-
" mand, and are then much surprised that the
" price of provisions continues rising. In this
" we act much in the same manner as if, when
" the quicksilver in the common weatherglass
" stood at *stormy*, we were to raise it by some
" forcible pressure to *settled fair*, and then be
" greatly astonished that it continued rain-
" ing *."

A general scarcity of work can only be remedied by increasing the funds for the support of industry; and no plan which has not this effect will in the least improve the labourer's condition. The employment of the poor in workhouses, which is the remedy provided by

* Essay on Population, Vol. II. Book III. Chap. V. p. 165, 166.

law, creates no new fund for the maintenance of labour. It merely diverts a portion of the old stock into a different channel. Even if there were no such establishments, the materials which are there worked up would set industry in motion, under the more careful inspection of the private manufacturer; and the effect of such projects is, not to increase the funds of industry, but to change their management—to take them from those who have an interest in faithfully administering them, and to place them under less careful overseers, where they may be abused or lost. This effect is clearly pointed out in an old treatise of Daniel De Foe, entitled, " Giving Alms no Charity," quoted by Mr Malthus and Sir F. Morton Eden, where it is observed, that for every skein of worsted spun in the workhouse, there must be a skein the less spun by some poor family that spun it before; and for every piece of bays made at London, there must be a piece the less made at Colchester, or somewhere else. This employment of the poor, he therefore adds, is " only transposing the manufacture " from Colchester to London, and taking the " bread out of the mouths of the poor of Essex,

" to put it into the mouths of the poor of Mid-
" dlesex*."

It is obvious that all such plans of general benevolence are inconsistent with the fixed order of human society. The calamities to which the labouring classes are exposed, arise from causes which legislation cannot controul; and no statesman therefore who knows the limits of his power will enter into schemes either for providing the labourer with work or for regulating his wages. In former times, however, the law seems to have been considered by the legislators of Europe as the efficient remedy for every grievance; and in place of leaving the labourer to depend on his own industry and prudence, they have generally endeavoured to fix his condition by arbitrary regulations.

In Scotland a legal provision was formerly established for the maintenance of the poor; but owing to the manners of the people, which attach disgrace to dependent poverty, the system has fallen into disuse, and the poor are now chiefly maintained by voluntary charity.

* See Extract from this performance, in Sir F. M. Eden's elaborate work on the Poor Laws, Vol. I. p. 261, 262.—See also Malthus on Population, Vol. II. Book III. Chap VI. p. 185.

In England the laws for the relief of the poor, in place of falling into disuse, have been carried far beyond the original plan. By the 43d of Queen Elizabeth, on which the present system is founded, the justices are required to set to work poor children, or those who are able to work and cannot find employment. They are also empowered to levy whatever assessment they may think necessary for the relief of the poor, and to judge who are fit objects of public charity. It is the opinion of Sir F. M. Eden, that this act of Queen Elizabeth had no relation to the able bodied labourer, but was only meant for the relief of those who either had not work, or who were unable to work. In later times, however, relief has been extended to all classes of labourers, and its amount has been regulated by the high price of provisions; although it is obvious that to add generally to the earnings of the labourer when wages are low, or when the price of provisions is high, is in effect the same thing as forcibly to raise wages, or to fix a maximum on the price of provisions.

According to these notions, we are informed by Sir F. M. Eden[*], that in 1795, the following

[*] Inquiry into the Poor Laws, Vol. I. p. 576.

plans were proposed in several counties: 1*st*, That in pursuance of the 5th of Elizabeth, the magistrates should either regulate the lowest rate of wages; or 2*dly*, That the money price of labour should be regulated by the necessities of the labourer; and that his earnings, where they were not sufficient for his maintenance, should be made up by a parish contribution. The second plan was adopted. A table was published for the direction of the magistrates and overseers, in which the wages of the labourer were computed according to the price of bread or the number of his family; and by this rule, a labourer with a family of seven children was allowed 25s. per week. During the scarcities of 1800 and 1801 this principle was generally acted upon; and Mr Malthus mentions, that he has known a labourer, whose earnings amounted to 11s. per week, receive 14s. from the parish. " Such instances," he observes, " could not pos-
" sibly have been universal, without raising the
" price of wheat very much higher than it was
" during any part of the dearth. But similar
" instances were by no means unfrequent; and
" the system itself of measuring the relief given
" by the price of grain was general." The result has been such as might have been expected.

The number of paupers, and the funds required for their maintenance, have rapidly increased, insomuch that, in the year 1801, the latter amounted to the enormous sum of ten millions, though formerly not exceeding three millions.

These facts fully prove the impolicy of the English poor laws, and indeed of any such extensive system for the maintenance of the poor. The enormous sums levied from the rich, and wasted in this ineffectual charity, form but a small evil in comparison of the general debasement of character to which it necessarily leads. The labourer being once taught the pernicious lesson of trusting to a public provision for his support, loses all the energy of honest independence, and in place of exhibiting the virtues of industry and prudence, his character degenerates into the opposite vices of idleness and mendicity. That the poor laws may mitigate cases of severe distress cannot well be questioned. But when it is considered that they necessarily require a system of harsh restraint—that they obstruct the free circulation of industry—that they are a constant source of tyranny, contention, and legal wrangling, and that they also give rise to alienation between the rich and the poor,—it may well be doubted whether the good which they produce is not far overbalanced by the evil which accompanies it. From the excellent remarks with which Bishop Burnet concludes his history, it appears that these considerations had not escaped that eminent writer. " It may be " thought," he observes, " a strange mo-" tion from a bishop, to wish that the act " for charging every parish to maintain their " own poor were well reviewed, if not taken " away; this seems to encourage idle and " lazy people in their sloth, when they know " they must be maintained. I know no other " place in the world where such a law was " ever made. Scotland is much the poor-" est part of the island; yet the poor there " are maintained by the voluntary charities " of the people. Holland is the perfectest " pattern for putting charity in a good me-" thod; the poor work as much as they can; " they are humble and industrious; they never " ask any charity, and yet they are all well re-" lieved."

Upon these and similar grounds, various plans have at different times been suggested for the gradual abolition of the poor laws, and some, looking chiefly to the pernicious effects of the system on the character of the labouring classes, have proposed as a remedy for the evil to establish schools, where the labourer may be instructed, and gradually so improved in his habits, as to be raised above the disgrace of receiving parish relief. But the radical error is, the maintenance of the poor at the public expence, which necessarily leads to dependence with all its degrading consequences; and as long as the exertions of industry are weakened by this assurance of public support, it is vain to expect any favourable change in the moral habits of the people.

Mr Malthus proposes a law for excluding from parish relief all lawful children born one year, and all illegitimate children born two years after its enactment. But this plan, however effectual for the gradual abolition of the poor laws, provides no remedy for the errors of their actual administration. These consist chiefly in extending to persons in health and strength the provisions of the original statute of Queen Elizabeth, which were intended only for the benefit of the sick and infirm, and in increasing the amount of the relief given in proportion to the high price of corn. The impolicy of such regulations has been already pointed out; and indeed it is sufficiently obvious, that any attempt to mitigate the calamity of a deficient supply of food by a rise in the money price of labour, can only aggravate the general distress. The necessary effect of such a deficiency is to throw a certain burden on the labourer, which no donations of money can possibly lessen; and with regard to those who are unable to work, as the object is merely to place them on a level with common labourers, the relief given should be measured not by the price of corn, but by the general rate of wages. If the poor laws were to be administered on this principle—if all sort of charity were, after due warning, to be denied to the common labourer who is able to work—and if in the recurrence of scarcity the practice of measuring out relief by the price of provisions were to be entirely forborn, the poor would be maintained in equal comfort at much less expence; and matters being thus regulated in the mean time, it might afterwards become a question whether, in place of any public provision for the relief of the poor, they should not be left, as in Scotland, to voluntary charity. Experience certainly proves the danger of abuse in all systems of public charity; and it is a question whether this can be sufficiently guarded against by any regulations, however careful. With respect to the quantum of relief given, it is clearly better to fall short than to exceed, as what is wanting in public may be supplied by private benevolence, while there is no remedy for excess.

But however necessary it may be from views of policy to limit public charity, no such rules apply to the benevolence of individuals; and Mr Malthus certainly carries his doctrines an unwarrantable length when he arraigns early marriages as immoral, and recommends that private benevolence should be sparingly administered to those who are burdened with a family which they cannot support *. To pity

* The following are the exceptionable passages here alluded to.

" After the public notice which I have proposed had been " given, and the system of poor laws had ceased with re- " gard to the rising generation, if any man chose to marry, " without a prospect of being able to support a family, he " should have the most perfect liberty so to do. Though " to marry, in this case, is in my opinion clearly an immo- " ral act, yet it is not one which society can justly take " upon itself to prevent or to punish; because the punish- " ment provided for it by the laws of nature falls directly " and most severely upon the individual who commits the " act, and through him, only more remotely and feebly on " the society. When nature will govern and punish for " us, it is a very miserable ambition to wish to snatch the

and relieve our suffering fellow-creatures, is one of the first social duties which nature teaches; and genuine benevolence extends its cares not to

" rod from her hands, and draw upon ourselves the odium
" of executioner. To the punishment therefore of nature
" he should be left,—the punishment of want. He has erred
" in the face of a clear and precise warning, and can have
" no just reason to complain of any person but himself,
" when he feels the consequences of his error. All parish
" assistance should be denied him; and if the hand of pri-
" vate charity be stretched forth in his relief, the interests
" of humanity imperiously require that it should be admi-
" nistered sparingly. He should be taught to know, that
" the laws of nature, which are the laws of God, had doom-
" ed him and his family to suffer for disobeying their re-
" peated admonitions; that he had no claim of *right* on so-
" ciety for the smallest portion of food beyond that which
" his labour would fairly purchase; and that if he and his
" family were saved from suffering the extremities of hun-
" ger, he would owe it to the pity of some kind benefac-
" tor, to whom therefore he ought to be bound by the
" strongest ties of gratitude." Essay on Population, Vol. II. p. 397—399.

" With regard to illegitimate children, after the proper
" notice had been given, they should not be allowed to
" have any claim to parish assistance, but be left entirely
" to the support of private charity. If the parents desert
" their child, they ought to be made answerable for the
" crime. The infant is, comparatively speaking, of little
" value to the society, as others will immediately supply
" its place. Its principal value is on account of its
" being the object of one of the most delightful passions
" in human nature—parental affection. But if this value
" be disregarded by those who are alone in a capacity to
" feel it, the society cannot be called upon to put itself
" in their place; and has no further business in its protec-

those only who have fallen into distress from no fault of their own, but to those also who have no plea to offer but that of actual wretchedness. It is scarcely necessary to add, that the charity of individuals is voluntary and precarious; that it affords no certain ground of dependence; and that it cannot therefore lead to the abuses which seem to be inseparable from a legal provision for the poor.

" tion, than to punish the crime of desertion or intentional ill treatment in the persons whose duty it is to provide for it.

" At present, the child is taken under the protection of the parish, and generally dies, at least in London, within the first year. The loss to the society is the same; but the crime is diluted by the number of people concerned, and the death passes as a visitation of Providence, instead of being considered as the necessary consequence of the conduct of its parents, for which they ought to be held responsible to God and to society." Ibid. p. 399, 400.

ON STOCK.

It is by means of its stock or capital that a country is supplied with the necessaries and luxuries which it consumes; and the extent of this capital is regulated by the consumption for which it has to provide. Every increase of consumption not only checks the farther accummulation of capital, but it adds to the employment of what is already accumulated. A rich nation not only consumes annually more capital than its poorer neighbours, but a greater capital is necessary to provide for its greater consumption.

The expenditure of a nation, to which its capital is always proportioned, naturally increases with its revenue, and it cannot permanently increase otherwise. An increase of revenue must either be saved, in which case it will be so much added to the supply of capital, or it must be spent; and this increased expenditure adding to the business which capital has to perform, will increase the demand for it. The saving of revenue thus increases the supply of capital, while the spending of it increases the demand; and in this way, the increasing revenue of a country may be partly saved and partly spent, in such equal portions, that the revenue saved may form a capital just sufficient to provide for the revenue spent. At first, though a small capital would sufficiently provide for the expenditure of a country, it cannot be procured; capital is scarce, and the high rate of profit is a standing inducement to its accumulation. Revenue is accordingly very rapidly converted into capital, and the supply gains upon the demand. The increase of capital soon reduces profit; there is less encouragement to parsimony; and those who in other circumstances would have added to their capital, will now by spending their revenue gratify their desire of enjoyment. Accumulation and expenditure, thus keeping pace with each other, may increase to any extent; because every increase of revenue may be partly saved and partly spent, and may thus add equally to the demand for capital as well as to the supply. In this way there is no limiting the increase of capital, as it may be employed to any amount in supplying the endless wants of luxury and taste.

The accumulation of stock is treated of at some length in the fifth volume of the Edinburgh Review; and the writer, after dwelling on the bad effects of its excessive increase, observes, that war, aside from its other mischiefs, is so far beneficial as it tends to repress this growing evil. But if the reviewer had been aware, that every increase of capital naturally finds employment in providing for the growing expenditure to which it leads, he would have seen that his alarm was altogether visionary. After remarking that the stock of Great Britain would probably have been doubled, if it had never been dissipated by war, he asks, where in that case it could have been invested with profit, since it is even difficult to find employment for our actual capital? This question has already been answered in the course of the preceding observations. The additional capital would, it is clear, have been partly saved and partly spent, and would thus have created employment for itself. What was saved would have been employed in providing consumable articles to meet the demand occasioned by what was spent. This increase of wealth would indeed have diminished the rate of profit; but by increasing the demand for all the finer manufactures, and for the ingenious industry by which they are furnished *, it would have raised wages; and to the labouring classes, therefore, who make the chief part of every community, it would have been eminently beneficial.

But though the capital of a country must always bear a certain relation to its expenditure, the same capital will provide for a larger expenditure where profit is high than where it is low. Capital and profit form two component parts in the price of all commodities, neither of which can be increased without diminishing the other. A capital of L.10,000, yielding a profit of 10 per cent., will provide for an expenditure of L.11,000; and if this capital be increased without any increase of expenditure, the consequence must be a diminution of profit, to the precise amount of the additional capital; because otherwise this capital cannot find employment. A larger capital than

* See observations On the Wages of Labour.

L.10,000, with a profit of 10 per cent. can never be employed in providing for an expenditure of L.11,000.

An increase of capital without any increase of expenditure, may be compared to an increase of currency without any corresponding increase in the demands of trade—the addition to capital causing a loss of profit, and the addition to currency a loss of value. A currency which amounts, we may suppose, to fifty millions, will lose exactly one half of its value by being suddenly doubled without any previous increase of trade; and in like manner, rating the profit of a country at ten millions, it must be reduced one half, by an addition to its capital of five millions, which, unless there has been some previous increase of expenditure, cannot be employed without a corresponding diminution of profit.

ON THE PRICE OF GOLD AND SILVER SINCE THE YEAR 1773.

Corn, from the steadiness of its own value, is employed by Dr Smith as a general standard for measuring the value of other things; and when its price rises, or when more gold or silver is given for it, he infers, not that the value of corn has increased, but that the value of gold and silver has fallen. Reasoning on this principle, Dr Smith is of opinion, that the precious metals, since their great depression by the discovery of the American mines, have been gradually rising in value, and that they were still rising in the year 1773, when his work was published. Since that time, however, if we are to judge by the prices of corn and of all other commodities, the value of the precious metals has been rapidly declining; and this fall in their value seems to have commenced about the middle of the last century; for we find that the quarter of wheat, which previous to the year 1745 was occasionally under 30s., was never afterwards at so low a price. It was in like manner never under 40s. after the year 1786; after the year 1793 it was never under 50s.; and after the year 1804 it was never under 60s. Its price has since risen still higher. But this rise of price seems to be owing rather to a fall in the value of the currency with which corn is purchased, than to any rise in the value of the corn. Since the Bank of England was freed from its obligation to pay in specie, its currency has been issued in excess*, and its value has fallen in proportion. The depreciation of Bank of England paper commenced about the year 1798, and has since greatly increased. In the British mint a pound of gold being coined into $44\frac{1}{2}$ guineas, should never bring a higher price in the market; and an ounce should therefore cost L.3. 17s. $10\frac{1}{2}$d. At this price, accordingly, it has always been and may be purchased with gold coin; but since the year 1798, its price in Bank of England notes has been considerably higher, having varied during the four following years, from

* See observations On Paper Currency.

L.4. 2s. to L.4. 10s. per ounce, and having in each year successively exceeded the price in gold coin by 11, 16, 10, and 8 per cent. Until the end of the year 1808 this evil seems to have made no farther progress; but at that time gold rose rapidly in its price, from L.4. to L.4. 9s. and L.4. 12s. per ounce, and continued rising throughout the year 1813, until it amounted to L.5. 10s. per ounce; which being an excess of about 40 per cent. beyond its price in gold coin, leaves the difference to be accounted for by the depreciation of the paper. The same nominal sum in gold coin was therefore 40 per cent. more valuable than the same nominal sum in paper; and consequently to ascertain the price of corn in gold and silver, 40 per cent. must be deducted from its price in paper.

The price of wheat in 1813 fell after the harvest to 85s. per quarter, which, deducting 40 per cent. for the depreciation of the paper, leaves the price so low as 51s. But the harvest of 1813 was abundant, and corn was unusually cheap. The average price during the previous year, *i. e.* before the harvest of 1813, was about 120s.; and making an allowance of about 33 per cent. for the depreciation of the currency, the price of gold being throughout that year about L.5. 6s. per ounce, the result shews the real price of corn to have been 80s. Taking the average of these two years, the one a year of dearth and the other of cheapness, the price of wheat in gold turns out to be 65s. 6d. per quarter, which is moderate, and is only 3s. higher than the average price for ten years previous to the year 1800*. For several years past, therefore, if we are to judge from the prices of corn, no material fall appears to have taken place in the value of gold and silver.

There can be no doubt, however, that since the year 1773 the value both of gold and silver has greatly declined; and the great increase of paper currency, setting aside its depreciation, very sufficiently accounts for the fact. It is principally for the purposes of commercial exchange that the precious metals are so much prized. But if in this capacity they are superseded by paper, they will be in less request, and will of course be less valuable. The invention of paper currency has the same effect as the discovery of a new and very productive mine; as currency is by this means supplied at little

---

* For the average prices of corn till the year 1813, see Vol. I. p. 423, &c.

expence and to any amount, leaving a greater stock of the precious metals for other purposes. In the year 1774, when a new coinage of gold was last issued in this country, it is stated by Lord Liverpool, that twenty-one millions of guineas were brought to the mint for recoinage, besides about six millions more estimated to be left in circulation. But it is not probable that there are now in circulation more than four or five millions; and the balance being thrown into the market of the world, must thus have tended generally to reduce the value of the precious metals. In the currency of Britain gold coin preponderates; but in most other currencies silver is the prevailing coin. If paper currency were therefore to become as common in other parts of the world as it is in Britain, a large quantity of silver would be thrown out of employment, and its value must of course fall proportionally.

The supply of the precious metals also from the American mines has, for the last 80 years, been greatly increasing. From about the year 1770, more especially, Spanish America has been rapidly advancing both in its trade and population; and the business of mining has been carried on with increased activity. The produce has been in proportion *. According to accounts inserted in the Mercurio Peruano†, a periodical journal published at Lima, containing much curious and accurate information respecting the state of the country, the annual coinage of Mexico, which is nearly equal to the produce of its mines, as very little bullion is exported, amounted, on an average of ten years, from 1762 to 1773, in silver, to 12,303,753 dollars, and in gold to 770,742 dollars, altogether to 13,074,495 dollars. On an average of ten years, from 1782 to 1793, it amounted in silver to 19,491,309 dollars, and in gold to 644,040 dollars, altogether to 20,135,349. In the year 1790, also 1½ million of dollars was remitted in bullion to Spain. In 1793, it amounted to 24,312,942 dollars; and on an average of ten years, from 1794 to 1805, it amounted in silver to 21,084,787 dollars. The produce of the Brazilian mines has for the last 60 years greatly decreased; but in general it is clear that, while the precious metals have been partly superseded

* For an account of the increasing produce of the Mexican mines since the year 1733, see Appendix, Note (B.)

† See Appendix to the Report of the Committee on the High Price of Bullion, p. 175.

by paper as an instrument of commercial exchange, the average supply throughout the world has been rapidly increasing; and this sufficiently accounts for the fall which has taken place in their value.

This great increase of the supply and consequent fall of price, will in time give rise to a quicker consumption both of gold and silver, which will gradually stop the progress of their declining value; and from the prices of corn for the last ten years, as already stated, it seems probable that this effect has either already begun, or is very nearly about beginning to take place.

ON PAPER CURRENCY.

The value of coin depends on its intrinsic worth; while the value of a paper currency depends on the promise which it bears to pay a certain quantity of coin. It is on the faith of this promise that it circulates, and without the promise it would be of no more value than waste paper. The gold or the silver, therefore, for which a bank note is a promise, should be the exact measure of its value. A promise for an ounce of gold should be exactly worth an ounce of gold, and its value should rise in proportion to the gold for which it is a promise. A rise or fall in the value of the gold should always be followed by a corresponding rise or fall in the value of the note. The gold, which is the thing promised, is the standard of value, from which the value of the promise ought never to vary.

The value of a paper currency will, however, vary from its standard, by reason either of discredit or of excess. Where the security is defective, the value will fluctuate with the risk of ultimate loss, which may at length be such as entirely to stop its circulation; and in like manner, where paper is increased without any increase in the business which it has to perform, it will experience a proportional loss of value. If we suppose the payments of a country perfectly well managed with 50,000 guineas, and its business suddenly doubled without any addition to its currency, it is quite clear that there will be a great want of money to carry on its trade; and this want can be supplied in no other way than by a rise in the value of the guineas. As a guinea will have double work to perform, its value must be doubled before the demand of the country for currency can be supplied; and the 50,000 guineas, therefore, will rise in their value until they bear the same relation as formerly to the business which they have to perform, *i. e.* until their value be doubled. In the same manner, if we suppose 50,000 guineas suddenly added to the currency of a country without any increase of its trade, in what manner can they be employed while they retain their value ? If a currency of 50,000 guineas was formerly sufficient for all its payments, there will be obviously no room for 100,000. It is quite certain, however, that it will not remain useless in the hands of those who have possession of it, but will circulate, and in making its way into circulation, it must lose precisely one half of its value ; so that in this instance the 100,000 guineas will be worth no more than the 50,000 in the other. In both cases the value of the currency will depend on the business which it has to perform. The value of a paper currency is regulated by the same principles ; and when it is multiplied beyond the demands of trade, the excess will occasion a fall of value.

A paper currency convertible into specie at the will of the holder, cannot suffer any loss of value either from discredit or excess, because the security may always be brought to the test by a demand of payment, and because, in case of an over-issue, the excess will be returned upon the bank for specie. A one pound note, for example, or a promise to pay one pound, will never be exchanged for less than its value in specie, so long as the original obligation to pay on demand remains in force. On the first appearance of its declining value, the bank will be called upon for the performance of its promise; its notes will be returned in exchange for specie, until by a diminution of their quantity they are restored to their former value. If the bank persists in re-issuing its returned notes, it will be exposed to a continual drain of specie, so long as there remains any excess of paper to encumber the circulation.

Where a bank is not obliged to pay in specie, the whole currency is regulated by the discretion of its managers; and where an over-issue is the consequence there is no remedy; because the bank, which has the power of refusing specie, is closed against any return of its superfluous and depreciated notes. But it is possible that a bank may not abuse such extensive powers; that it may still regulate its issues by the demands of trade; and that reserving its privilege of refusing specie for a case of extreme pressure, it may pay cash for such of its notes as are returned in the ordinary course of business; in which case, if there be no suspicion of its credit, there will be no depreciation of its paper. The immediate convertibility of paper into specie is not, therefore, absolutely essential to its value. It affords indeed the best security against excessive issue, one sure cause of depreciation. But where paper has the security of ample funds, and is not issued in excess, it will still retain its value, though convertible into specie only at the discretion of the bank.

Paper being provided at little expence, gradually increases in the circulation of a country to the exclusion of specie, which is at length stored up by the bankers for answering their occasional demands. In the currency of this country specie has been almost entirely superseded by paper, the circulation of which seems greatly to have increased during that short interval of peace which followed the American war; and about this period, accordingly, banks were established in all parts of the country.

There are now in London, besides the Bank of England, 75 private banking houses, and 803 in other parts of the country *. The currency of London consists of Bank of England notes; but in the country each bank supplies the cir-

* According to an account laid before Parliament, the number of licences granted in 1812 for the issue of promissory notes, amounted in England to 825 (of which 66 were for new banks); and in Scotland to 53. There are in London 75 banks; and there remain of course for the country 803.

culation of a certain district. The chief business of those bankers is to manage the money dealing of distant places, and to issue their notes for the accommodation of trade by discounting bills of exchange; and their whole management is calculated to promote the dispatch of business, and the economy of cash. The nature of their arrangements for this purpose may be shortly explained.

When merchants reside in the same town, their cash transactions may be managed without the assistance of a banker; but when they reside in distant places, they cannot make payments without remitting cash, and each separate transaction requires a separate remittance. To avoid those payments in detail, the business is transferred to a particular class of dealers, who bring the whole of those transactions to a common balance, for which one general remittance is sufficient; and in this way the extensive dealings of trading towns will be settled with a comparatively small remittance of cash. Thus the exports of Edinburgh to London, amounting annually, we may suppose, to L.1,000,000, and its imports to L.1,010,000, are, by the agency of the bankers, brought to a general balance; and it is only for the small surplus of L.10,000 that Edinburgh has to remit cash. In the event of the exports and imports being more equally balanced, even this small quantity of specie may be sill farther diminished.

But when the transactions of trading towns lead to no intercourse between their respective money-dealers, their mutual payments will be made through the medium of some third place, by drawing on which, their occasional balances being transferred to a more general fund of debt and credit, will ultimately be brought to a common balance. The transactions of Edinburgh and Bristol, for example, occasion no regular money dealing between the two places; and were the former, therefore, indebted to the latter, the balance would be discharged, not by a remittance in cash, but by a draft on London, which would thus come in place of Bristol as the creditor of Edinburgh, the debt being transferred to the general cash account of those two places. But Edinburgh may be the creditor of other towns, as well as the debtor; and London being credited with the money to be received, as it was formerly charged with the money to be paid, the two sums may be nearly equal; in which case the general balance bearing no proportion to the mass of the account, the most extensive money dealings between distant places may be settled with a very small remittance of specie. The scattered balances arising on the transactions of the country will thus be collected into new accounts by the bankers of the wealthy and populous towns, in which it is found convenient to settle the money dealings of the neighbourhood; and the metropolis, the centre of intercourse and trade, will grow up to be the centre also of this great system, where the respective debts and credits of the inferior towns, which cannot be settled otherwise, will be brought to a final balance.

It is thus that, by the improvements of the bankers, the money dealing of this country in so far as it cannot be settled without remitting specie, is transferred to London, which, from its extensive commerce with the country, has its debtors and creditors in all parts, and on which bills invariably sell for a premium, as the balance of trade is generally in its favour. All the other currencies of which the circulation is composed, being limited to certain districts, are unfit to serve as a common medium of payment between distant places. But money in

London is in universal request; and bills for its payment form a species of currency common to the whole island.

All money dealers require a provision of this common currency to carry on their business; and for this purpose they procure a credit on the metropolis, on which they sell drafts at all times. In this manner both the expence and trouble of settling the cash transactions of distant places has been greatly diminished. In the year 1780 it was stated in evidence, before a Committee of the House of Commons, by several of the collectors of the public revenue, that for about forty years before this period the premium on London bills had varied from 2s. 6d. to 20s. per cent. in proportion to the distance from London. In 1764 a premium of 7s. 6d. per cent. was paid on money remitted from Wales. In 1774 the public revenue was remitted from Dorsetshire to London, by bills payable at forty days, and procured for a premium of 2s. 6d. per cent. Nor was there any channel through which those remittances could be regularly made; so that the collectors were under the necessity of procuring drafts on London, on the best terms they could, from such manufacturers or merchants as had dealings with the metropolis. In the progress of commerce and of money dealing, the premium on London bills was gradually diminished, and it was altogether abolished in the year 1778, the term of payment being shortened at the same time *.

The cash transactions of the country, which are transferred to London, are finally settled by the London bankers, with specie or with the notes of the Bank of England, it being agreed to use no other currency in the payments of the metropolis; and the economy with which they use both bank notes and specie is apparent from their arrangements for this purpose. A clerk, it appears, is dispatched at an appointed hour in the afternoon, from every banking house in London; and a meeting of the whole having taken place in a room provided for the purpose, the day's transactions are collected into one general account, which being finally settled, it is only for the several balances then remaining due that cash is required; for which purpose a much smaller quan-

* The evidence of those collectors, as far as it respects the remitting of money from the country to London, will be found at length in the Appendix, Note (C.)

tity will obviously be sufficient than if all those transactions were settled in detail. Thus, if we suppose A to be debtor for L. 30,000, and creditor for L. 35,000, his claims being transferred in extinction of his debts, cash will only be required for the small balance still remaining due of L. 5000 ; and the same process being repeated with each individual, all those transactions will be finally settled *.

From the preceding remarks, the advantages of paper, as a medium of exchange, are sufficiently obvious; but it must be observed, that it is by no means so safe an instrument for this purpose as specie, because it depends wholly on credit, the failure of which must be followed by a general derangement of trade. It is chiefly by discounting bills of exchange that paper is circulated; and the merchant who receives cash for his bills, enlarging his dealings in proportion, gradually becomes dependent on the banks for money to carry on his business, while the banks in their turn depend on the public confidence for the circulation of their notes. The banker provides a cheap instrument of exchange in place of a more expensive one, and as his profit consists

* Thornton on Paper Credit, p. 55.

in lending it on the same terms, he is naturally induced to increase the circulation of his paper, and on the faith of his credit, to diminish the specie reserved for its payment. While general confidence prevails, no evil will result from this complicated system of credit; bank notes will circulate freely; there will be no great demand for specie; and the bills of the merchant will be readily convertible into cash. But when confidence fails, the banks are exposed, by the necessary discredit of their paper, to continual demands for specie. To avoid this pressure, they diminish the circulation of their notes; while the merchant, no longer receiving the same accommodation as before, is left without the means of maintaining his credit, and is thus involved in the greatest possible embarrassment. The demand for specie in the country gradually centers in the metropolis, the bankers converting into cash the property which they usually hold in the public funds and other government securities, and repairing to the Bank of England for the specie which they require. Embarrassed by the increasing drain of its cash, the bank reduces the circulation of its paper; the transactions of the metropolis, hitherto managed with the smallest possible quantity of currency, are in consequence deranged; and the disorder thence arising in the centre, quickly extends to the remotest parts of this great system of money dealing. In the mutual dependence created by credit and confidence, every merchant involves others in his fate; the contagion of bankruptcy spreads, and in the general commotion the greatest mercantile establishments may be overthrown.

All those consequences were fatally exhibited in this country during the mercantile alarm which prevailed in the year 1792. The scarcity of cash and the discredit of paper occasioned numerous bankruptcies, as well as a general demand for specie, which the Bank of England was ultimately called on to supply. As this demand proceeded from the alarm by which the paper was discredited, it was obvious that while the alarm lasted, specie to any amount might be drawn from the bank by the most limited circulation of its notes, continually issued, and continually returned; and it was therefore the evident policy of the bank to increase the issue of its paper, for the purpose of restoring mercantile confidence, by which alone the demand for specie could have been checked.

But in place of assisting trade, either by an increased issue of its paper, or by any other means, the bank refused to accommodate such of the country banks as applied for assistance; and in these circumstances Parliament interposed for the relief of such merchants as were in want of cash, offering to lend, on proper security, exchequer bills to the amount, if required, of L. 5,000,000. Of this sum applications were made for L. 3,855,624, great part of which being either rejected or withdrawn, the sum finally granted amounted to L. 2,202,000; which was repaid, a considerable part before it was due, and the remainder at stated periods, without apparent difficulty or distress.

This seasonable measure soon restored mercantile confidence, which experienced no farther interruption until the year 1795, when the directors of the Bank of England having in the course of that year made large advances to government, found it necessary to diminish the sum allotted for the accommodation of trade. The transactions of the metropolis were in consequence deranged, and the menace of invasion continually held out by the enemy during the year 1796, diffused a general panic, which was quickly followed by the discredit of bank notes, and a demand for specie.

In the north of England several banks were under the necessity of suspending their cash payments, and the effect of these failures rapidly extended to the metropolis; in consequence of which, about the commencement of the year 1797, the Bank of England experienced an alarming demand for specie, occasioned at first by the efforts of the country banks to support their declining credit, but afterwards by the return of its own discredited notes. Before this period the directors had frequently stated to the Chancellor of the Exchequer how much the bank was embarrassed by the drain of its specie; but being now seriously alarmed, they communicated to him, on Tuesday the 21st of February, the precise reduction which had taken place in its cash, in order that he might the more freely devise the measures which so difficult a crisis required. During the remainder of the week demands continued to accumulate with such rapidity that, though the loss of specie for the first four days had been immense, it was exceeded by that of the two subsequent days, and to the last hour the demand continued increasing at this accelerated rate *. The necessity of relieving the bank from this ruinous drain of specie was now obvious ; and on Sunday, the directors having by appointment met the Chancellor of the Exchequer and the other ministers, an order in council was issued, prohibiting all farther payments in specie.

But though the difficulties of the bank thus originated in the alarm and the demand for specie at home, they were undoubtedly increased by the great foreign expenditure of the country occasioned by the war. The foreign expences of a nation may be provided for by an exportation either of specie or of goods; and where time is allowed for some previous arrangement, such transactions should not necessarily disorder either its currency or its trade. A rich country abounding in the various produce of land and labour, affords a supply of goods for every market ; and in whatever part of the world funds are required, the demand may be speedily answered by an exportation of

* See Appendix, Note [D.] Extracts from the Minutes of the Secret Committee of the House of Lords, appointed to inquire into the Affairs of the Bank in 1797 ; containing the Evidence of Mr Raikes, Governor, and Mr Giles, Deputy-governor of the Bank.

its produce. We find that the great expenditure of this country in Germany, on account of the war which commenced in 1793, was speedily discharged by a suitable exportation of goods, the exports to that country which had in the previous years of peace amounted only to L.1,900,000, suddenly rising to L.8,000,000 *.

Where commodities cannot be found for the entire discharge of those foreign expences, a trading country may easily provide, from its general intercourse with the world, bills or specie for any outstanding claims; and the inconvenience, which amounts merely to an unfavourable balance of trade, should never exceed a temporary depression of the exchange. In the trade of Europe to India specie is regularly exported; and neither the collecting nor the exporting of this treasure is ever found to disturb the domestic transactions of the country. In the several years of 1790, 1791, and 1792†, when there was no war expenditure abroad, specie was exported from this country to the

* See Report of Lords' Committee, p. 143.

† For an account of the specie exported from this country between the years 1790 and 1796 inclusive, see Note [E.]

amount of L.1,571,364, L.1,338,742, and L.2,250,121,*; and in the year 1795, the imperial loan, amounting, after deduction of interest and other charges, to L.4,000,000, was remitted to Germany by a mercantile house in London, partly in bills on different trading countries, and partly in bullion, without even materially affecting the course of exchange. Mr Boyd, to whose house this great remittance was intrusted, specifies in his evidence before the Secret Committee of the House of Lords the mode in which the business was managed. It was necessary, it appears, frequently to change the mode of remittance, and for this purpose, to watch the varying exchanges of Europe, for the favourable moment of remitting through those different channels. Bills direct on Hamburgh were occasionally sent; at other times it was found expedient to remit by bills on other places, such as Madrid, Cadiz, Leghorn, Lisbon, Genoa, &c.; and bullion to the amount of L.1,200,000 was employed. " It " was not by forcing," Mr Boyd observes, in

* A great proportion of the specie thus exported, went to Holland and France, probably for the purpose of supplying in the latter country the want of currency, occasioned by the discredit of the assignats.

his very instructive evidence before the Committee, " any of the means of remittance be-
" yond what it could well bear, that we had
" the satisfaction of completing so unparalleled
" a remittance with so very small a variation in
" the course of the exchange*." In the war of 1763 also, the expenditure of Britain on the continent of Europe amounted, within a period of seven years, to twenty millions, and funds for its final discharge, whether specie or goods, seem to have been collected and sent abroad without occasioning any inconvenience at home †.

A public bank may, however, be exposed by an unusually large and urgent demand for money abroad, to an inconvenient drain of its specie, as the high premium on foreign money, by encouraging the exportation, raises the value of specie, which it becomes profitable in that case to draw from the bank by a return of its notes. On this principle we may account for the drain of specie to which the Bank of England was exposed from about the year 1793 to 1797. According to accounts laid before Parliament, the

* See Report of the Lords' Committee of Secrecy, Minutes of Evidence, p. 64. † Ibid, p. 104.

foreign expenditure of Britain amounted, during this period, in subsidies paid to foreign powers, and in the expence of maintaining troops on the continent of Europe or in the West Indies, to L.33,510,779 *. The only safe mode of providing for those enormous demands from abroad, would have been by previous remittances from home, as the time and the mode of remitting might then, as in the case of the imperial loan, have been selected with all due care. But they were chiefly provided for by drafts from abroad, on the treasury and other public offices, which were generally made payable at the bank. On the treasury alone the foreign drafts amounted to L.13,582,844; and those demands, in place of being provided for beforehand, were frequently so little expected, that Mr Pitt, after stating to the bank directors that they could not last longer than two months, was alarmed by the sudden appearance of bills from St Domingo to the amount of L.700,000 †. By thus drawing from abroad, therefore, all discretion both as to the time and the mode of

* For an account of those remittances and drafts, see Appendix, Note [F].
† See Report of Lords' Committee of Secrecy, p. 92.

payment was necessarily lost. The bank or the government were bound to pay cash by a certain day; while to those who received the cash, the subsequent and important business of remitting was altogether left. Those bills seem to have been finally paid, partly with goods, and partly by clandestine exportations of specie, a great proportion of which would naturally be drawn from the bank by a return of the notes in which the bills were originally payable. And accordingly during the whole period of this foreign expenditure, the bank experienced demands for specie to a considerable amount.

But though a great expenditure abroad will always occasion some demand for specie at home, it was chiefly by involving the bank in large advances to government, and by thus diverting its funds from the support of trade, that the foreign expenditure of this country proved indirectly so injurious to its credit. In the year 1796, the bank notes circulating in the metropolis amounted to between 10 and 11 millions. They were gradually reduced as the bank became involved with government; and in 1797, previous to the suspension of its cash payments, they amounted only to L.8,640,250. So sudden a reduction of its circulating cash must at any time have created an alarm and a demand for specie in the metropolis; and we find, accordingly, from the previous history of the bank, that a drain of specie has always been occasioned by a diminution of its notes. In March 1782, for example, the circulation of the bank amounted to L.9,160,470; in March 1783, to L.7,338,230; and in October it was reduced to L.5,894,520. From April to October 1783, the bank accordingly experienced a great loss of specie, insomuch that its cash was considerably lower than in 1797, previous to the suspension of its payments, and the alarm of invasion was only wanting to produce a similar result. The directors were so alarmed that they refused to accommodate government with the usual advances on the loan of that year. But the advances to government were only prejudicial as they encroached on the ordinary accommodation of trade; and unless this reserve of the bank to the government had therefore produced an increase of liberality to the merchant, it could be of no use. In 1784 the bank was relieved from the drain of its cash, by the improvement of credit, the natural effect of the recently concluded peace*.

The directors of the bank, for about two years previous to the suspension of its payments, were alarmed by the unprecedented accumulation of demands from abroad, and frequently stated to Mr Pitt their apprehensions of the result, insisting at the same time that some part at least of their advances on treasury bills and other securities should be immediately repaid. On the 11th of February 1796, about a year before the bank suspended its cash payments, they even went the length of formally recording it as their opinion, founded, as they stated, on the experience of the effects of the last imperial loan, that any farther loan or advance to the emperor of Germany or any foreign state would be fatal to the bank. Notwithstanding this resolution, advances were made to the emperor in the course of the year 1796, and of the two first months of 1797, to the amount of L. 1,420,000. But so limited a remittance, even though it had consisted wholly of bullion, could hardly have occasioned such an alarming

* See Appendix, Note (G.) Evidence of Mr Bonsanquet before the Lords' Committee of Secrecy.

demand for specie; and it is besides clear, upon other grounds, that the bank was exposed to no serious danger until its notes were discredited by the alarm at home; for it appears from the concurring evidence of all those concerned in the management of its affairs, that the drain of specie from abroad had lasted for two years without injuring its credit, while the suspension of its cash payments was the consequence of a single week or little more of domestic alarm; nor was it so much the actual drain of its specie, (its cash having been lower both during the American war and in the year 1782) as the rapidity with which the drain increased, that clearly denoted the nature of the impending danger*. The resolution adopted therefore by the directors in February 1796, appears to have been the result of undue apprehension; for if the pressure, arising from domestic alarm, could by any means have been removed, the credit of the bank would certainly have survived all the other casualties either of commerce or of war.

(*) See Appendix, Note (D.) Evidence delivered before the Secret Committee of the House of Lords, by Mr Giles, Governor, Mr Raikes, Deputy-Governor of the Bank, and Mr Pitt, then Chancellor of the Exchequer.

The year 1810 was remarkable for numerous bankruptcies, as well as for a general failure of confidence and a scarcity of cash, which it was proposed to relieve, as in 1792, by an issue of exchequer bills. But the mercantile distress of 1810 was entirely different from that which occurred in 1792, inasmuch as it arose from the more substantial evil of an almost ruined trade. The commerce of the world experienced about this period such an interruption from the hostility of the belligerent powers of Europe, that the surplus produce of trading countries was either confined to the place of its production, or left to reach its destination by the uncertain channel of a contraband trade. The merchants of this country being in consequence oppressed by a load of unsaleable goods, were in many cases ruined, and manufacturers were thrown out of employment. The evil was not merely a scarcity of cash, but a depreciation of stock, and a stagnation of trade, which could be in no respect relieved by the temporary accommodation of exchequer bills. As a scarcity of cash, however, never fails to aggravate every case of mercantile distress, it was of some consequence that the merchant of real property should know where to find money for his immediate demands; and in this view the proposed accommodation might certainly have proved beneficial.

It may be remarked in general, that where paper circulates, commercial confidence, which is its great support, will occasionally be carried to excess; for however anxiously the banker may discourage rash speculation, his confidence will still be abused, by the well known device of accommodation bills. This evil is inseparable from the circulation of paper, and its correction must be entirely left to the vigilance of those who are exposed to its effects.

The Bank of England, while possessing the privilege of refusing specie, is under no restraint as to the issue of its notes; and the discretion of its directors is in that case the only security for the due limitation of its currency. But this security is necessarily imperfect, as, independent of the convertibility of paper into specie, there exists no standard by which the supply of currency can be adapted to the demand. The price of bullion and the state of the exchange afford indeed the best rule for regulating the issue of a currency not convertible into specie; because when the market price of bullion is permanently high, or the exchange permanently unfavourable, it may be certainly inferred, that the paper is issued in excess, and ought to be diminished. But it was very fairly avowed by those concerned in managing the affairs of the bank, in the evidence which they gave before the committee of the House of Commons, that they neither regulated their issues by the price of bullion nor by the state of the exchange; being of opinion, that the public would never call for more paper than was necessary to the wants of trade; and that so long, therefore, as the notes of the bank were advanced on the security of good bills, there was no possibility of excess*. In maintaining this doctrine they do not seem to have been aware that paper acts in the double capacity of currency and of capital, and that a merchant may very naturally desire to borrow capital from the bank in the form of paper, though the public may

* The Report of the Committee of the House of Commons contains some extracts from the evidence of the Governor and Deputy-governor of the Bank, which are inserted in the appendix; and from these the reader will perceive how confidently they maintain, that there can be no excess of bank notes while they are issued only in exchange for good bills. See Note [H.]

have no need of any addition to its currency. The paper however is soon exchanged for commodities by the merchants who borrow it from the bank. It thus forms an addition to the mass of currency, which though it now consists of a greater number of notes, is not on this account of greater value, the aggregate value of a currency being in all cases fixed by the business which it has to perform. If there be no increase of business there will be no increase of value; and in that case an addition being made to the number of notes in circulation, the consequence is, that each particular note falls proportionally in value. The effect of an excessive issue of paper is not, as this doctrine seems to suppose, to encumber the circulation; for though the number of notes is increased, the aggregate value is still the same, and the only difference is that, by the excessive multiplication of notes, the currency is now divided into a greater number of parts, each part being of course of less value than before. In this manner the depreciation of the note is the only inconvenience produced by the excessive issue; and it is only by means of its immediate convertibility into specie, that the quantity can be reduced and the value restored.

Since the suspension of its cash payments,

the Bank of England seems to have carried its circulation beyond the due limit. The market price of bullion has in consequence risen above its mint price, and the exchange has become unfavourable; while each of those symptoms of depreciation has exactly corresponded to the increased issue of bank notes. From the year 1773, when a new coinage of gold was issued, till the year 1799, two years after the Bank of England suspended its cash payments, the market price of standard gold in bars remained with some trifling variations, at L.3. 17s. 6d. per ounce. During the same period, the price of silver was about 5s. 1d. and 5s. 4d. per ounce, while the foreign exchanges were almost uniformly in favour of this country. From the year 1789 to 1799, the exchange with Hamburgh, of which the par is between 34s. and 35s. varied generally from 34s. to 36s. rising or falling occasionally to 37s. or 33s. The notes of the Bank of England in circulation for three years previous to the year 1795 amounted on an average to L.11,975,573. In 1795 they varied from about 13 to $10\frac{1}{2}$ millions. In 1796 and 1797 they amounted to between 9 and 10 millions; and in February 1797, immediately previous to the suspension of its cash payments, they were reduced to 8,640,250*. In the course of the year 1799 they were increased to 14 millions, when the exchange with Hamburgh fell to 32, the price of silver rising at the same time to 5s. 8d. per ounce, and that of gold in proportion. The bank continued gradually increasing its circulation, which amounted in the year 1801 to L.16,169,549, the exchange with Hamburgh falling to 31s. 10d. and the price of silver rising to 6s. per ounce. In the year 1809 the circulation of the bank amounted to 19 millions, in 1810 to 22 and 23 millions, and in 1812 to 21 and 25 millions. The price of bullion and the state of the exchange were soon affected by this great additional issue of paper. The price of silver rose in 1811 to 6s. and in 1812 to 6s. 6d. ; that of gold to L.4. 14s. and L.5. 10s. per ounce. The exchange with Hamburgh also fell to 26s. and 24s. while paper now began to be exchanged for specie at a regular discount, 25s. and 26s. in paper being the current price of a guinea. Since this period the price of gold bullion has remained at about L.5. 10s. per ounce, and the circulation of the Bank of England at about 25 millions.

---

* See Appendix, to the evidence taken before the Committee of the House of Commons, 1810, p. 180. No. 34.

But the exchange with Hamburgh has become more favourable, having risen to about 29s.; and hence it has been argued, that there is no necessary connection between the depression of the exchange and the high price of bullion. But though the exchange must necessarily be depressed when the price of bullion is high, it may still fluctuate partially from the influence of other causes. A country, for example, where the currency is depreciated and the price of bullion high, may have the balance of trade either favourable or otherwise. Where it is favourable, the exchange will not be so much depressed as where it is unfavourable, as in that case the effect of the depreciated currency in depressing, will be counteracted by the effect of the favourable balance of trade in raising, the exchange; but where the balance of trade is unfavourable, or where the imports of a country exceed its exports, the two causes which affect the exchange, namely, the state of the trade and the state of the currency, in place of opposing, mutually concur in aiding each other's effect. From the evidence of the merchants examined by the select committee of the House of Commons, it seems probable that throughout the year 1810 the balance of trade with the continent of Europe was against Great Britain*, and this circumstance must have aided the effect of the depreciated currency in depressing the exchange. The balance of trade has since become favourable, and a partial improvement of the exchange has taken place. But these facts, so far from invalidating, rather serve to confirm all general reasonings on the subject.

While paper continued to exchange at par for specie, its depreciation was on this ground plausibly questioned; but this argument of course lost its force when guineas were currently exchanged for 25s. and 26s. in paper. A discount on paper, however, when exchanged for specie, though decisive as to the depreciation of the paper, is not its necessary consequence, since a currency, though depreciated, may still circulate at par. It is generally for the purpose of being converted into bullion that specie is preferred to paper; and the price received for the bullion, into which the specie is converted, will necessarily regulate the price at which it will be purchased. The price of bullion rises with the depreciation of the currency, being indeed the measure of that depreciation, and an inconsi-

* Report of the Committee, p. 12.

derable depreciation of paper will therefore occasion an equally inconsiderable rise in the price of bullion; in which case it may not be worth while to give a premium for specie to be converted into bullion. If we suppose, for example, the paper to be depreciated 2 per cent. a quantity of bullion formerly worth L.100 will now cost in depreciated paper L.102; and 100 guineas, therefore, exchangeable at par for 105 one pound bank notes, will, when converted into bullion, be worth 107 one pound bank notes and two shillings. The profit on the transaction, thus amounting only to two guineas, will, after compensating the risk and trouble of collecting and melting, leave nothing remaining for a premium on the specie. In that case the melter, who cannot afford a premium, will endeavour to stop the circulation of those heavy pieces, which, though intrinsically more valuable, still circulate at par for depreciated paper. In these circumstances specie will always be scarce; as though it cannot be bought up at a premium, it will be secretly withdrawn from circulation, and converted into bullion.

The state of the currency, subsequent to the suspension of cash payments by the bank, was frequently brought under the consideration of

Parliament; and a committee of the House of Commons, appointed in the year 1810 to inquire into the cause of the high price of bullion, concurred, after a laborious examination of evidence, in ascribing it to an over-issue and a consequent depreciation of bank paper. The reasons of this opinion will be found at length in the report, which exhibits a clear and comprehensive view of the subject; to which in the appendix many valuable details are subjoined.

In opposition to the report of its committee, the House of Commons passed various resolutions, declaratory of the causes of the high price of bullion, and of the actual value of the currency; as if Parliament could restore by its votes the value which the currency had lost by reason of its excess. Other proceedings followed, however, which conferred substantial privileges on the depreciated paper.

When the Bank of England first suspended its cash payments, the law so far encouraged the circulation of its notes, that a debtor who offered them in payment was protected against arrest, though his creditor, by a common action of debt, might still exact payment in guineas, the legal currency of the country. In 1810 bank notes, owing to the progress of the depreciation, began to be currently exchanged for less than their nominal value in specie, 25s. and 26s. in paper being given for a guinea; and though Parliament had just voted the paper to be of its original value, a law was nevertheless found necessary, to prevent its being openly exchanged at a discount for specie. Severe penalties were accordingly imposed on the exchange of paper for guineas at the market price; and tenants who offered bank notes in payment of their rents were at the same time protected against distress, though they were still liable to a common action of debt or of ejectment. In 1811 an act was passed protecting a debtor who tendered payment in Bank of England notes against all farther proceedings; by which last regulation the depreciated paper became legal tender for all existing debts, without regard to its value; and all creditors were accordingly injured precisely in proportion as the currency in which they were paid had varied from its standard.

As it has been questioned in the recent discussions on this subject, how far a rise in the market price of bullion above the mint price, joined to an unfavourable state of the exchange, and how far even the exchange of paper for specie, at less than its nominal value, are to be regarded as indications of a depreciated currency, it will be proper shortly to point out the connection of the state of the currency with the price of the bullion and with the exchange.

The precious metals being universally used as the medium of exchange, have in all countries been divided into pieces of a specific weight and fineness, of which the value has been certified by the authority of a public stamp. In the British currency a pound of gold is divided into $44\frac{1}{2}$ pieces or guineas, which bear the public stamp as the warrant of their weight and fineness; and a pound of gold thus warranted cannot possibly be inferior in value to a pound of gold in any other form. To say otherwise is to maintain that one pound of gold may be of greater value than another pound of gold of the same weight and fineness. But when by rubbing and wearing the gold coin is diminished in weight, $44\frac{1}{2}$ guineas which will no longer weigh, will no longer purchase a pound of gold; and according as one, two, three, or any greater number of guineas are necessary to make out the weight, one, two, three, or any greater number of guineas must necessarily be added to the price. When in this country, therefore, the market price of the pound of gold rises above $44\frac{1}{2}$ guineas, its mint price, it may be fairly inferred that $44\frac{1}{2}$ guineas will no longer purchase, because they will no longer weigh, a pound of gold ; and consequently, that the rise in the price of gold is only the necessary compensation for the deficient weight of the coin.

But if the price of bullion indicate the value of the coin, it must, when paid in paper, indicate the value of the paper with equal accuracy ; for what is paper, but a promise to pay on demand a certain quantity of coin ? Paper must consequently be considered as coin ; and coin, as already remarked, is bullion of a known weight and fineness. Forty-seven one pound bank notes are therefore so many promises to pay on demand something more than a pound of bullion ; and when L.47 in paper will not purchase a pound of bullion, is it not clear that the paper has varied from its standard, and that the promise which it bears is no longer of the same value with the thing promised ?

The state of the exchange between different countries is another sure test of the value of their respective currencies. In exchanging coin for bullion the price is fixed by the intrinsic worth of the currency in which it is paid; and the exchange between different countries is substantially the same transaction, the currency of the one being exchanged for that of the other, on a fair computation of the quantity of pure metal which they respectively contain. Thus, in computing the par of exchange between Hamburgh and London, one pound sterling is reckoned something more than 34 Hamburgh shillings; and when a bill for L. 100, drawn on Hamburgh by a banker in London, produces for each pound sterling 34 Hamburgh shillings, the exchange is said to be at par, and is generally supposed to denote that the exports of the two countries are equal to their imports.

But when by an excess of imports London is left indebted to Hamburgh, money must be provided to discharge this debt; and the demand in London for money in Hamburgh being greater than the demand in Hamburgh for money in London, bills on Hamburgh will, in the money market in London, sell for a premium. This premium, however, should never exceed the price of remitting specie from London to Hamburgh, as the demand for money in Hamburgh may in this manner be supplied to any extent. At this price the debtor country may always procure bills on the creditor country, and the expence of transporting specie, from the one to the other, must consequently form in all cases the limit of an unfavourable change.

But by a change in the value of either of the currencies exchanged, the rate of exchange may appear to vary to any extent, though it is really at par. The par of exchange between London and Hamburgh is 34; a British pound sterling being reckoned worth 34 Hamburgh shillings. But if we suppose those Hamburgh shillings to lose one half of their weight, a British pound sterling will then be worth precisely double its former nominal value in this debased currency, and will accordingly exchange for 68 Hamburgh shillings. The exchange being computed on the former value of the Hamburgh shilling and the par stated at 34, will then appear to be 100 per cent. against Hamburgh, though it is really at par; since although a greater number of Hamburgh shillings are in consequence of their diminished value exchanged for a pound sterling, any quantity of bullion paid to a

Hamburgh banker, and converted into a bill in London, will still purchase the same quantity of bullion in the London market; and it is evident that the fact of so unfavourable an exchange could not be otherwise explained; for if 68 shillings in Hamburgh, of their standard value, were exchanged for one British pound sterling, money would be doubled in value by the simple process of remitting it from the one place to the other; and by the enormous premium thus gained, the difference of exchange would soon be reduced to the necessary expence of transporting specie from the debtor to the creditor country.

The merchants and bankers who were examined by the Committee of the House of Commons relative to the high price of bullion, ascribed the fall in the exchange to an unfavourable balance of trade. But this notion was sufficiently refuted by the facts contained in their own evidence; from which it appeared, that in the existing state of the exchange, a pound of gold, worth $44\frac{1}{2}$ guineas, remitted from Paris to London, produced in bank paper L. 59. 8s., about L. 12 more than its value in coin; and that the L.59. 8s. in bank paper, purchased in London one pound and one ounce of bullion, with a small fraction. A pound of bullion, remitted from Paris to London through the respective bankers of those places, thus produced one pound and one ounce, and the premium of one ounce gained on the transaction, equal to $8\frac{1}{2}$ per cent., expresses the real amount of the exchange in favour of Paris. In like manner, a pound of gold remitted from Hamburgh to London yielded a premium of 13 dwts., and from Amsterdam a premium of 16 dwts., shewing the exchange to be $5\frac{1}{2}$ and 7 per cent. in favour of those countries, when bullion is exchanged for bullion. But a pound of gold remitted from Hamburgh to London, produced in bank notes L. 58. 4s., the premium thus amounting to L.11. 10s. 6d., equal nearly to 3 ounces, in place of 13 dwts., the premium paid on the exchange of bullion for bullion*. It is only of course when things known to be of equal value are exchanged, that the result will express the real state of the exchange; for if things differing in value be exchanged under a notion that they are of equal value, the exchange will appear to vary though

* See Appendix, Note (H.) where the reader will find some of the most material parts of the evidence of the bankers and bullion dealers respecting the high price of the precious metals at this period.

really at par. Now we find, from the evidence of the merchants and money dealers, that when things known to be of equal value are exchanged between Hamburgh and London, namely bullion for bullion, the difference in favour of Hamburgh is only about $5\frac{1}{2}$ per cent.; but when paper, the value of which is the point in dispute, is exchanged for bullion, the difference is increased to something more than 25 per cent. This difference between paper and bullion cannot obviously arise from any unfavourable balance of trade, which must indifferently affect the exchange both of paper and bullion. Whence can it arise therefore but from the depreciation of the paper, in consequence of which more of it than formerly is exchanged for the same quantity of bullion?

As the circulation of paper generally exceeds out of all proportion the specie reserved for its payment, it is obvious that a bank may in all cases be drained of its gold, by an unusual return of its notes; and it was for the purpose of preventing this evil that the cash payments of the Bank of England were suspended in 1797, the measure being evidently justified by the necessity of the case. By several successive acts, however, the power of refusing specie, which should naturally have ceased with the alarm in which it originated, has been continued to the bank till six months after the conclusion of a general peace; chiefly as a security against the drain of specie which may arise from the great expenditure abroad. But though from this cause the bank may no doubt be subjected to a demand for specie, I have endeavoured to show that the suspension of its payments was the consequence of the alarm and the demand for specie at home, and that with some exertion every other casualty might have been duly provided for. It does not appear necessary, therefore, that the bank should be exempted during war from the obligation of paying in specie; more especially as experience seems to prove, that such a privilege cannot be exercised without occasioning an excessive issue and a consequent depreciation of paper. In the event of a definitive treaty of peace, however, of which there is now happily every prospect, it might not be possible to resume payments in specie in so short a period as six months.

The Committee of the House of Commons, in their report on the high price of bullion, propose, that the bank shall be allowed two years to prepare for this necessary measure, and the expediency of such an indulgence is obvious; because in the present state of the currency, encumbered as it is with depreciated paper, the immediate resumption of cash payments by the bank would be followed by the return of the whole of its superfluous notes in exchange for specie; which might be the cause of serious embarrassments. But in the course of two years the measure might surely be adopted with perfect safety, as there would be ample opportunity, during that period, of gradually withdrawing the superfluous currency from circulation; and in this case, all unnecessary delay is the more impolitic, as by the gradual progress of the evil, the remedy, the more necessary it becomes, will be found the more difficult.

ON PRODUCTIVE AND UNPRODUCTIVE LABOUR.

Dr Smith's distinction between productive and unproductive labour, though it appears to be simple and obvious, has been perplexed by the ingenuity of subsequent reasoners, who maintain every species of industry to be equally productive which contributes, however remotely, to the general wealth. According to this doctrine, the soldier and the judge are reckoned productive labourers, because they raise the value of the national stock by protecting it, the one from plunder and the other from injury; for if the artificer of bolts and bars, who protects property in detail, be termed a productive labourer, much more, it is argued, should those be placed in the productive class who protect property in the mass, and add to every portion of it the quality of being secure*. In his ex-

* Edinburgh Review, Vol. IV. p. 357.

planation of this subject, Dr Smith expressly states, that he does not mean to undervalue the utility of the labour which he denominates unproductive; and the preceding argument seems to proceed upon the fallacy of maintaining, that labour because it is useful must necessarily be productive. But while the utility both of justice and of defence is freely admitted, the labour which is subservient to production ought not therefore to be confounded with the labour which actually produces; since by such a mode of reasoning, the plainest distinctions might be subverted. If the soldier, for example, be termed a productive labourer because his labour is subservient to production, the productive labourer might, by the same rule, lay claim to military honours; as it is certain that without his assistance no army could ever take the field to fight battles or to gain victories.

It is farther to be observed, that protection does not improve the value of property, its object being merely to preserve property to its actual possessors. There is surely, therefore, some distinction between the labour by which the value of a subject is increased, and that of which the sole object is not to increase the value, but to secure the possession.

The case of the menial servant is still more decisive in favour of Dr Smith's distinction. It seems quite plain that the wealth of an individual who maintains ten menial servants will be diminished exactly by the expence of their maintenance; while by maintaining ten labourers who reproduce their maintenance with a profit, he will be richer by the whole amount of this profit. In answer to which it is observed, " that there is no such difference as Dr Smith
" supposes between the effects of maintaining
" a multitude of those several kinds of work-
" men. It is the extravagant quantity, not the
" peculiar quality of the labour thus paid for,
" that brings on ruin. A man is ruined if he
" keeps more servants than he can afford to em-
" ploy, and does not let them out for hire;—
" exactly as he is ruined by purchasing more
" food than he can consume, or by employing
" more workmen in any branch of manufac-
" tures than his business requires, or his pro-
" fits will pay *." It is only therefore when workmen or productive labourers are multiplied without necessity, and maintained in idleness, or in other words, when they are not productive labourers, that they are compared by this

* Edinburgh Review, Vol. IV. p. 355.

writer to menial servants; for it is clear that while they reproduce their maintenance with a profit, they cannot be multiplied to the injury of their employer. Here then Dr Smith's distinction between productive and unproductive labour is plainly recognised; since it appears that a master loses only by maintaining workmen without employing them, or in other words, by maintaining unproductive labourers.

According to the theory of the French Economists, agriculture is reckoned the only productive employment; because its produce, after replacing the capital and paying the wages of the labour employed in cultivation, leaves a rent or clear surplus to be added to the national capital; while the manufacturer, who is represented as merely reproducing the value of his own maintenance, is on this account considered an unproductive labourer.

But the neat surplus by which the Economists estimate the utility of agriculture, plainly arises from the high price of its produce, which, however advantageous to the landlord who receives it, is surely no advantage to the consumer who pays it. Were the produce of agriculture to be sold for a lower price, the same neat surplus would not remain, after defraying the expences of cultivation; but agriculture would be still equally productive to the general stock; and the only difference would be, that as the landlord was formerly enriched by the high price at the expence of the community, the community would now profit by the low price at the expence of the landlord. The high price in which the rent or neat surplus originates, while it enriches the landlord, who has the produce of agriculture to sell, diminishes, in the same proportion, the wealth of those who are its purchasers; and on this account it is quite inaccurate to consider the landlord's rent as a clear addition to the national wealth.

The supposed pre-eminence of agriculture being founded on the neat surplus which arises from the sale of its produce, manufactures are reckoned unproductive by the Economists, because the price for which they are sold leaves no neat surplus, after paying wages and profit. Their whole theory is thus founded on the same fallacy. They never seem to consider that the neat surplus which they maintain to be the true criterion of productive labour, necessarily implies a high price; and that if manufactures yield no neat surplus, it is in consequence of their low price, which is advantageous to the community in exactly the same proportion as it is disadvantageous to the individual manufacturer. In every improving society, the price of manufactures is gradually reduced by the use of machinery. But if manufactures, though produced cheaper, were still to be sold for their former price, a large surplus would then remain after paying wages and profit, and according to the theory of the Economists, manufacturing industry would in such a case be productive. It is obvious, however, that by this high price, the manufacturer profits at the expence of the community; and that while the price is low, the community is benefited at the expence of the manufacturer. The only difference, therefore, between agriculture and manufactures appears to be, that owing to certain general causes, already explained *, the produce of the one is uniformly sold for a higher price than the produce of the other, in consequence of which, it yields a rent or surplus above wages and profit.

* See observations On the Price of such Commodities as yield a Rent.

ON THE PROGRESS OF NATIONAL OPULENCE.

It is remarked by Dr Smith, that the great commerce of every civilized society is that carried on between the inhabitants of the country and those of the town; the country supplying the town with the means of its subsistence and the materials of its industry, and receiving in return the manufactured produce of the town. The trade carried on between different countries is in no respect different from the trade carried on between the inhabitants of the same country; and the trade of the world accordingly consists in a great degree of the exchange of rude produce for manufactures, or of manufactures for rude produce. When a nation wants capital and industry to manufacture, or to supply an equivalent for the whole of its rude produce, the surplus must be sent abroad for the manufactures of richer countries; while the population and industry of the exporting country improving in the mean time in proportion to its abundant means both of subsistence and of employment, the surplus produce formerly sent abroad is soon required for the employment and support of domestic industry. If the country still continue to advance in population and industry, its produce will no longer supply the wants of its inhabitants, and rude produce and subsistence will in that case be procured from abroad by an exportation of manufactures. Agriculture, encouraged, in the mean time, by the great demand for subsistence, the consequence of improving industry and increasing population, will rapidly advance, and its increasing produce will again become sufficient both for the support and employment of the whole population. In this manner, in every improving country, agriculture and manufactures will alternately take the lead, the supply of rude produce and subsistence sometimes exceeding, and at other times falling short of the demands of population and industry.

In England, owing to the want of manufacturing industry, we are informed, that wool was formerly exported in its rude state for the wines of France and the fine cloths of Flanders, and corn appears also to have been alternately exported and imported. It is stated by Lord Bacon*, " that whereas England was wont to be fed by " other countries from the east, it sufficeth now " to feed other countries." Hume also observes, that during the reign of James I. the nation was still dependent on foreigners for bread, and that " though its exportation of grain now forms a " considerable branch of its commerce, notwith- " standing its probable increase of people, there " was in that period a regular importation from " the Baltic, as well as from France; and if " ever it stopped, the bad consequences were " sensibly felt by the nation†." In the mean time, as the agriculture of the country improved, its increasing produce gradually became sufficient for the support of the whole population; and about the years 1707 or 1708, a surplus remained for exportation; which surplus, by the subsequent progress of population and of manufactures, was again required for the support of domestic industry; and about the

* See Edinburgh Review, Vol. V. p. 205.

† Hume's History, Appendix to the Reign of James I.

year 1780, the exportation of grain from this country appears to have ceased. Since this period, owing to the rapid progress of manufactures, it has been found necessary to import both rude produce and subsistence; and great part of the foreign trade of Great Britain, accordingly, consists in the exchange of her manufactures for the rude produce both of Europe and America.

The capital and industry of America being chiefly engaged in agriculture, its produce exceeds the demand at home in the same proportion as the produce of industry fails. The rude produce of America is accordingly exchanged for the manufactured produce of Britain; and thus, while America is assisted by the wealth and industry of Britain, the surplus produce of British manufactures finds an outlet in the continually increasing demands of the American market. From the less improved parts of Europe also, such as Poland, Russia, Denmark, and Sweden, Britain imports provisions and rude produce, for the employment and support of her overgrown population; while the produce of those countries is exported for want of capital and industry to manufacture it at home. And were it not for the demands of other countries for more rude produce than their own soil affords, the agriculture of these poorer nations would be checked, by the want of a market for its produce.

If, as Dr Smith states*, the natural order of improvement was reversed by the policy of Europe, which favoured commerce at the expence of agriculture; the country where improvement ought to commence, advancing only in consequence of the prior improvement of the town; we should naturally expect to find the industry of the country in continual arrear to the industry of the town, for a supply of subsistence and of rude produce; and this scarcity of the produce of the country would no doubt be a decided mark of its inferior improvement. We find, however, from Dr Smith's own account of the commerce of those times, that rude produce was exported from England for the wines of France, and the fine cloths of Flanders; and he states generally, that the trade of Europe consisted in the exchange of its own rude, for the manufactured produce of more civilized nations. But if in Europe the rude produce of the country was in greater plenty than the finished work of the town, does not this greater plenty

* Vol. II. Book III. Chap. I.

of its produce clearly prove its superior improvement; and what then becomes of Dr Smith's hypothesis respecting the prior improvement of the town? The inaccuracy of this hypothesis is apparent, indeed, in every view in which it is considered. The country, as Dr Smith himself states, being the original source of all improvement, it seems an inconsistency to speak of the prior improvement of the town; to obviate which, Dr Smith remarks, that the town, by its commerce with distant countries, may flourish while the neighbouring country is in poverty. But though a particular town may thus improve by means of foreign commerce, a great continent, such as Europe, to which Dr Smith's reasonings apply, must always furnish the means of its own increase, and its towns can only improve in consequence of the prior improvement of the country. As their subsistence and the materials of their industry must principally consist of domestic produce, an increase of this produce must clearly precede every other species of internal improvement.

In contrasting the progress of America with that inverted order of improvement, which he states to have taken place in Europe, Dr Smith has overlooked the very peculiar circumstances which influenced the condition of the New World*. The progress of America has always been assisted by the capital and industry of Europe; by which a supply of manufactures being provided, the capital of the country was left free for the cultivation of the soil, and agriculture rapidly advancing, a few scattered inhabitants have grown up, almost within the memory of man, to be a great people. But in a less improved state of the world, the demand of America for manufactures could not have been supplied from abroad; her capital must, in that case, have been divided between agriculture and the manufacture of her own rude produce; and population must have slowly advanced, as in other countries, in proportion to the diminished supply of subsistence.

In every country the state of manners will greatly depend on the nature of the equivalent given for the surplus produce of the soil. Where that equivalent consists in manufactures, wealth and industry will flourish; but where there are no manufactures to give to the landlord for his surplus produce, it will generally be consumed by idle retainers. Such, accordingly, was the

* Vol. II. Book III. Chap I.

state of manners under the feudal system; the landlord distributing his surplus produce among a train of dependants, and receiving his equivalent in military service. The feudal system has declined throughout Europe with the progress of trade and manufactures. In the Highlands of Scotland this change is not yet fully accomplished, though the ancient state of property is daily subverted by the progress of modern manners. The landlord, without regard to the hereditary tenant, now offers his lands to the highest bidder, who, if he is an improver, instantly adopts a new system of cultivation. The land, formerly overspread with small tenants or labourers, was peopled in proportion to its produce; but under the new system of improved cultivation and increased rents, the largest possible produce is obtained at the least possible expence; and the useless hands being, with this view, removed, the population is reduced, not to what the land will maintain, but to what it will employ. The dispossessed tenants either seek a subsistence in the manufacturing towns, or, if they can afford the expence of the voyage, emigrate to America for a more congenial mode of life. But though emigration is their last and only resource, and is indeed the necessary consequence of those improvements by which the landlords profit, it is notwithstanding generally discouraged throughout the Highlands, and it has even been represented as an evil which it might be proper, in some cases, for the law to restrain; as if those who are outcasts at home could, with any justice, be denied the poor privilege of exploring the world for a new settlement *.

Among a people of simple manners, the necessary supply of food and manufactures will be more easily provided than where luxury prevails, and a larger surplus of industry will consequently remain for other purposes. It is in such a state of society that a nation can most freely use its population as an instrument of war; and on this model were formed the ancient military communities both of Greece and Rome. The surplus produce of agriculture was engrossed by the state for the support of soldiers, who had no leisure to provide for their own sustenance. Luxury was also checked by sumptuary laws, the legislators of those days easily perceiving that by the pre-

* For an account of the present state of the Highlands of Scotland, with the causes of emigration, see Lord Selkirk's judicious treatise on the subject.

valence of luxury, the surplus produce of the soil would soon be diverted from the support of soldiers to that of artificers. Thus accordingly it happened. The simplicity of republican manners was corrupted by the wealth of the conquered countries. The lands which formerly supported soldiers and freemen were engrossed by the opulent senators, who spent the surplus on slaves and artisans, the ministers of pride and luxury; and the strength of this warlike community gradually declined under the same change of manners which subverted the feudal aristocracy of modern Europe.

ON THE LAWS FOR REGULATING THE EXPORTATION AND IMPORTATION OF CORN.

In the early legislation of most countries, it has always been accounted a capital object to keep down the price of corn; and with this view, such penalties were formerly imposed on its transportation from one place to another, that the supply of the market was materially obstructed. In this country an act was passed in the reign of Charles II. which, though it sanctioned those prejudices, the evils of which it was intended to correct, gave to the inland trade in corn the freedom which it now enjoys; and this act, as Dr Smith justly remarks, with all its imperfections, has done more for the encouragement of agriculture than all the other acts ever passed on the subject.

But while the legislature was thus providing for the freedom of the inland trade in corn, the foundation was at the same time laid for that system of laws of which the object is ultimately to make corn cheap, by restraining importation, and encouraging exportation by means of a bounty. In pursuance of these views, corn was subjected, on importation, to a duty of 16s. per quarter, unless when the price exceeded 53s. 4d. to which it never rose but in consequence of extreme scarcity; and exportation was at the same time permitted at 40s. per quarter, and afterwards at 48s. per quarter. At last, a bounty of 5s. per quarter was granted in the reign of William III. on all corn exported, at whatever price.

This system continued until the year 1765, when, in consequence of a course of unfavourable seasons, importation was allowed duty free, and exportation was prohibited. In 1773 it was provided, that the high duties on importation, imposed during the reign of Charles II., which amounted to a prohibition, should be taken off when the price of wheat rose to 48s., and that the bounty on exportation should cease when it rose to 44s. In 1791 a new law was made, by which the high duty of 16s. was paid on all wheat imported under 50s.; above 50s. and under 54s. a duty of 2s. 6d. was paid; and above 54s. the duty on importation was lowered to 6d. The bounty of 5s. on exportation was payable only when wheat was under 44s. per quarter, and when it rose to 46s. exportation was prohibited. In 1804, the prices at which wheat became liable to a duty on importation were raised; the high duty of 16s. being payable until the price rose to 63s.; above 63s. and under 66s. the duty was reduced to 2s. 6d.; and above 66s. it was still further reduced to 6d.

The practical effect of these various laws was, from the time of Charles II. to the year 1765, to prohibit importation, while exportation was, from the reign of William III., encouraged by a bounty. From 1765 to 1773, exportation was prohibited and importation was allowed. By the laws in force from 1773 to 1791, importation was free during eight years of this period; corn being in these years always above the price at which the duties on importation were exigible; and for a like reason, during thirteen years of the same period, there was no encouragement to exportation; the price during these years being always too high to warrant the payment of the bounty which the law allowed. After the year 1791, exportation and importation were generally free, as corn was almost always above the price at which the high duty was exigible, or the bounty payable. In several scarce years also, which occurred after that period, special bounties were granted for the encouragement of importation.

Various plans have been subsequently proposed for reviving into greater efficacy the laws for restraining the importation of corn into this country, by raising more or less the prices at which the duties are exigible; and in the year 1813, it was suggested by a committee of the House of Commons appointed to inquire into this subject, that the high duty of 16s. per quarter on the importation of wheat should be continued until the price rose to 105s.; and that above 105s. and under 135s. a duty of 2s. 6d. should be imposed. Under those regulations it is clear, that, as the country does not produce what is sufficient for its consumption, wheat would never fall under 105s. per quarter; and even when corn rises above this high price, the duty of 2s. 6d. would still operate as a check to importation. Other plans have been since proposed, of which, as they have all one object, namely, to regulate the price of corn by restraining importation and encouraging exportation, it is unnecessary to enter into the details.

In favour of this system it is urged, that while the exportation of corn was encouraged by a bounty, and while importation was prohibited, prices were comparatively low and remarkably steady; and that after the year 1773, when the encouragement to exportation, and the restraints on importation were virtually diminished, they gradually rose higher and were also liable to greater fluctuations. But it is not very easy to believe that prices were reduced in the home market by the law, which, by encouraging exportation, manifestly tended to reduce the supply in that market, and thus to raise the price. It has been always understood that the price of commodities is fixed by the proportion between the demand and the supply. Increase the demand or diminish the supply, and the price rises. Now, exportation surely tends to diminish the supply in the home market; and how then can it lower the price? By encouraging agriculture, say the advocates of the system. Here then the inconsistency of the argument manifestly appears. Agriculture, we are told, is encouraged by a high price of corn; by restricting importation and encouraging exportation, this high price is produced—and yet the project is recommended on account of its tendency to produce low prices. Where then is the encouragement to agriculture? The prices must either be high or low. If they are high, where are the boasted advantages of the system to the community? If they are low, where is the encouragement to agriculture?

As the fact however is undoubted, that the money price of corn was low while importation was prohibited and exportation encouraged, and that it rose while the trade was less restrained; and as it is evident that such effects could not be produced by the law, it is proper to inquire to what other principle they may be traced.

It may be remarked, in the first place, that a rise in the price of corn may be occasioned as much by a fall in the value of the money as by a rise in the value of the corn. Because more money is given for corn than heretofore, it does not therefore follow that its real value has risen, as the same effect may be equally produced by another cause. From the time of the Revolution, to the year 1773, the period when the bounty on exportation was in force, prices were comparatively low. From the year 1773 to the present time they have been much higher; but it is well known that the value of money has greatly fallen during the latter period, and that every article of consumption, as well as corn, has consequently risen in price. Here then is a reason for the rise which has taken place in the money price of corn, and one every way sufficient to produce the effect. More money is given for corn, not because the corn is of more value, but because the money is of less value; so that there is no occasion for ascribing it to the law prohibiting importation, more especially as the fact cannot in this manner be accounted for.

But were it even true that the real value, and not the money price of corn, were lower in the former than in the latter period, there are other causes to which it must be ascribed. The great trade of every community consists in the exchange which takes place between the town and the country, of manufactured produce for the produce of the soil ; and in the progress of national wealth, it happens at one time, that the value of what is produced exceeds the value of what is manufactured, and at another, that the manufactures exceed in value the produce of the soil ; in either of which cases, an exportation will take place at one time of manufactures, and at another time of corn. Now, at the time when the laws were passed granting a bounty on the exportation of corn, the agriculture of the country had got the start of its trade—there was more corn produced than the population required*. Corn was of course plenty, and its price reasonable. Far from being lower, however, on account of the bounty granted on its exportation, it must have been higher on this account; the quantity in the market must have been diminished by the quantity exported; and according to the rule by which prices are invariably adjusted, a higher price must have been the consequence of this diminished supply.

Since the year 1772, the trade and manufactures of the country have taken the lead of its agriculture. There has been such an increase of capital, and such an improvement of industry in all its branches, for the last thirty or forty years, that its produce has exceeded in value the produce of the soil, and it has in consequence been exported for the produce of other countries, where there is not such an overflow of wealth and industry. This state of things, too, has been attended with an increase in our population, for the maintenance of which we

* See observations On the Progress of National Opulence.

are in part indebted to other countries. There has thus been a great demand for industry—a great demand for an increase of people—and a great demand for provisions for their support. It is natural to think, therefore, that in this latter period, the real value of corn must have risen, and it is by means of this higher price, that an adequate supply has been procured from other countries.

By violently checking this necessary supply, a great hardship must in the first instance be imposed on the consumer; the natural course of the country to improvement must be checked, and one great stimulus to agriculture, namely, the improvement of manufactures, must be partially counteracted. It is probable that those effects may not go any great length; because there is in every community a principle of internal vigour sufficient to remedy the effect of faulty legislation; and because also, in all those laws that regard the exportation and importation of corn, a dispensing power has been, from time to time, exercised by the Privy Council, by which the law has been suspended, when it was likely to produce any bad effects; an undeniable proof, as Dr Smith justly remarks, that a system thus continually interrupted by exceptions, must have been defective in its principle. It now seems, indeed, to be generally admitted, that a community will flourish most when trade is left perfectly free; and there seems little doubt that the trade in corn, far from being an exception, would be benefited in a most especial manner, were it left to find its level under the operation of this excellent principle.

It has been stated, indeed, by those who recommend the policy of restraints on importation, and bounties on exportation, that if commerce were left perfectly free, agriculture would require no special encouragement; but that as commerce has in every country been favoured by extraordinary encouragements, it is but fair that agriculture should be treated with the same indulgence*. That laws exist in most countries for the encouragement of trade is undoubtedly true. But I have endeavoured to shew †, that the practical effect of this system has been greatly overrated by Dr Smith, and that commerce has received no real encouragement from those laws enacted in its favour. Admitting, however, that

* Malthus on Population, Vol. II. Book III. Chap. 10. p. 272, 273.

† Vol. I. p. 196. Vol II. p. 141

certain branches of trade have been encouraged by particular statutes, those who admit the impolicy of all such expedients, surely act with singular inconsistency in endeavouring to establish a system in regard to agriculture which they condemn when applied to trade; and there is indeed an end of all sound legislation, if one abuse is thus to be made the ground of another. If the laws for the encouragement of trade are impolitic, this is a good reason for abolishing them. But it is surely no reason for extending the system to other branches of industry, and for thus giving it a greater degree of permanence. It is only besides to certain branches of trade that those extraordinary encouragements are stated to be granted; and upon the same principle that agriculture claims peculiar privileges, every other trade which is not already encouraged, might with equal propriety lay claim to the especial favour of the legislature. It is obvious, in short, that if we once leave the sure ground of policy and reason, we cannot consistently reject any project of monopoly however pernicious or absurd.

With regard to the steadiness of price which is stated to have taken place in consequence of the bounty, it does not appear that prices were more steady when the bounty was in force, than after it was repealed. The bounty was granted in the year 1688; and in the several years of 1705, 1706, and 1707, the price of wheat was L.1. 10s., L.1. 6s., and L.1. 8s. 6d. per quarter. In 1709 and 1710 it was L.3. 18s. 6d. and L.3. 18s. In 1728 the price was L.2. 14s. 6d. In 1732 it was only L.1. 6s. 8d. In 1740, 1741, and 1742, it was L.2. 10s. 8d., L.2. 6s. 8d., and L.1. 14s. per quarter. In the three succeeding years it was only L.1. 4s. 10d., and L.1. 7s. 6d. In 1757 it was L.3. In 1761 it was L.1. 10s. The highest prices here stated are generally about double the amount of the lowest prices; and from the period when the law which granted the bounty on exportation was repealed, no greater fluctuations of price appear to have taken place.

In arguing against this measure, Dr Smith maintains, that the rise which the bounty occasions in the price of corn is no advantage to the farmer, because the price of corn regulates the money price both of labour and of commodities; and the farmer, therefore, if he receives a higher price for his corn, pays a proportionably higher price for the labour which he employs, and for the commodities which he purchases. I have already endeavoured to shew that the price of corn has no effect whatever either on the wages of labour or on the price of commodities * ; and that in whatever degree the bounty raises the price of corn, it increases the farmer's profits, and thus gives a real encouragement to agriculture. The question, therefore, comes to be, whether agriculture ought to be encouraged by violently raising the price of produce? And if we judge of measures of this sort as they affect not merely the interest of the landlord, but that of the community at large, they will all appear to be highly unwarrantable. A perpetual famine would undoubtedly afford the best encouragement to agriculture; but, though no one would recommend any measures tending to produce so great a calamity, in what respect do laws for preventing importation differ in their principle? Their effect is to shut corn out of the country, that it may be scarce and of course dear; and it is not easy to conceive upon what principle, either of policy or justice, such a measure can be defended. It can neither be maintained that, of late years, the price of pro-

* See observations On the Wages of Labour.

visions has in this country been too low, or that agriculture has not been most flourishing; and though trade and manufactures have gone beyond it, this implies no backwardness in agriculture—it is a state of things which will speedily work its own cure; as the great stimulus which it always offers to cultivation, will soon bring it back to the level of trade and industry.

ON COMMERCIAL TREATIES.

The ancient policy of Europe imposed such restraints on commerce, that in later times special treaties have been found necessary to restore the free intercourse of trading countries.

The principal treaties of this nature of which it is necessary to give any account, are, 1*st*, The Commercial Propositions made by Great Britain to Ireland in 1785, and afterwards carried into effect in the year 1800, when the two countries were united under one parliament; and 2*dly*, the Commercial Treaty concluded between France and Great Britain in 1786.

OF THE IRISH COMMERCIAL PROPOSITIONS.

By the early policy of this country, the commerce of Ireland was subjected to the most ruinous prohibitions. It was excluded from the British colonies in North America and the West Indies by the navigation laws, and it was circumscribed both in Europe and Asia by the privileges of the English trading companies, and by particular statutes. The Irish woollen and glass manufactures were injured, and at length ruined, by a series of hostile enactments, the object of which was to prevent the importation of the raw material, and afterwards the exportation of the finished manufacture. The same system of prohibition was extended, with some trifling exceptions, to the exportation of cattle and provisions of all sorts; and while the British manufacturers were allowed free access to the Irish market, the introduction into Britain of the Irish manufactures was either obstructed by heavy duties, or entirely prohibited *.

In the year 1782 the Irish parliament, hitherto the organ of a British party, became the successful advocate of its own independence and a free trade; and from this period, Ireland

* The effects of this system of restraint in cramping the trade and industry of Ireland, are truly and eloquently described in the speech with which Mr Pitt introduced to parliament his plan for a free intercourse between the two countries. See Appendix, Note [K.]

maintained an unrestrained intercourse with other nations. But her trade with Britain was still subjected to all its former restraints; and for the purpose of removing these, Mr Pitt brought forward, in 1785, a series of commercial propositions, which being agreed to by the Irish parliament, only required the sanction of Britain to form the law of the two countries.

By these regulations, it was proposed to remove all the prohibitions on the reciprocal exchange of produce between Britain and Ireland, and to equalize all existing duties on importation, by reducing them in the country where they were highest, to the amount payable in the country where they were lowest, except where a commodity was liable in either country to an internal tax; in which case it became necessary to impose a countervailing duty on its importation. It was also agreed, that in future neither country should impose prohibitions on the importation of the produce of the other, nor grant bounties on the exportation of its own.

This enlightened system for the free trade of two neighbouring countries, was opposed by merchants who disliked competition, and by statesmen hostile to the existing administration; and unhappily with so much success, that Mr

Pitt, to satisfy the British manufacturers, found it necessary to introduce various alterations inconsistent with the independence of Ireland. By the new clauses the British parliament was empowered to regulate the trade and navigation of Ireland; and in many cases the exportation of Irish produce was subjected to the burden of the high duties payable in Britain, for the avowed purpose of protecting the British against the competition of the Irish manufacturer with his low duties. The measure thus altered being regarded by the Irish legislature as an encroachment on its rights, was on this ground finally rejected. From this period the intercourse of the two countries continued under all its former restraints till the year 1800, when the legislative union which then took place naturally suggested the policy of a freer trade. It was accordingly proposed to withdraw all duties, prohibitions, and bounties, both on exportation and importation, with the exception of countervailing duties, corresponding to the internal taxes established in each country, and to impose a duty of 10 per cent. for 20 years on the importation from either country into the other of certain enumerated commodities. Duties were also imposed on the importation of calicoes, cottons, and muslins, and on cotton yarn and cotton twist; which were to be gradually abolished, and altogether to cease in the year 1816.

To impose heavy duties on the importation of foreign manufactures is certainly not the most eligible mode of encouraging domestic industry; but, as the protecting duties agreed to by this treaty were not to be permanent, no great fault can be found with this part of the arrangement.

The trade between two countries, subject to different and unequal taxes, must of course be regulated by drawbacks and countervailing duties; it being necessary, in justice to the domestic dealer, where a commodity is liable to an internal tax, to subject it to a similar tax when brought from abroad, and in like manner to allow a drawback of all internal duties on its exportation. To this interruption the intercourse of Great Britain and Ireland is necessarily exposed, as in consequence of the different modes of taxation which they respectively pursue, certain commodities are taxed in the one country which are not taxed in the other; and on this account they can neither be exported nor imported, without either paying duties or having duties drawn back. It is, however, provided by the 7th article of the union, that if the debt of Great Britain and Ireland should be in the proportion of their respective contributions to the common expences of the empire, or nearly so, *i. e.* as 2 to 15, the united parliament might then proceed to extend the same system of taxation to both countries; in which case there would be no farther necessity for drawbacks and countervailing duties, and the trade between Great Britain and Ireland would be carried on with the same freedom as the internal trade of Great Britain.

The proportions here stated can only take place in consequence either of the decrease of the British, or the increase of the Irish debt; and we have no data to calculate when the debt of either country may be so far diminished or increased.

But though the common revenue of the empire cannot be raised by one uniform system of taxation, while different parts of it continue so unequally burdened, it seems no way necessary to retain the taxes peculiar to Ireland. The sum for which Ireland is liable, whether on account of her own debt, or for the general expences of the public service, might, without difficulty, be raised by taxes on the same articles which are taxed in Britain; and there would be then no other difference between the two countries, except that the one would be more heavily taxed than the other. Certain articles would be taxed in Britain which would not be taxed in Ireland, and the drawbacks and countervailing duties connected with such articles, would form the only obstacle to a free trade.

If by new-modelling the system of taxation in either country the revenue of Ireland could be thus raised, such an arrangement would establish the freest intercourse that can possibly take place between the two countries while they continue so unequally burdened.

OF THE COMMERCIAL TREATY CONCLUDED BETWEEN FRANCE AND GREAT BRITAIN IN 1786.

The conclusion of this important treaty formed a new era in the history both of France and of Britain. They had for centuries before been rivals and enemies; and their commercial policy was dictated by the same spirit which prompted their unhappy wars; insomuch that though they possessed the materials of a most extensive commerce, the one abounding in all that art and industry can supply, and the other in the productions of a more favoured soil and climate, the exchange of their peculiar produce was discouraged by a complicated system of restraints and heavy duties. The object of the commercial treaty concluded by Mr Pitt in 1786 was to abolish all those pernicious restraints, and connecting the two countries in the bonds of a reciprocal trade, to pledge them, by their mutual interests, to an oblivion of their ancient animosities.

All the heavy duties formerly imposed on the importation, into either country, of the produce of the other, were accordingly reduced. The importation of French wines was permitted at the same duties as the wines of Portugal, according to the stipulations of the Methven treaty *, or at one-third less than the duty formerly paid. The duties on various other articles, the produce of France, were materially

* It was stipulated in the Methven treaty, that the wines of Portugal should be imported into Britain at duties one-third under those of France. A reduction of one-third part of the duty on the importation of French wines, necessarily required, according to the agreement entered into with Portugal, a reduction of one third on the importation of Portuguese wines; a condition which, after the amicable adjustment of the pending negociations with Portugal, was carried into effect.

reduced; beer was subjected to a duty of 30 per cent., and on various other commodities a duty was charged, according to the sixth article of the treaty, of from 10 to 12 per cent. which could evidently be no impediment to the trade of the two countries. On such commodities as were not specified, it was agreed that no higher duty should be levied than on the same commodities imported from the most favoured nations. The ships of both nations were exempted from the port duties which they formerly paid, and creditors in the one country were allowed the important privilege of sueing for debts in the other. In several important particulars, the maritime law of Europe was altered by this treaty, the list of contraband articles of war being extended only to such as were necessary to a land war, while France was allowed to trade with the enemies of Britain in every thing belonging to a naval war. The right of search was also abandoned by both parties, a certificate, signed by the proper officer, being held to be a sufficient warrant of the legality of the cargo.

The views in which this treaty originated were explained by Mr Pitt when it was submitted to parliament; and the sentiments which he expresses give to this measure a remarkable character of moderation and of wisdom. In reply to an argument inculcating constant jealousy of France, he enquired, whether " in using the " word *jealousy*, it was meant to recommend to " this country such a species of jealousy as " should be either mad or blind; such a species " of jealousy as should induce her either madly " to throw away what was to make her happy, " or blindly grasp at that which must end in " her ruin? Was the necessity of a perpetual " animosity with France so evident and so press- " ing, that for it we were to sacrifice every com- " mercial advantage we might expect from a " friendly intercourse with that country; or " was a pacific connexion between the two " kingdoms so highly offensive that even an " extension of commerce could not counter- " poise it?" Towards the close of the same speech, he observes, " The quarrels between " France and Britain had too leng conti- " nued to harass not only those two great " and respectable nations themselves, but had " frequently embroiled the peace of Europe; " nay, it had disturbed the tranquillity of " the most remote parts of the world. They " had, by their past conduct, acted as if they

"were intended for the destruction of each
"other; but he hoped the time was now come
"when they should justify the order of the uni-
"verse, and show that they were better cal-
"culated for the more amiable purposes of
"friendly intercourse and mutual benevo-
"lence."—" Considering the treaty," he continued, " in a political view, he should not
"hesitate to contend against the too frequently
"advanced doctrine, that France was and must
"be the unalterable enemy of Britain. His
"mind revolted from this position as monstrous
"and impossible. To suppose that any nation
"was unalterably the enemy of another was
"weak and childish. It had neither its founda-
"tion in the experience of nations nor in the
"history of man. It was a libel on the consti-
"tution of political societies; and supposed
"diabolical malice in the original frame of
"man *."

It is only when the policy of states is guided by such liberal and enlightened views, that nations can hope for permanent repose. Before the conclusion of this memorable treaty all friendly intercourse was discouraged between France and Great Britain. The statesmen of

* Debrett's Parliamentary Register, Vol. 21, anno 1787.

this country seem to have imagined, that because Louis XIV. disturbed the peace of Europe each succeeding ruler must necessarily possess the same ambitious views; and acting on those suspicions, they in part provoked the enmity of which they complained. A different policy was now pursued. The rulers both of France and of England, far from acquiescing in the necessity of eternal enmity between the two nations, resolved to try the experiment of a sincere and lasting union ; and it is in this view, as a political as well as a commercial measure, that this treaty will ever remain a monument of policy and of wisdom—the discourse of men of reflection in after ages, and the theme of the historian's praise *.

* A copy of this treaty will be found in the Appendix, Note [L.]

ON NATIONAL DEFENCE.

The events of war are decided by discipline, numbers, and military skill; and wherever one army conquers another, it must be owing to its superiority in some one or other of those essential points.

Discipline consists in habits of prompt obedience to command, and in that courage which naturally arises from the practice of war. It seems to be evident both from reason and experience, that a regular army, bred to duty and obedience under the severe sanction of military law, and trained to warlike habits amid the perils of actual service,—the soldiers full of confidence in their officers, and they in return glorying in the achievements of their troops, must in battle possess a decided superiority over a body of peaceful citizens, occasionally employed in military exercises, but wholly unpractised in war. With the outward appearance of soldiers, such troops must be deficient in all the essential qualities and habits which are formed by the discipline of armies, and the duties of the field; and which, as they chiefly contribute to the gaining of battles, constitute the perfection of a military force. The distinction between regular troops and bodies of citizens occasionally trained to the use of arms, but neither subject to military law, nor exposed to the hazards of war, is accordingly recognised by all military writers. It has been acted upon by the most skilful generals, and is sanctioned by universal experience; since it has always been found that, where irregular troops have been rashly exposed to the attack of a veteran force, they have been irrecoverably broken and dispersed at the first onset, while in these circumstances panic generally aids the sword of the enemy, and numbers only augment the confusion.

A commander, therefore, who invades a country at the head of a regular army, and who is fully aware of its power, will naturally endeavour, if he is acting against new levies, to bring on a battle; and having, by the bravery of his troops, driven his adversary from the field, he will hasten to complete his ruin, by a bold and rapid pursuit, pushing forward into the invaded country with his victorious troops, attacking and dispersing the flying bodies of the routed army, and crushing resistance wherever he appears. So long as an army exists to check, however imperfectly, the adversary's force, there is always some hope of repelling his attack. But the destruction of the army is an irreparable blow; as it leaves a country defenceless and open to the conqueror. It is to the army that the peaceable inhabitants look for protection, while they are preparing for defence, and are yet unable to protect themselves, and they afford in return, to the army, the constant means of renovation under the losses of the field. The army and the population, while they are thus united, form a sure and solid defence; but their union once broken by the overthrow of the army, the country is lost. The army is the rallying point for all those who are disposed to unite against the enemy. It is the basis on which every arrangement must naturally rest, and if it is once shattered and thrown down, the people must yield without a struggle. Resistance confined to secret plots and petty insurrections will then assume the character of treason against established power, and the ruin and punishment of its authors will give the last blow to an expiring cause.

If the invader, in place of carrying on a daring system of attack, wastes his time and the energy of his troops in timid and indecisive warfare, he allows the country that precious interval of leisure, which if duly improved may be sufficient for its defence. His policy consists in dispatch, that he may subdue his enemies before their arrangements for defence are complete; but if he neglect the first fair opportunity of success, he cannot rationally calculate on finding another.

A commander who undertakes the defence of a country with troops which he cannot on equal terms expose to his adversary's attack, will naturally seek for his inferior force the shelter of strong positions, where, if he be attacked, he may hope to escape a ruinous defeat, while his adversary attacking at a disadvantage, may suffer such a loss of men as may not only disable him from any further prosecution of his enterprize, but may lead to his final overthrow. If the invading army refuse to attack, its progress is stopped, which is a great step to the successful defence of the country; for as in general its population far exceeds in physical power the force by which it is attacked, it is not so much the means of defence that are wanting as time to call them into activity and use. In war nothing is so valuable as time; and a country, by wisely improving every interval of leisure, will finally overpower the most formidable assailant. When Sertorius, the Roman general, had recourse to bribery, to gain the passes of the Pyrenees, and was reproached with a conduct so little congenial to the feelings of a Roman soldier, he laughed at these scruples, adding, " that he never scorned to buy time of an enemy at any price." It is in this view that a well trained army is so formidable an instrument, being ready to overwhelm a country, while it is providing for its defence. But if an invading army be once involved in a contest of indecisive movements, this peculiar advantage is lost; the invaded country has time for defence; and its newly raised force, gradually inured to war, becomes formidable in the field, covering the population from the inroads of the enemy, and drawing in return from the population supplies of men to any extent. A country may thus be defended against the superior discipline of an invading army, by a skilful use of its natural advantages; or the invader may fail in his enterprize, from the want of means, or from his own timidity or misconduct.

A country which is defended by a numerous, brave, and well commanded army, can only be conquered by an army braver and better commanded, and either more numerous, or with greater means of repairing the ravages of war. In such a contest, no easy nor very decisive advantages are to be looked for; every inch of ground will be obstinately disputed; and the invader, to succeed, must push his force through a course of desperate service, in which doubtful victories will be gained at a very high price. If he has not abundance of means, his force will perish under the waste of service, and every battle will bring him nearer to destruction.

A country which is still further strengthened by a chain of fortified towns, will by that means acquire an additional security against any sudden inroad; as the enemy's force, arrested at the frontier, may be engaged in a destructive warfare of battles and sieges, in which army after army may waste away, without any visible progress in the work of conquest.

An invader who has not the means of supporting such ruinous warfare must be foiled in his attack. His army, pushing on in the full career of its exploits, must be exhausted at length by a succession of dear bought victories. His scheme of conquest must fail for want of the means necessary to carry it into effect. He cannot pay the fair price for success—he cannot hazard any of those daring attacks, in which victory must be purchased by an enormous sacrifice of men. No harrassing marches,—no sanguinary battles can be tried. The enthusiasm of his troops is suffered to languish under a system of timid and protracted warfare; and the country, relieved from the vigour of his attack, has leisure for defence.

A well supported army, however, pushed on with vigour and skill, will pierce through every opposing barrier, either of strong positions or of fortified towns. The utility of these defences consists in wasting both the time and the strength of an invading force. But an invader who can repair this waste, who can instantly bring into the field a crowd of new assailants, and who, to gain time, can lavish the blood of his troops in a series of incessant attacks, eager for the prize, and regardless of the cost, will, in the end, triumph over the natural and artificial strength of any country.

The invasion of Greece by the Persians is the first great military enterprize of which there is any authentic account. The battles to which this expedition gave rise were fought between the numerous and tumultuary armies of Persia and the small but well disciplined bands of Greek patriots. Courage and skill were thus fairly matched against superior numbers, and in the end they completely triumphed. In the battles of Marathon and Platea, the vast armies of Persia fled before a handful of Greek troops. The general effeminacy of manners among the Persians had corrupted the discipline of the army, which was besides attended by a train of idle followers, that added to its numbers, though not to its strength. The institutions of Greece, so wisely contrived to make a nation of warriors, were at this time in their full vigour; and the Greek troops, bred in so admirable a school, excelled the Persians as much in valour as they fell short of them in numbers. They accordingly gained a complete victory with a trifling loss. The Persians were routed and dispersed, and were never able afterwards to make the least show of resistance in the field. So complete a victory, so easily gained, plainly shewed that no serious resistance had been made. The wars which afterwards broke out among the states of Greece were carried on with troops nearly equal in discipline. There was, accordingly, in every action an obstinate struggle for victory; and the armies on both sides being equal in bravery, the skill of the generals usually decided the contest. The celebrated battles of Leuctra and Mantinea were gained entirely by superior science; Epaminondas the Theban general having, by a masterly manœuvre, suddenly broken the Lacedemonian centre, and thrown it into irreparable disorder. In the war of Greece, with Philip of Macedon, both parties seem to have had brave troops; and the battle of Cheronea, so fatal to Greece, was lost, not by any want of valour in the soldiers, but by the incapacity of the generals. The Greeks, though they fought well, were so unskilfully managed, that they were routed and dispersed.

The subjection of the states of Greece under one great power made way for the long threatened invasion of Persia. This great enterprize was accordingly undertaken by Alexander the Great, who, having defeated the Persians in several decisive battles, made himself master of the whole country. In this war the veteran troops of Macedon were matched against the effeminate and ill-trained armies of Persia, which, though greatly outnumbering their enemies, were routed in four great battles, and were at last entirely dispersed. These decisive victories, so cheaply gained, insured to Alexander the conquest of the country. If he had been more skilfully opposed, and had in consequence lost more men, he would have had great difficulty in recruiting his armies; and it seems doubtful, however ably he had managed his force, whether he could have supported a destructive warfare, so far from his own territory.

The rise of the Roman power forms an interesting era in history. The policy of Rome was directed to freedom and glory, to which her government and civil institutions were entirely subservient. By the laws of the republic, the Roman territory was shared among a race of soldiers and freemen, ready to second with their blood the warlike views of the state. Their martial spirit was debased by no servile industry. Agriculture was the sole pursuit; and the leisure of peace was filled up with the discipline of war. The Roman youth were familiarised by the daily task of military duty to the toils of actual service, and hardened by such a process of domestic training, they excelled both in body and mind the troops of every other nation. Rome, with her whole population, trained and disposable for war, was in this manner the most perfect model that can be conceived of a military community.

To guide this mass of strength, the popular institutions of the republic, which placed with the people all civil and military appointments, insured an able government. The choice of the people always implies some peculiar merit or fitness in the person chosen. Public opinion is in truth the test of merit—it is the great market in which men are estimated at their true value; and where it guides the appointments of the state, it is sure to place in the public service the whole talent of the community. Such was the system established at Rome; and under its favouring influence, ability naturally rose to its level; capacity for service was the sacred principle which governed the distribution of public trusts; and the result was such a display of power as subdued the world.

The continual warfare in which this state was engaged, preserved and improved the military science. Every branch of knowledge connected with war was diligently studied; instruction was sought from friends and foes; and the art of war was thus gradually brought to perfection. With abundance of brave men, therefore, with able generals, and a complete knowledge of war, the armies of Rome went forth conquering and to conquer; and her enemies being inferior in warlike strength, were, each in their turn, overpowered by the weight and violence of her attacks.

During her progress to empire, the power of Rome was exposed to many rude attacks. The causes of her greatness were, however, so firmly rooted in the constitution and manners of the people, that victory was still the result of each new struggle. The invasion of Italy by Pyrrhus was the first great trial of her strength. This warlike prince took the field with brave troops, and gained the first battle that was fought; but with such a sacrifice of men, as clearly presaged the ultimate failure of his enterprize. A seasonable defeat completed his dismay, and forced him with disgrace from the Roman territories.

Hannibal, a more formidable assailant, penetrated into Italy by a daring march across the Alps; and having gained three great battles, spread everywhere the terror of his arms. The Romans, foiled in the field, had recourse to defensive war; and having raised new armies, succeeded in occupying positions which Hannibal could not have carried without a ruinous waste of his troops. His progress was thus checked; and while he was wasting his force without forwarding his object, Rome was embodying her whole population against his declining strength. He wanted men to carry his army through such a series of destructive battles as would have insured the conquest of Rome. He had drawn out a fair scheme of conquest, and had assembled a fine army; but while he grasped the precious instrument of victory, he wanted the means of keeping it in repair till its work was finished. Success was to be obtained by the most prodigal sacrifice of men, while the want of men was precisely the defect for which he had no remedy. The road to conquest was thus shut against him. His advance was impossible; and time, which was wasting his strength, was daily multiplying the resources of his enemies.

The power of Rome declined with that state

of property and manners which placed the whole population at the disposal of the state. In every nation, the surplus produce of the soil is the great fund either of enjoyment or of power*. The Romans, hitherto intent on power, had disposed of it in the maintenance of soldiers. But when the senators came to ingross the lands of the poorer citizens, they substituted for the soldiers, who were the original possessors of the soil, a race of slaves and artizans, the ministers of pride and luxury. The foundation was thus laid for enjoyment, at the expence of power; and Rome, though ruling over a larger population, possessed fewer citizens, and of course fewer soldiers. The decline of freedom and of the national character, kept pace with the progress of luxury; and the degenerate Romans, disgusted with the perils of war, were content to owe their safety to the sword of the barbarians rather than to their own courage.

In transferring the seat of government to the east, a pure despotism was established with all its manifold corruptions; and in the decline of warlike habits, and of every manly virtue, the materials of an army were no longer

* See observations On the Progress of National Opulence.

to be found. Military discipline was relaxed; the science of war was neglected; and, in this lamentable condition, the Greek empire was assaulted by the vigour of the Turkish power. From this period commences a long era of national calamity, in which the loss of the capital, after being stript of its dependent provinces, concludes the tragical story of imbecility and ruin *.

* The circumstances which hastened the decline of Rome, are so simple and obvious, that in place of inquiring why the empire was destroyed, we ought rather, according to Mr Gibbon, to be surprised that it lasted so long. The remark is just; and to solve the problem of its duration, the following causes may therefore be suggested.

I. It was the policy of Augustus, when he assumed the government, to conceal the extent of his power under a shew of freedom; by which means he preserved, along with the forms of the ancient constitution, some remains of the national spirit. From this source was derived the martial ardour of the Roman legions, which, while it lasted, was more than a match for the untutored valour of the barbarians, and preserved the frontiers from their inroads.

II. The decline of Rome was arrested by the vigour of her elective system. The Roman emperors, though they frequently owed their dignity to the basest motives, were often chosen for their public services or their martial virtues. At other times, the competition for supreme power was decided by the sword; and the contest which ensued, however destructive of the peace and happiness of the community, was a fair trial of skill, in which the sovereignty was the prize of superior talent. The losing can-

In the wars of the middle ages, there is nothing to fix the attention of a rational inquirer. The contests between the barbarians of those times were usually mere exhibitions of courage; and it was not until civilization had made greater progress, that science resumed its influence over the fate of battles. The Turks, flushed with their triumph over the declining empire of the Greeks, carried on, for a length of time, some fierce wars with the states of Christendom. But the superiority of European science at length decided the struggle and circumscribed the conquests of these modern barbarians. In Europe the art of war was studied and improved in common with all other arts and sciences, while in this, as in other matters, the Turks retained their original ignorance. In the wars of

didate was condemned to obscurity, on a fair comparison of merit with his more fortunate and able rival. By whatever path, therefore, the Roman emperors rose to their high station, there was generally some question of their capacity for the discharge of its great duties. Hence arose a succession of able princes, whose talents imparted new vigour to the declining state. Nerva, Adrian, Trajan, and the two Antonines, and in later times, Severus, Probus, Aurelian, reviving the ancient discipline of the troops, scattered dismay amongst the enemies of Rome, and upheld with a firm hand the tottering fabric of her power.

Europeans with each other, different nations have acquired military renown, according as the practice of war happened to improve their armies, or the skill of their generals, beyond that of their opponents. But the successes gained in this way were partial and short lived, and made no material change on the political state of the world.

The ambition of Louis XIV. gave rise to the first serious enterprize against the independence of nations. Relying on his great resources, this vain and restless monarch invaded Holland with a force fully sufficient to have subdued the country had his generals pursued their first advantages with vigour. But they committed the capital error of wasting their time; while the Dutch recovered from their first dismay, and in the interval their troops, under the Prince of Orange, acquiring all the habits of soldiers, fought at last an equal battle with their enemies, and repelled their attack. In the wars which were afterwards carried on against France, the armies on both sides appear to have been equally matched. It is related of king William, by bishop Burnet, that he committed great errors of conduct; but that he had a heroic courage, which, in the moment of action, inflamed all around him; and it seems likely that this talent of communicating enthusiasm to his troops, had redeemed the faults of his management. The jealousies of the European powers soon produced a new contest, in which the armies of France maintained an obstinate but unavailing struggle against the talents of Marlborough. Defeated wherever they could be brought to action, and forced to abandon all schemes of offensive hostility, they were at last reduced to a doubtful conflict on their own territories, in the course of which the chief fortresses of the country successively fell into the enemy's power. But after six years of success France remained still unsubdued, and her armies, though frequently defeated, occasionally withstood in defensive positions the farther progress of their victorious adversaries. The invading army thus checked, was forced to turn away to safer though less decisive operations, and the invaded country acquired the necessary interval for defence. Had this interval been duly improved, France might have overwhelmed her enemies by her vast resources; but on neither side was this contest carried on with an ardour suited to the great interests at stake. It was a struggle between rival governments, in which the respective armies consisted of such precarious supplies as could be brought together without system or perseverance to fight the battles of ambition. The genius of the age was not warlike. The employments of peace were not yet drained to supply victims for the field, and the commanders on both sides were afraid to waste, even for important objects, what they found it so difficult to replace. The want of men was the true reason of Marlborough's caution. He was forced to suit his mode of warfare to the state of his supplies, and to reject even success, unless he could attain it on his own terms. The attack of the French position at Malplaquet, in which he succeeded, with the loss of 18,000 men, was his boldest enterprize. For this action he was violently censured, though it is through a succession of such desperate battles that the natural course of an invader lies; and unless he can bear the unavoidable waste of this sort of warfare, it is vain to attempt the invasion of any country.

The effect of science against numbers was displayed in the wars of Frederick of Prussia, who, against powerful enemies, maintained a long and unequal contest, by the rapid movement and skilful distribution of his limited force. The victory of Prague was the result of wise combinations, by which he united his whole army, before an Austrian corps which was advancing from Moravia could join the main body. The same principle will be found to pervade his whole system, and indeed every other system where the resources of talent are matched against superior force.

In the contest of Great Britain with her colonies, a well disciplined army was opposed to a whole people; and its exploits in the field attested its superiority over the popular army of America. The Americans were never able to stand an equal battle with the British troops; and their general, conscious of inferiority, sought protection from the higher grounds, where his antagonist did not think it prudent to attack him. The country in truth abounded in the most impregnable positions. It was one continued natural fortress; and an army beaten from one post, would have soon found another equally advantageous. These positions were still further strengthened by every species of artificial intrenchment; for it was the boast of the American general, that he never spared the mattock and the spade; and had the invading army at such a distance from its supplies, and with so many obstacles to encounter, commenced decisive operations, they must have speedily terminated in its own ruin. In the battle of Bunker's Hill, so great a proportion of the assailants were either killed or wounded, that the result, while it proved the Americans, with every advantage of position, unable to withstand the onset of the British troops, fatally demonstrated, at the same time, that the invading army must perish under a succession of such victories. The British general may have missed some fair occasions of success: he may have managed his attack unskilfully. But the strength of the country, the union of the people, the talents of the general, and the small number of the assailants, sufficiently account for the failure of the enterprize.

To the same general causes may be ascribed the failure of the invasion of France in 1792. When the hostile armies advanced into the country it was in a great measure unprepared for defence; its weak and undisciplined levies were broken and dispersed by the veteran troops of the allies, and a decisive system of attack, with ample means of renovation under the losses of the field, would have insured the final triumph of the invading force. But the assailants were in no haste to profit by their first advantages. They delayed to advance until the defenceless country collected its strength, and they were finally overwhelmed by the desperate energies of a united people. To avert the calamity of a foreign yoke, the French nation, under the powerful sway of a popular government, flew to arms, and Europe beheld, for the first time, the whole talents and resources of a civilized country devoted to war. The singular events of a revolution in its first aspect favourable to freedom, called forth a spirit of enthusiastic devotion to the public cause. Under the influence of this popular feeling, all the necessary materials of war were instantly provided, and such vast resources collected, that the French generals were enabled to overwhelm their enemies, by a succession of sanguinary attacks. Far from pausing to count the sacrifice that was to be the price of success, it was their glory and their policy to engage in general battles; and having exhausted their adversary by repeated attacks, to pursue him, with restless activity, through all the disasters of retreat or flight, until his ruin was complete.

It was soon found, however, that in those

decisive but sanguinary operations, the waste of men was greater than the supply ; and in the first years of the revolutionary war, a short era of brilliant success was accordingly followed by a series of striking reverses. But the grand experiment was made; the system had displayed its power, and the means were only wanting for carrying it into effect. With this view new and more effectual arrangements were adopted by the rulers of France for the renovation of their wasted force; and the French generals, thus assured of supplies, were left to pursue their successes, through scenes of carnage, such as no armies ever before encountered. Offensive war was now displayed in all its tragical perfection. The cautious policy of former ages was forgotten ; and Europe was astonished by a new system of warfare, which, while it led to the most prodigal sacrifice of life, was, beyond all former example, decisive in its results.

But modern war is not more remarkable for its bold and decisive operations than for the science by which its vast armies, though extending over a line of several hundred miles, still preserve the most perfect concert in all their diversified movements.

When two hostile armies are opposed to each other on so extensive a line, it is obvious that the general who can suddenly collect a commanding force may overwhelm his adversary at the point which he selects for attack, and pursuing his blow until the hostile army be broken and its communications lost, he may finally overpower and destroy it in detail. In such operations, the commander who waits for an attack must necessarily be defeated; since the particular point being left to the choice of his antagonist, he will naturally fix it where the strength of his own and the weakness of the opposite line enable him with certainty to penetrate to the enemy's rear. It avails nothing to the party attacked that he is strong at some distant point—a circumstance which can be of no advantage to him after his line has been penetrated, and part of his army driven from the field; since if he were to advance against the weak parts of his adversary's line, the latter would retreat, making a defence suited to his limited means, while the victorious part of the line, after clearing its front, and guarding against annoyance from that quarter, would proceed to take such positions as to cut off the retreat of the advanced part of the enemy's force, and expose it to a double attack both in front and rear. The science of modern generals appears therefore to be displayed in the management and distribution of their force—in weakening themselves where it is not their interest to be strong, that their whole strength may be collected where the decisive blow is to be struck *.

* The history of the wars subsequent to the French revolution, furnishes many examples where, by concentrating their strength at particular points, modern armies have succeeded in defeating superior forces; and the system is strikingly exemplified in the plan of operations adopted by the Archduke Charles in the campaign of 1796, when with inferior numbers he compelled the combined armies of Jourdan and Moreau to retreat from Germany and to recross the Rhine. At this period the counsels of France were occupied with the dazzling scheme of uniting in the heart of Germany the triumphant armies of Italy and the Rhine; and with this view Jourdan and Moreau advanced into Germany from different points for the purpose of attacking the Austrian army with superior forces. In these circumstances, the Archduke Charles plainly perceived that if he waited for the combined attack of the enemy, his army must be destroyed. He continued therefore slowly to retire, disputing the position of every important post, and patiently waiting for an opportunity of commencing a bolder and more decisive plan of operations. When the favourable moment arrived, he instantly collected his whole force, and leaving a sufficient number of troops for carrying on in his absence a defensive war against Moreau, he proceeded with great secrecy, and by forced marches, in search of Jourdan's army. A battle was fought near Amberg, in which the French general was totally defeated;

The advantages which an invading army derives from this system of extended hostility are obvious and striking, since, in place of ap-

and, by the boldness and rapidity of the Archduke's movements, the road through which he was retreating being preoccupied, he was driven by cross-roads to Bamberg, where being again defeated, and forced from the line of his retreat, he was finally compelled to retire across the Rhine, with the loss of nearly half his army, in the course of a disorderly flight of about 300 miles, from the frontiers of Bohemia to the walls of Dusseldorf. Moreau in the mean time, ignorant of the fate of Jourdan, had advanced into Germany, until he was in his turn surrounded by superior forces; and he extricated himself by precisely the same system which the Archduke had followed on a larger scale and with such decisive success.

This campaign, so memorable for the salvation of Germany, was distinguished also by the loss of Italy, and in both cases success was the result of the same skilful combinations, which enabled a force inferior on the whole to engage in every decisive battle with a local superiority. The French army which invaded Italy in 1796, under the command of Bonaparte, is generally estimated at 80,000 men, and it was opposed by an equal number of Austrian and Piedmontese troops. The hostile armies were extended over a space of about eighty or ninety miles, and it was the plan of the French general, by piercing the enemy's line, to disunite his force and to destroy it in detail. With this view, after alarming the whole position by a series of feints and manœuvres, and sending forward a corps to threaten Genoa on the left, which instantly attracted thither a large detachment of the Austrians, he suddenly concentrated his main force and directed a decisive attack against the right and centre, which being defeated in several obstinate battles, were at length completely disunited, and thrown into such disorder, that the right was only saved from de-

proaching the invaded country by one route, it may threaten its whole frontier, and attacking the weak and unguarded points, may leave struction by an armistice; and the centre, after various disasters, was forced to relinquish the defence of Italy, and finally driven into the Tyrol.

These decisive events were followed by the siege of Mantua; and the new army which advanced under General Wurmser to relieve the place, shared the fate of the former by copying its errors. The Austrian general, in place of manœuvring with his united force, divided it into separate columns, of which the right making a circuit round the lake of Garda, menaced the rear of the enemy's line, while the left and centre were to attack it in front. By these movements the position of the besieging army was threatened on both sides; but the opposite force was at the same time disunited; and the French general seeing his own danger, as well as the error of his antagonist, precipitately raised the siege, and having fallen upon the Austrian right with his whole force, overwhelmed and dispersed it in a series of obstinate battles. Wheeling round with his victorious troops he then encountered the centre, which being thus involved in a general action with a hopeless disproportion of numbers, was defeated at all points, and after a disastrous flight forced to seek safety in the Tyrol. Undismayed by these reverses, fresh armies advanced to contend for the prize of Italy. But in spite of all the lessons of experience, the Austrian generals persisted in the same fatal policy of dividing their strength, while their skilful adversary overwhelmed them in detail by the surer game of rapid manœuvres with a commanding force.

In the civil wars carried on in England during the reign of Charles I. many opportunities occurred where a judicious concentration of force would have insured the triumph of either party. But it is justly remarked by Hume, that in these wars there was no display of science. Previous to

those which are stronger and more defensible to fall of their own accord, as they are successively flanked by the irruption of the victorious force. Against such hostility the natural strength of a country affords no defence, as all its strong points may be gained by manœuvres executed on more accessible ground. The in-

the battle of Naseby, so fatal to the royal cause, the king had an army of 8000 men engaged in the siege of Taunton, which if it had been united to the main army by a rapid march, would have given him a decisive superiority; and if he had beaten his enemies in that decisive battle, the partial advantages which they might have gained in the mean time, in other parts, owing to the absence of his force, would have been of little avail. ' By his reluctance to forego minor objects, he lost the great game in which all those objects were involved.

The celebrated march of Marlborough from Flanders to the Danube, previous to the great battle of Blenheim, affords a most remarkable example of military science; and the secrecy, rapidity, and admirable combination of his movements, may challenge a comparison with some of the finest manœuvres of modern times. The Bavarians were already masters of the Danube as far as Passau, and it was the plan of the French, after forcing their passage through the defiles of the Black Forest, to unite with their allies and penetrate to Vienna. A great effort being necessary to rescue Germany from this formidable irruption, Marlborough resolved to unite his force with the imperial armies on the Danube; and his plans were concerted and executed with such secrecy and decision, that having gained several marches on the French armies, he succeeded in concentrating a commanding force, with which he fought the decisive battle of Blenheim, and thus saved the German empire.

vader, by extending and combining his force according to the rules of modern science, may assail a hostile frontier, not where it is strong, but where it is weak; by which means, evading the doubtful attack of difficult positions, he will bring the contest to the issue of a battle on ground of his own chusing. The defence of the country will thus rest not on its strong frontier but on its army, the ruin of which must instantly decide the struggle in favour of the invader. In modern war, the armies of Europe manœuvred upon those great principles have frequently extended, in one immense chain of posts, from the Adriatic to the Rhine: and against a force thus arranged, and manœuvred upon the sure maxims of science, what vigilance could guard so extensive a line? Where is the frontier of such uniform strength as to withstand the policy of those formidable combinations? In so vast a scheme of hostility, of what moment is the strong country of Switzerland, when it can be won by movements made in Germany; or the fine positions of the Italian territory, when powerful and unbroken armies may be forced from their ground by battles fought at the distance of several hundred miles * ? No example of such combination and science, is to be found in the past scenes of military history.

* In the campaign of 1805 the hostile armies of Austria and France occupied positions both in Italy and in Germany. The Austrians were posted near Ulm on the Danube, and were guarding the defiles of the Black Forest, when Bonaparte, crossing lower down the Rhine, at different points, between Manheim and Strasburg, made a circuitous sweep with the greater part of his vast force, which, after a series of astonishing marches and great manœuvres, crossed the Danube at Donawerth and other points, and was extended over the adjacent country, while the Austrian force either retained its original position in the vicinity of Ulm, or was endeavouring to effect a doubtful retreat. The two armies were thus in the rear of each other, in the same manner as in the campaign of 1800, previous to the memorable battle of Marengo; but the Austrians, in place of following the bold example of General Melas, who concentrated his force for a decisive action, endeavoured to retreat, and being attacked and beaten in detail, the greater part of their army was either dispersed or taken. By the destruction of the Austrian army in Germany, the Archduke Charles, who commanded a force in Italy, though distant more than 200 miles from the scene of action, found it necessary to provide for the safety of his army by an immediate retreat, though apparently in a condition to maintain his ground against the French force, to which he was immediately opposed. Had he remained in his position, however, the rapid advance of the grand French army into Germany, by cutting off his retreat, would have exposed him to certain destruction. It may be also remarked, that Massena, who commanded the French army in Italy, states, as his reason for ordering his army to advance and to attack the enemy, that " it was with

The armies of former times, when engaged in distant points, followed no common principle of action, nor were they ever affected by the result of battles in which they were not immediately engaged. But the plans of modern war, however extended or apparently complicated, present a series of orderly manœuvres, artfully arranged for the accomplishment of one simple design. There is no waste of strength in useless operations; nothing is sacrificed to show or parade. In every movement, policy still directs what valour executes, and the whole force in the field is manœuvred in such exact subordination to the main plan, that no story in romance will be found more happily combined, according to the rules of critical unity, than the incidents of a well conducted modern campaign.

This union of force and policy has abundantly displayed its power during the wars which, with occasional intermissions, have agitated Europe since the period of the French revolution; and in the course of those eventful contests, a series of unparalleled successes enabled the rulers of

a view of conforming to the progress of the grand army, and because he was always impressed with the policy of rendering his movements subordinate to it."

France to extend their influence over the finest kingdoms of Europe. From the immense population which was placed at their absolute disposal, they drew unlimited supplies of men, while a severe and impartial promotion called forth ability into active service through all the gradations of command. Science and discipline thus gave irresistible weight to superior numbers, and the chief powers of Europe fell in a succession of unavailing struggles for their independence.

In place of joining in one scheme of resistance to the progress of the French arms, the sovereigns of Europe either passively beheld the contest, or were ranged on the side of the common enemy, while those whose arms and counsels were united under a different policy, were by their slow or injudicious combinations crushed before their joint force could take the field. In 1805, Austria was overwhelmed before Russia could lend her aid ; and in 1806, Prussia was swept from the field while the Russian troops were in Poland. The whole Prussian force was annihilated in a single battle, while the French armies, with all the losses which the rapid pursuit and the operations of the succeeding winter must have cost them, continued their advance and outnumbered the Russian force in the proportion of three to two upon its own frontiers. The victory of Friedland was the consequence partly of this superiority, and partly also of superior skill. In the war of 1809, Prussia was a passive spectator of the fall of Austria, while Russia was leagued against her. The destruction of that vast army which, in the year 1812, was engaged in the stupendous project of conquering Russia, gave the first great blow to the military power of France; for although in the succeeding campaign fresh armies enabled her to resume the attitude of victory, the great powers of Europe had, during the interval, coalesced for their common defence, and by a singular combination of circumstances, their armies were already united in the field of battle. No unexpected blow could therefore be struck,—no project devised for insulating any part of the opposing force and destroying it in detail; and France, forced at length to encounter the united strength of Europe, was overthrown in the unequal struggle. Her victorious adversaries, pursuing their success, advanced into the country before an adequate force could be collected for its defence, and having penetrated to the capital, they terminated the contest by the subversion of the government.

France, which had so long triumphed over the nations of Europe, was thus at length overthrown by their united power; and the causes both of her elevation and of her fall are simple and obvious. When the new republic first arose in the vigour of her strength to triumph over all her enemies, mankind were astonished; the revolution seemed to have developed some new and secret principle, which set at defiance all the boasted calculations of policy, and a succession of triumphs was achieved which spread far and wide the illusion of irresistible power. But when the first alarm passed away, and when those astonishing results began to be traced to their causes, it was soon found that Europe had to deal with an armed nation, which poured its population into the field, which supplied men faster than the sword could cut them down, and thus continually replenishing the field of battle with new victims, carried her armies with undiminished strength through destructive battles and through restless marches. In such an emergency, the old system of military policy in Europe was of little avail, and the armies which it produced were quickly borne down by the torrent of conquest and revolution. The want of concert also among the European powers, exposed them to be destroyed in detail by this new power which it would have required all their combined force to resist. Since this period, however, Europe began gradually to adapt its military policy to the emergencies of the world; its states disunited by jealousies, united their strength; their population was more effectually called forth; their armies became more numerous; the new science of war was studied and practised; and France thus found herself matched at length in all the great requisites of military power.

OF THE AFFAIRS OF THE EAST INDIA COMPANY.

Dr Smith's view of the East India Company's affairs is imperfect in many respects; and in pursuance of the plan of his work, I have therefore added the following account of the more recent transactions of the company in Europe, and of its commercial and political transactions in India.

OF THE CONSTITUTION AND TRANSACTIONS OF THE COMPANY IN EUROPE.

In 1784, the company possessed a nominal capital of L.3,200,000, of which only a part, amounting to L.2,800,000 was subscribed, the directors retaining the power of calling for the remainder. In 1786, an additional capital of

L.800,000 was subscribed at L.155 per cent. which produced L.1,240,000. In 1789, a million more was added to the capital stock, at the rate of L.174 per cent.; and in 1793, the capital was still farther increased by another million, at the rate of L.200 per cent.; so that the nominal capital of the company, on which a dividend is payable, amounts to L.6,000,000, for which cash has been paid into the company's funds to the amount of L.7,780,000 *.

The original constitution of the company has received some important amendments. When first instituted, its affairs were managed by twenty-four directors, who were continued in office for one year. They were afterwards elected for four years, six of them vacating their offices by rotation every year. Those directors were not only accountable for their whole management to the proprietors, but all their appointments were liable to be reversed by their authority; and it frequently happened that the proprietors overruled not only the resolutions

* In addition to this capital, the company advanced, at different times, to government, L.4,200,000; for which interest was paid at the rate of three per cent. But as the annuity payable on this account was sold by the company, they in effect borrowed the whole sum lent to government.

of their own directors, but those of parliament also.

The year 1783 was distinguished by the political contests between the rival parties of Mr Fox and Mr Pitt, who rested their claims to public confidence on the merits of their respective systems for the government of India. On Mr Fox's accession to the ministry, he submitted to parliament a plan for the reformation of the East India Company's affairs; by which it was proposed to vest in seven commissioners or directors, to be appointed in the first instance by parliament, and afterwards by the crown, the whole management of the company's concerns. Those commissioners were to be assisted by nine others, proprietors of India stock to the amount of L.2000, and removable by the seven principal commissioners; and, under their joint controul, both the trade and the government were to be managed for the benefit of the company; they were vested with the power of nominating to all offices, both civil and military; all the books, papers, and documents, as well as the money, merchandize, and ships, belonging to the company, were committed to their charge; and for the due execution of their trust, they were responsible both to parliament and to the company. The receipt of bribes, under the name of presents, was strictly prohibited; and the restoration of the landholders to the estates of which they had been deprived, was specially provided for. The powers of the executive government in India were also more strictly defined; and various provisions were added for preventing war, or the farther extension of the company's territories.

The object of the plan thus devised by Mr Fox was, not so much to change the company's institutions, as to remedy the evils arising from the admitted inefficiency of the government at home; for though the directors generally disapproved of the conduct of their servants in India, their votes and resolutions were attended with no practical effect. The servants not only retained their offices and pursued the same system, but they had secured an influence in the court of proprietors, by which they were enabled to counteract the views both of the directors and of parliament. By abolishing the influence of the proprietors, by vesting the whole management in the commissioners or directors, and by placing the appointment of those directors in the recognised authorities of the state, Mr Fox proposed to place the government on a firmer basis.

This system being finally rejected, a new measure was introduced by Mr Pitt, who had succeeded to the administration of public affairs; by which it was proposed to leave with the court of directors the entire management of the trade, and to institute a board of commissioners, consisting of two secretaries of state and three privy councillors, appointed by the king, and removeable at his pleasure, for the controul of the government. With the directors was still placed the power of nominating to all civil and military appointments; but they were bound, in every proceeding which affected the government or territorial revenues of their dominions, to submit their whole correspondence with the resident administration to the board of controul; which might alter, amend, or altogether withhold any letter or order deemed improper to be sent to India. The directors had the privilege of an appeal to the king in council, provided the commissioners should interfere in matters purely commercial; and any civil or military officer might be removed, either by their authority or by that of the king. The proprietors still retained the privilege of electing the directors; but the power which they formerly possessed of over-ruling their proceedings, was abolished.

It was proposed, as in Mr Fox's bill, to reinstate the landholders in their respective properties, and to make a permanent settlement of the land rents. The receipt of presents was also declared illegal, and the governor-general and council were declared incompetent to make war, except in case of actual invasion or of preparations for hostilities. A new system of judicature, composed of a certain number of peers and commoners, chosen by ballot, was at the same time proposed for the trial of crimes committed in India.

It may be generally remarked of those plans for governing India by a controul established in Europe, that the object which they have in view appears to be impracticable; for although Great Britain may hold the nominal sovereignty of those remote dependencies, it is obvious, that all power must substantially reside with those who are delegated to rule in India. The distance of the two countries necessarily places with the resident government the power of acting according to circumstances as they arise; and the European sovereigns of India can only exercise their controul, either by changing a system of administration already established and acted upon (and such alterations will seldom be found expedient) or, where criminality appears, by censuring and punishing the guilty. But for this purpose a criminal process becomes necessary; and when the disadvantages are considered under which a proceeding of this nature must be carried on, as well as the various means which exist both of evasion and delay, it seems obvious that such restraints will be of little avail in practice, and that, however the constitution of the company may be regulated in Europe, the prosperity of India must be finally committed to the discretion of its own local government.

In 1793, the charter of the company expired, and it was renewed till the 1st March 1814; with the usual provision, that on three years notice, and the discharge, by government, of its debt of L. 4,200,000 due to the company, the exclusive privilege might be annulled. The provisions of the plan of 1784 were at the same time re-enacted, and various other regulations were added. It was provided that if any surplus of territorial revenue should remain, after defraying all the necessary expences of the trade and the government, it should be employed in the provision of the company's investment, to the extent of not less than one crore of rupees, or one million sterling; and that if any further surplus remained, it should either be applied to the discharge of debt, or should remain at the joint discretion of the commissioners and directors.

In Europe the company's profits were to be employed in paying a dividend to the proprietors of 10 per cent., amounting on six millions to L. 600,000. To meet the bills drawn on the company, for the purpose of transferring debt contracted in India to Britain, the sum of L. 500,000 was to be annually allotted, and a like sum was to be annually paid into the exchequer, unless such annual payment should be suspended by the lords of the treasury. If a surplus should still remain, it was to be employed in the discharge of debt at home, or in the reduction of the debt in India, until it should be diminished to L.2,000,000; in which case, and provided the bond debts in Britain did not exceed L. 1,500,000, one-sixth of the surplus was to be applied to augment the dividend, and the other five-sixths were to be paid into the bank, until they should accumulate to twelve millions; after which the surplus was to become the property of the public. This fund of twelve millions was to be employed in securing to the proprietors, in the event of the company's dissolution, L. 200 for every L. 100 of their capital stock. On the first payment of L. 500,000 into the treasury, the company might increase their dividend to 10½ per cent.

From the subsequent account of the company's transactions in India, it will be found, that the territorial revenues in place of affording any surplus for the benefit of the proprietors in Europe, have generally proved inadequate to defray the expences of the resident government; and the various provisions enacted at different times, for the purpose of enabling the public to participate in the revenue expected to arise from the company's territories, only serve to show the fallacious views entertained respecting those remote and apparently useless acquisitions. The sum of L.500,000, which, according to the terms of the charter, should have been annually paid into the public treasury, was only received for the first year; and the company having in consequence become entitled to raise their dividend to 10½ per cent., immediately made use of this privilege.

In 1813, the company's charter was renewed for twenty years; and the exclusive privilege of trade, which formerly extended between the Straits of Magellan and the Cape of Good Hope, was now limited to the dominions of the emperor of China. The monopoly of the trade in tea was still reserved to the company. The other provisions of former acts were at the same time renewed.

OF THE TRANSACTIONS OF THE COMPANY IN INDIA.

The East India Company, before acquiring territory, carried on their trade on the common principle of exporting some suitable equivalent to the foreign market, and of bringing back a supply of its produce in return. This equivalent consisted chiefly of bullion, which was in greater request in India than any sort of European produce. Upon this footing, aided by the monopoly, the company's affairs prospered, yielding an annual dividend of from 5 to 10 per cent *. To encourage their trade, the Mogul government granted an exemption from the internal duties levied on the passage of

* The following is an account of the dividends of the company at different periods.

1708	5 per cent.	1766	10 per cent.
1709	9 ..	1769	11 ..
1711	10 ..	1770	12 ..
1722	8 ..	1771	$12\frac{1}{2}$ ..
1732	7 ..	1773	6 ..
1743	8 ..	1777	7 ..
1755	6 ..	1778	8 ..
		1793	$10\frac{1}{2}$ ..

goods through its territories; and this privilege was secured by the company's passport at the various toll-bars and customhouses of the country. The servants of the company were also allowed to make up their deficient salaries, by trading under the same indulgence.

While the native governments preserved their authority, this indulgence could always be kept within due bounds; and there was little risk of its seriously injuring the general trade of the community. But, in 1757, when the company began to acquire political power, their servants took advantage of the exemption from custom, to undersell the native merchant, and gradually to engross the whole commerce of the country.

Cossim Ali Khan, a sovereign set up by the company, seeing his subjects thus excluded from every market, resolved to place both parties on an equal footing; and with this view, he published a general immunity from all internal duties. For this equitable measure, he was deposed by the servants of the company, who set up a new ruler in his stead, on the well understood condition of subservience to their views. The country now became the scene of monopoly and abuse; the only object being to acquire wealth by whatever means.

"The servants," says Mr Burke, in the Ninth Report of the Committee of the House of Commons on India Affairs, "for themselves or "for their employers, monopolised every article "of trade, foreign and domestic; not only the "raw merchantable commodities, but the manu- "factures; and not only these, but the neces- "saries of life, or what in these countries habit "has confounded with them; not only silk, "cotton, piece-goods, opium, saltpetre, but "not unfrequently salt, tobacco, betel-nut, "and grain of most ordinary consumption. In "the name of the country government they "laid on or took off, and at their pleasure "heightened or lowered, all duties upon goods; "the whole trade of the country was either "destroyed, or in shackles."

The acquisition of the territorial revenues of Bengal by the company, in 1765, changed completely the state of its affairs, and afforded the means of still farther extending these ruinous practices. After defraying the charges of the civil government, the residue of the revenues was claimed by the company; and it became necessary to devise some profitable expedient for sending home this surplus wealth. As bullion was more in request in India than in Europe, a loss would have been incurred, by sending it from the better to the worse market; so that the only mode of remitting the tribute of India was through the medium of Indian produce. In place of exporting bullion and other goods, as formerly, to India, in return for its commodities, the land and labour of India were now to be laid under contribution, for the supply of Europe, without any return. The trade thus became a vehicle for tribute. India was to be drained of its wealth for the benefit of a trading company in London, and the most convenient mode of transporting it was therefore to be contrived *.

With this view, the numerous agents of the company were dispersed through the country to select whatever was most suitable to the demands of Europe; and that they might buy cheap goods, they claimed the right of pre-emption in all markets. Thus, secured against all rivalship, they had the market under their controul. They could prevent the holders of goods, who refused to sell at their price, from bargain-

* See Ninth Report of the Select Committee on India Affairs.

ing with other purchasers; by which means they were always enabled to supply their wants on their own terms. The authority of the state was thus employed to destroy the freedom of trade. It was the policy of those mercantile sovereigns, in dealing with their subjects, to place the seller at the mercy of the buyer. For this object, all the powers of government were called forth; and, to gain a profit on a trading adventure, they sacrificed their interest as sovereigns, in the permanent welfare of their dominions. Under this mistaken system of trade and policy, commerce and manufactures soon began to decline, and the company's agents, who were commissioned to make money for their masters, and vested with such extraordinary powers for the purpose, could hardly be supposed to miss so fair an occasion of profit to themselves. They accordingly forestalled every market, carrying on, under the sanction of the public service, a large illicit traffic of their own, and always using authority, where it was wanted, to facilitate their bargains. Whether they traded for themselves or for the company, they gave no equivalent for what they received, and their trade was in this manner a constant drain on the wealth of the country*. It seems a sufficiently hard condition of the company's government, that India should pay an annual tribute to Britain; and to lighten this hardship, the

* When the provincial councils were established in 1773, for the management of the revenues, it was proposed that those who were chosen for this duty should forego the privilege of trade, for which they were to be compensated by an increase of salary; and the reasons for this arrangement, as stated by Mr Hastings, in a revenue consultation at Fort William, 23d November 1773, clearly shew the oppressive practices of the company's servants. " If allowed the li-
" berty of trade," he observes, " while they possess an un-
" bounded power, (and who shall bind those who constitute
" the government itself?) their trade will be a monopoly
" and an oppression. If forbidden to trade, without some re-
" paration for the loss, and some allowed means of acquiring
" a livelihood, and even the prospect of a competency, the fee-
" ble words of a public edict will not hold them; but they will,
" with little scruple, break through them, and obtain those
" ends, by unhallowed means; because they will think, that a
" decree which imposes upon them the necessity of perpetual
" penury, could not have been really intended for their rigid
" observance; such having been, in many instances, the fatal
" practice of this service—we say " Fatal," because laws and
" restriction which have no coercion, and bear too hardly on
" the passions or the common sufferance of mankind, inevita-
" bly defeat their own purpose: they become totally disre-
" garded, nor is it deemed an impeachment of morality to
" transgress them. And, it is a consequence as infallible,
" that when men are once allowed to pass the line of their
" prescribed duty, at their own option, they will, by de-
" grees, extend the latitude to the farthest extremes of cor-
" ruption, embezzlement, and rapine." See also Ninth Report on India Affairs.

least that could have been done was surely to adopt some easy mode of contribution. But the mode of contribution turned out to be the worst evil; since, for the inferior object of converting the tribute with a profit into Indian produce, the clearest rules of policy and justice were subverted.

In addition to the privilege of pre-emption, claimed in all the Indian markets, other devices, not less injurious, were set on foot for raising money. Some of the most essential articles of consumption, such as opium, salt, betel-nut, and saltpetre, were held under strict monopolies for the benefit of individuals in the first instance, and ultimately for that of the state, whose agents frequently compelled the production of the monopolised articles, under the severest forfeitures and punishments *. Monopolies, wherever they exist, must necessarily be destructive both of freedom and industry; nor is it easy to imagine, why it should be necessary in India, to raise the national revenue by such expedients rather than by taxes. A monopoly is the device of improvidence, which for a present advantage, wastes

* For some further account of those monopolies, see Appendix, Note [M].

the resources of futurity; and no circumstances can be imagined to justify a policy so pernicious.

While such abuses existed in the management of the company's trade, the same principle, namely, the desire of present gain, seems also to have prevailed in the administration of the land revenues.

Under the Mogul government, the public revenues arose from the produce of the soil ; its owners being bound to the state for the payment of a stipulated tax or quit rent on their various properties. The lands were held by different descriptions of proprietors, under the titles of Rajahs, Zemindars, Jaghiredars, Talookdars, and Ryots.

The Rajahs or Nabobs were originally provincial governors, ruling with a temporary and delegated jurisdiction, which, on the decline of the Mogul empire, naturally grew into an independent right of sovereignty. The authority of the superior was recognised by a tribute, either in money or in military service; while in some cases, even this badge of dependence was thrown off.

The Zemindars were the original proprietors of the land, and their rights were confirmed to them by the Mogul government, when the country was conquered, for a fixed and moderate rent, the punctual payment of which was the common tenure of property throughout the empire, and had been hitherto found sufficient for every purpose either of transmission or of enjoyment. The landholders had lived for centuries in great splendour, on the produce of their estates, which had quietly descended, under the existing tenure, through successive generations; and though, under a despotic government, arbitrary ejectments might occasionally occur, they were universally regarded, both in law and usage, as the illegal stretches of abused power. The zemindars being the immediate obligants for the revenue, were necessarily invested with the power of collecting the land tax from the subordinate landholders and tenants. They united in this manner legal authority with the possession of property, while, as judges and magistrates, they administered both civil and criminal justice, and were held responsible for all crimes committed within their respective boundaries. They were generally looked up to with unbounded devotion; and, being frequently of a high cast of Bramins, sentiments of piety mingled in the homage paid to their family and rank. Religion and manners were thus brought in aid of law and government, and the influence of the aristocracy, the source of so many abuses in other countries, became in India the guarantee of civil order. The people yielded a willing obedience to their chiefs; and any indignity offered to them was resented as a national, and even as a species of moral dishonour, which it was devotion to revenge *.

The tenure of Jaghire appears to have originated with the Mogul government, and to have been a military grant for the maintenance of a body of cavalry, the command of which, being a mark of royal favour, entitled the possessor to suitable rank. This dignity was termed ' Munsub;' and the station of the Munsubdar was fixed by the number of horse for which he had lands or money assigned. But, though he was bound by the terms of his grant to military service, and to appear also in the retinue of the court with due splendour, the number of cavalry which he ac-

* See Appendix Note [N.] containing the evidence of Messrs Vansittart, Boughton Rowse, Edward Baber, and Captain Gabriel Harper, before a Committee of the House of Commons, on the rights and conditions of the Zemindars. See also " Plan of Mr Francis, relative to the system to be adopted in letting or disposing of the lands in Bengal, dated Fort William, 22d Jan. 1778," which contains a most able and interesting view of the state of property and manners in India.

tually maintained had no relation to the extent of his land, and seems merely to have been specified in his tenure as a form for conveying the property. As the Mogul government, when the country was conquered, confirmed for a fixed rent the rights of the landed proprietors, this rent constituted its only fund for the reward of meritorious service; and a jaghire was accordingly an assignment to a certain portion either of rent or of zemindary property, for which the proprietor was allowed a suitable deduction from his annual tax. When the land was improved, the government, or the individual, gained by the bargain, as it seems to have been for ever alienated from the zemindar, though his original right was still recognised by the payment of a nominal rent. Jaghire lands were occasionally attached to certain great offices of state, the possessor holding the property through the medium of the office, for the temporary support of his rank; at other times, the grant was personal, reverting to the crown with the death of its possessor [*]. The land being, like feudal property, held on an express contract for military service, its reversion to the superior on the death of the

[*] See Minute of Sir John Shore on the Rights and Privileges of Jaghiredars.

vassal, and the consequent failure of service, seems inherent in the nature of the title. In time, however, it became hereditary, and a new sunnud, or grant, was only required, as a matter of form, to confirm the succession.

The Talookdars and Ryots held subordinate rights, the first of property, and the latter of occupancy; and while the government looked to the principal landholders for the discharge of its demands, the inferior proprietors and tenants were bound, each to his immediate superior, for their several proportions of the stipulated tax. The regular payment of this tax was universally considered as the sure guarantee of possession, though it is uncertain how far the title depended on usage or on positive law. The property of India appears, at this time, to have been held on principles analogous to those of the feudal system; and a state of manners somewhat similar seems also to have arisen. The ryot was bound to the zemindar by affection and hereditary respect; and though he claimed a right of occupancy without any definite title, he held the security of immemorial usage for the soil which he laboured, so long as he paid his proportion of the general rent.

The land tax was discharged in monthly payments, advances being for this purpose made to the landed proprietors, by the bankers, which were regularly repaid with the produce of the harvest; and this arrangement, which united the landed and the monied interest in a mutual system of credit and confidence, indicates the state of improvement to which the country had arrived. The collection of the tax was superintended in each province by an officer, who possessed a special jurisdiction distinct from that of the civil government, and who, after defraying the local expences of the empire, remitted the surplus to the imperial treasury. The subordinate detail of the revenue was managed by hereditary canongoes, or clerks, who were established in each village, where a register was also kept of all transfers and conveyances of land, and of the rights of property, both public and private. The canongoe was reckoned the head man of the village; and all the petty differences of the inhabitants were settled by his arbitration. For these various duties, he was paid by an assignment of the village lands [*].

Under the well ordered constitution of the

---

[*] See Mr Francis on the Revenues of India. See also Memoir of Sir J. Shore, 1789.

Mogul government, and during the prevalence of ancient manners, every right, whether founded in law or usage, was duly respected, the land tax was easily collected, and the country flourished. But in the decline of that empire, along with its peculiar laws and usages, the zemindars and under-tenants were exposed both to tyranny and extortion; a larger tribute being exacted, under the severer penalties of imprisonment and the lash, and other tortures still more cruel. To the original ground rent various other taxes were added, some permanent, and others occasional, consisting of duties on the transit of goods through the country, of taxes on shops and manufactures, and of fines and exactions of various sorts; the zemindar, who was the immediate obligant for the revenue, being empowered, in proportion to these requisitions, to increase the contribution of the tenants [*]. To such a length were these exactions sometimes carried, that they exceeded the surplus produce of the land; and in such a case the only resource of the proprietor consisted in oppressing the tenant.

But in any inquiry into the ancient maxims or

[*] Mr Francis on the Revenues of Bengal, &c.

practice of the Mahometan law, a distinction must always be made between those casual outrages of despotism, and the settled form and order of the Mogul constitution. Failing to make this necessary distinction, some, otherwise well informed, have raised doubts as to the validity of zemindary tenures, and, confounding in their researches practice with principle, have drawn generally a very dark picture of the ancient government. They seem to dwell on the contrast of former abuses, and on the imaginary sanction thus given to their own subsequent proceedings; as if violence could ever subvert the sanctions of law, or as if the transactions of those disorderly times were any argument against the spirit of the Mogul institutions.

The conquest of India by the Mahometans was completed in the reign of Akbar, in the year 1573; and it was not the policy of the conquerors to dispossess the hereditary proprietors of the land, nor even to oppress them by heavy impositions. A general rent-roll was formed for all Hindostan, by Rajah Torrel Mull, minister of finance to the emperor, as well as a scheme of division, fixing the separate proportions of districts and villages, the individuals of which were sometimes held bound, jointly and severally, for the common rent. According to this plan, a settlement was concluded with the native proprietors, fixing the amount of the tax, which yielded, according to the accounts in the institutes of Akbar, 1 crore 49 lacks 61,482 rupees *, or nearly L.1,500,000. Its produce was in this manner inferior in amount by about one million sterling, to the assessment imposed on the land by the government of the company in 1775; while, in the reign of Akbar, the country being also in a more flourishing condition, there seems every reason to conclude that the tax was moderate. That it was fixed, and liable to no increase, appears from the authenticated rent-roll of the Mogul treasury, according to which it amounted, in 1728, to 1 crore 42 lacks, 45,562 rupees, or to L.1,425,000 sterling; thus varying from the original standard, only about 7 lacks of rupees, or L.75,000, in the course of two centuries.

The original land tax was first augmented by the arbitrary assessments of Aliverdi Cawn, who succeeded to the throne in the year 1741; but

* The current rupee is generally converted into British money at the rate of 2s. A lack of rupees is one hundred thousand; a crore is one hundred lacks, or ten millions.

the rights and privileges of the land owners and tenants were in general respected till the reign of Cossim Ali Cawn, in 1761, whose government is described as being in the highest degree illegal and oppressive. In place of adhering to the assessment fixed by the ancient policy of the empire, he instructed his agents to ascertain, by an exact survey, the actual produce of the land, and he claimed for the treasury the whole surplus which remained after maintaining the cultivators. In the course of his tyrannical reign, laws and usages were disregarded; the ancient state of property and manners was subverted; and the country exhibited generally the appearances of poverty and decay.

It was in these circumstances that the East India company acquired, by a grant from Shah Allum, the Mogul emperor, the territorial revenues of Bengal, Bahar, and Orissa; and their servants, dazzled by so splendid an acquisition, were more eager to pursue their own schemes of profit and ambition, than to promote the improvement of the country. In place of the profit formerly gained by the trade between India and Europe, an ample revenue was now expected to arise from the dominions of which the company had acquired the sovereignty;

and this revenue being invested in the produce of the country, was to be transported to Europe, without any return. To realize this project, the whole attention of the local government was now directed; and not content with the former revenues of the native rulers, the servants of the company contended for the right of their masters, as sovereigns, to the whole produce of the soil. By the constitution of the Mogul empire, it was maintained, that the sovereign was absolute proprietor of all the lands, and that the zemindars were mere tenants, liable to be removed at any time by his arbitrary mandate. On this convenient and readily admitted theory, an exorbitant assessment, consisting of the original ground rent, with all the subsequent impositions of Aliverdi Cawn and Cossim Ali, was imposed on the land; and where the zemindar hesitated to become bound for the required rent, he was displaced by a farmer of the revenue, who could only fulfil his engagements to the public, by extorting from the country the means of its future improvement. Under this system, the revenue contracted for in 1765 amounted to L.1,607,826; in 1766 and 1767 it amounted to L.1,713,677, from which deductions were afterwards granted, as it was found impossible to collect so large a tribute from an impoverished people. But the revenue actually realized exceeded the surplus formerly paid into the Mogul treasury, when the country was in a flourishing condition. The new sovereigns of India were resolved to profit by their recently acquired power. It was their great object to draw the largest possible revenue from their subjects, while, owing to their inexperience in the laws and usages of the country, they were incapable of fixing, by any just standard, the amount of the public claims. Disputes were continually arising with the land owners and tenants, which they were unable to decide; and, in these circumstances, the claims both of fraud and of justice were too frequently silenced by the over-ruling plea of the public necessities. The land owners, failing almost universally in their engagements, were left to the discretion of the revenue officer, who was invested with the most extensive powers over their persons and properties, while the civil institutions of the country were in the most imperfect state, and seem rather to have been devised for the convenience of taxation than for the protection of the people; all questions regarding the public revenue being left to the decision of its collectors, that no pretence might exist, in a matter accounted of such vast importance, either for evasion or delay*.

The obvious tendency of a land tax, variable in this manner at the discretion of government, was, by diminishing the interest of the land owner in the improvement of his estate, to discourage generally the cultivation of the country, and this effect was soon visible, in the desertion of the villages by the ryots, and the consequent desolation of the land. Those evils were still farther increased by a grievous famine which prevailed in Bengal in the year 1770, and by which it is supposed that nearly one-third of the inhabitants perished. But the sovereigns of India were so intent on revenue, that they re-assessed the deficiencies occasioned by this calamity upon the wretched survivors; and this new exaction was so strictly levied, that the land revenue for that year, in place of a defalcation, exhibited an increase above the produce of the preceding year. By such a series of heavy impositions, industry was depressed; the cultivators deserted the lands; and all subsequent accounts of the country

* See Appendix, Note [O.]

concur in the same story of its misery and decline. " The tax," it is stated in a letter to the directors, from the governor-general and council, dated 3d November 1772, " not " being levied by any fixed rate or standard, " fell heaviest upon the wretched survivors of " those villages which had suffered the greatest " depopulation, and were of course the most " entitled to the lenity of government. It had " also this additional evil attending it, in com- " mon with every other variation from the regu- " lar practice, that it afforded an opportunity to " the farmers, or sheidars, to levy other contri- " butions on the people under colour of it, and " even to increase this to whatever magnitude " they pleased, since they were in course the " judges of the loss sustained, and of the pro- " portion which the inhabitants were to pay to " replace it*."

* In the preceding part of the letter, it is observed, that the influence of the famine on the revenue was unfelt by those for whom it was collected. " For notwith- " standing (it is added) the loss of at least one-third of " the inhabitants of the province, and the consequent de- " crease of the cultivation, the neat collections of the year " 1771 exceeded even those of 1768, as will appear from " the following abstract of accounts of the Board of Reve- " nue at Moorshedabad, for the four last years:

To the same effect Mr Middleton, who was employed in superintending the collection of the public revenue, observes,—" It is too

Bengal Year.		Crore. Lacks.		
1175 or 1768, Neat collections		1,52,54,856	9 4 3	
1176 or 1769, The year of dearth, which was productive of the famine in the following year		1,31,49,148	6 3 2	
1177 or 1770, The year of the famine and mortality		1,10,06,030	7 3 2	
1178 or 1771,	1,57,26,576 10 2 1			
Deduct the amount of deficiencies occasioned in the revenue by unavoidable losses to government	3,92,915 11 12 3			
		1,53,33,660 14 9 2		

" It was naturally to be expected, that the diminution
" of the revenue should have kept an equal pace with the
" other consequences of so great a calamity ; that it did not,
" was owing to its being violently kept up to its former stand-
" ard. To ascertain all the means by which this was effect-
" ed will not be easy. It is difficult to trace the progress
" of the collectors through all its intricate channels, or
" even to comprehend all the articles which compose the
" revenue in its first operations. One tax, however, we will
" endeavour to describe, as it may serve to account for the
" inequality which has been preserved in the past collec-
" tions, and to which it has principally contributed. It is
" called ' Najay,' and is an assessment upon the actual in-
" habitants of every inferior division of the lands, to make
" up for the loss sustained in the rents of their neighbours,
" who are either dead or have fled the country. It had
" not the sanction of government, but took place as a mat-

"melancholy a truth, that the whole coun-
"try suffered a very dreadful depopulation in
"the time of the famine; and that the pre-
"sent thinness of the inhabitants manifests very
"clearly, that the effects of that calamity still
"remain.

"Had the most proper measures been pur-
"sued after the event, probably the effects of
"it might by this time have been felt in a much
"less considerable degree; but too much re-
"gard having been then and thereafter paid to
"the realizing as considerable a present reve-
"nue as possible, these effects have of course
"continued aggravating.

"When a very considerable portion, sup-
"posed even a third of the whole inhabitants,
"had perished, the remaining two-thirds were
"obliged to pay for the lands now left without

"ter of course. In ordinary cases, and while the lands
"were in a state of cultivation, it was scarcely felt, and
"never or rarely complained of. However irreconcileable to
"strict justice, it afforded a reparation to the state for occa-
"sional deficiencies. It was a kind of security against de-
"sertion, by making the inhabitants thus mutually respon-
"sible for each other, and precluded the inferior collector
"from availing himself of the pretext of deserted lands, to
"withhold any part of his collections. But the same prac-
"tice, which at another time, and under different circum-
"stances, would have been beneficial, became at this period
"an insupportable burden upon the inhabitants."

" cultivators. The country has languished ever
" since, and the evil continues enhancing every
" day. The first remedy, without the adoption
" of which all other measures will be fruitless, is
" an universal remission of some considerable
" portion of the revenue throughout the pro-
" vinces. Such remission should have been
" made immediately on the famine. Its not
" taking place then has made it more and more
" necessary every day; and the longer it is de-
" layed the more ruinous the consequences
" must be to this country and its revenue."—
Mr Barwell, a member of the general council
at Calcutta, speaking of the over-valuation of
certain districts, observes, that this error proceeded from a desire to obtain the highest
possible revenue; and that in almost all
the districts of Bengal the lands were overvalued, and many of the renters ruined. " I
am convinced," says Mr Francis, in his admirable remarks on this subject, " it will be
" found, that for some years past, the govern-
" ment of this country has been living upon its
" capital; that is, they have annually taken
" a portion of the existing wealth which
" ought to have been reserved for future pro-
" duction."

An annual land tax, variable at the discretion of the government, was so obviously injurious to the cultivation of the country, that it was at length resolved to make a settlement of the land revenues for five years, commencing from the year 1772. But the grievance by which agriculture was oppressed, consisted not so much in the uncertain and arbitrary nature of the tax, as in its excessive amount; from which an abatement was the more necessary, as it was now to be fixed for a term of years. The policy, however, was still to increase rather than to diminish the revenue, and for this purpose a committee was appointed, named the " Committee of Circuit," consisting of five principal servants of the Company, who, in the event of the land owners refusing to comply with their conditions, were empowered to let the lands in lease, by public auction, to the highest bidder. These persons proceeded in their circuit, through the country; and, where the landlord hesitated to contract for the assessment proposed, his estate was publicly advertised, and let in farm for the highest rent that could be obtained. A great proportion of the landed property throughout Bengal was thus exposed to auction; and, in the general sale, the ancient owners and hereditary nobility of the country being outbidden by adventurers, to whom property was acceptable on any terms, were generally dispossessed of their estates, from the surplus produce of which a provision was assigned them by the indulgence of the revenue committee.

In this manner, the arbitrary claims of the state were made to assume the equitable form of a permanent tax fixed by voluntary contract; but this tax being founded on an exorbitant estimate of the land, the surplus produce of the proprietor was found unequal to its discharge. A large and increasing balance of arrears was accordingly accumulated, for the payment of which it was generally agreed, by those concerned in the management of the revenue, that no funds were to be found in the already exhausted country. " I believe," says one of the collectors, " the " amount of the settlement exceeds the abi- " lity of the district; and if the farmer was not " a responsible man, he would, I apprehend, " fall greatly in arrears; the common distresses " attendant on the famine are again to be " quoted as the cause of its decay." Mr Vansittart also, one of the committee of circuit, observes, " I attribute the collections falling "short of the settlement, to the settlement's "having in some places been over-rated, and "in almost every place fixed as high as could "be afforded in a favourable season; so that "every extraordinary accident unavoidably oc- "casioned deductions or balances. This I re- "gard as the general cause throughout the Ben- "gal provinces. I apprehend there is no imme- "diate remedy, no possibility of realizing the "settlement, unless by reducing it to the actual "value of the lands. No one will assert, I be- "lieve, that Bengal is in as flourishing a state "as in the year 1757, when first we acquired an "influence; its decline arises from the decay "of commerce, the want of specie, and the loss "of inhabitants." Under this system of management the country appears to have rapidly declined, and, in 1789, its condition is described by Lord Cornwallis, in the following terms:— "I am sorry," he observes, "to be obliged "to say, that agriculture and internal com- "merce have for many years been gradually "declining; and that at present, excepting "the class of Shroffs and Banyans, who re- "side almost entirely in towns, the inhabit- "ants of these provinces are advancing has-

" tily to a general state of poverty and wretched-
" ness. In this description I must even include
" every zemindar in the company's territories;
" which, though it may have been partly occa-
" sioned by their own indolence and extrava-
" gance, I am afraid must also be in a great
" measure attributed to the effects of our for-
" mer system of management."

Admitting the plea urged in favour of those measures, namely, that land was held under the Mogul government by a loose and ill defined tenure, it was the duty of those who had now succeeded to the sovereignty of India, to reform so great a defect in the laws and policy of the country, and, by improving possession into a solid title, to secure the community against the shock inseparable from the violent subversion of ancient rights. So wise and equitable an arrangement, while it would have produced universal content and happiness, would have proved a most auspicious commencement for a newly established government. But such views were inconsistent with the policy of the Indian administration, which was chiefly occupied with schemes for increasing the revenue; and by this standard, indeed, the merits of those who have been delegated to govern India have in most cases been estimated. The question has generally been, not how far they have succeeded in promoting the happiness of the people, but what proportion of their wealth they have been able to remit to the company in Europe. A flourishing revenue has been the continual boast of each successive administration; and we can scarcely wonder if a government, intent on this favourite object, should have harrassed its subjects by excessive and arbitrary taxation *.

The attention of the British parliament had frequently been directed to the state of India

* The principle which regulated the management of the revenues in India, and the effects of the system on the minds of the people, are very fairly described in the following passage from a letter of the governor-general and council to the directors, 28th March, 1775:—
" The continual variations in the mode of collecting the
" revenue, and the continual usurpations on the rights of
" the people, which have been produced by the remissness,
" or the rapacity, of the Mogul government; and, in the
" English, by the desire of acquiring a reputation from the
" sudden increase of the collections, without sufficient atten-
" tion to remote consequences, have fixed in the minds of the
" ryots so rooted a distrust in the ordinances of government,
" that no assurances, however strong, will persuade them that
" laws, which have no apparent object but the ease of the
" people and the security of property, can be of long dura-
" tion, unless confirmed by a stronger pledge than the reso-
" lution of a fluctuating administration. Even with the
" sanction of the honourable court of directors, time will
" be required to reconcile their belief to so extraordinary
" a revolution in the principles of this government."

and to the transactions of the resident government; and in 1784 a new system was established in Britain for the controul of the local administration, under which Lord Cornwallis being chosen governor-general, was specially directed by the act of parliament, to " inquire
" into the alleged grievances of the landholders,
" and, if founded in truth, to afford them re-
" dress, and to establish permanent rules for
" the settlement and collection of the revenue,
" and for the administration of justice, founded
" on the ancient laws and local usages of the
" country."

The settlement of the land revenues, concluded by the committee of circuit in 1772, expired in 1777; and, until the necessary arrangements could be completed for a permanent land tax, the former plan of annual assessments was adopted. But, in the course of the years 1789 and 1790, an assessment was imposed, for ten years, on the lands of Bengal, Bahar, and Orissa, which being acceded to by the zemindars, and confirmed by the directors in 1792, was declared to be perpetual, the land being guaranteed to its proprietors and their heirs for ever, under the burden of the stipulated rent. Other important reforms were at the same time introduced into the domestic policy of the country. In the administration of justice, the functions of judge, magistrate, and collector of the revenue, formerly exercised by the same person, were now separated; and to avoid all unnecessary severity in the collection of the revenue, the process against defaulters was confined to imprisonment and to a sale of their properties, while the produce of the inferior tenants could in like manner be attached for arrears by the principal landholders; except in disputed cases, where a decision of the contested claim was previously required. The police establishments of the country were also new modelled, the zemindars, from time immemorial the superintendants of the public peace, being superseded by a new system of magistracy, consisting of Europeans, with native officers acting under their orders.

According to the terms of this agreement, which has been usually distinguished by the name of the decennial settlement, the landed property of India is still held, and the same arrangements have been since extended to the conquered countries*. But this system,

* See Appendix, Note [P.]

though introduced under the fairest professions of moderation and policy, afforded no relief to the landed proprietor, because it granted no abatement of the tax by which he was oppressed. The proportion of the surplus produce claimed by the state was fixed at ten elevenths of the actual rent payable by the occupiers of the land*; and the proprietor having become bound for an equivalent money rent, was, on these conditions, confirmed in the possession of the land. By this arrangement, the zemindar was reduced to the condition of a farmer, or land steward, employed by the state, and receiving for his trouble and risk an uncertain reversion from the surplus produce of his own hereditary estate. In other essential points also the system was defective; for while the process against the land owner for outstanding balances was prompt and efficient, his proceedings against the under-tenants might at any time be impeded by an appeal to the courts of justice, where, from defective arrangements, a large arrear of undecided causes had already accumulated †. While the zemindar was in this manner exposed to the

* Fifth Report of the Select Committee on the Affairs of the East India Company, p. 59.

† See Appendix, Note [Q.]

summary demands of government, he was left to seek recourse against his tenants through the medium of endless litigation.

The consequences of those ill-digested measures soon appeared in the failure of the land owners to fulfil their engagements, and in the sales of land which took place in order to discharge their outstanding balances. In the years 1797 and 1798, the lands sold on this account bore an annual assessment of L. 164,576. and L. 262,938 *; and among the defaulters were numbered some of the most ancient nobility in the country, " the dismemberment of " whose estates, at the end of each succeeding " year, threatened them, (according to the " statement contained in the fifth report of " the select committee), with poverty and " ruin, and, in some instances, presented dif-

* The purchase money amounted to L. 207,688, and to L. 248,313. From these transactions we may estimate the proportion which the assessment imposed on the landed property of India bears to the surplus produce of the soil. If the landed property of India be valued at fifteen years purchase, a capital of L. 207,688 will be found equivalent to a land revenue of about L. 14,000, and one of L. 248,313 to a revenue of L. 17,000. While the government tax thus amounts to L. 164,576 and to L. 262,938 per annum, the revenue to the proprietor can only be estimated at L. 14,000 in the one case, and L. 17,000 in the other.

"ficulties to the revenue officers, in their en-
"deavours to preserve undiminished the a-
"mount of the public assessment." The revenue, however, in consequence of the measures adopted for its collection, has been hitherto realised; and, in the year 1799, the average produce of the land revenues of Bengal, since the decennial settlement, exceeded, by five lacks of rupees, or by about L. 50,000, the estimate formed in the year 1786, which amounted to L. 2,600,000 *.

In Bengal, the zemindary tenure prevails almost universally. But in Berar, land to a considerable amount is held under the tenure of jaghire; and though the grants under which this property was possessed had undergone three several revisions in 1766, 1771, and 1783, upon which occasions they had been successively ratified, it was about this period proposed, on the ground that the land was only heritable in certain cases, to institute a new scrutiny into the title deeds of those estates, with a view to their resumption by the company, on the demise of the existing proprietors. Considerable agitation was at different times ex-

* For a general account of the revenues and expences of the resident government, see Appendix, Note [R.]

cited among the land owners by those proceedings, while the only ground which existed for questioning the hereditary nature of the title, appears to have been the practice of confirming each succession by a new grant from the crown. This, however, though it may prove the original nature of the tenure, or the precarious state of property peculiar to a rude age, seems to have been a mere form, no way affecting the security of private rights; and the same forms will be found to prevail in the transmission of feudal property, without in the slightest degree invalidating the succession. The truth is, that the form under which property is held throws no light on the real nature of the tenure; and by a legal scrutiny, conducted on this principle, the rights of property might be subverted in all countries. From the various inquiries made at different times by the government of the company, respecting the nature of the jaghire tenure, it clearly appears, that in practice the property was hereditary, under whatever forms it may have been transmitted *.

* Sir John Shore questions the heritable nature of jaghire property, chiefly on the ground of some supposed informality in the grants, of which, however, he produces no evidence, and on the probability that they were sometimes fraudulently or surreptitiously obtained. In opposition, however, to those vague insinuations, he observes, first, that these grants

From the preceding account of the transactions of the East India company, it will be remarked, that an Indian revenue has been the leading object of its policy. The company, though raised to the sovereignty of an immense empire, seem never to have relinquished the mercantile notion of profit; and, as it appears that the inhabitants of India have with this view been subjected to heavy taxation, it will be proper to inquire, what advantage the company in Europe have ever derived from the contributions thus levied by the resident government.

It will readily be admitted, that a revenue so much out of the controul of those who claimed it, and for the expenditure of which, reasons and arguments could never be wanting, ought not at any time to have been reckoned upon as a certain resource. It is difficult, under any circumstances, to provide sure checks

have already undergone three several revisions, and have been confirmed each time. Secondly, that under the sanction of those confirmations, the jaghiredars have enjoyed the rents of the lands made over to them in perfect security; and thirdly, " That the persons who held these lands have " not any other means of subsistence, and if they were re- " sumed would be driven to poverty and distress."—[Minute on the rights and privileges of Jaghiredars.] After so clear and conclusive a statement, it is singular, that Sir John Shore should for a moment question the rights of the jaghire proprietors.

against the profuse expenditure of a nation's resources, the greatness and public nature of the concern naturally inducing prodigality in every part of its management. The rulers of India had, however, peculiar temptations to a waste of the public resources. They were separated by the distance of half the globe from those to whom they were to account; they had an overflowing treasury under their controul, and in such circumstances the practice of rigid economy was prescribed to them, that they might have a surplus of revenue to remit to their masters in Europe,—an object which, with adventurers in the eager pursuit of rapid fortune, was expected to outweigh the powerful temptations of private interest. Such fidelity would have been laudable, but was not to be looked for, and certainly was never practised. From the period when the company acquired the territory, the correspondence of the directors with their servants in India is filled with unavailing complaints of their extravagance, the enormous expence of their civil establishments, and the most urgent injunctions to retrenchment and economy; while their servants, on the other hand, always hold out fair promises of their future management, only

to be broken, and flattering statements of revenue, to be regularly overturned by the expence of the succeeding year. " We do not
" hesitate (the directors observe, in a letter to
" the governor-general and council, dated 1783),
" to pronounce that your late regulations for
" the management of the customs appear to
" us to have been made rather with a view to
" creating lucrative posts for a certain descrip-
" tion of men, than with any design either of
" increasing the revenue or of promoting com-
" merce. And we are confirmed in this opi-
" nion, by the enormous per centage you have
" fixed for the commission on the amount of
" the collections." In the same strain they express themselves to Lord Cornwallis in 1786.
" On reviewing the conduct of our revenue for
" some years back, we have seen a disposition
" to innovation and experiment, without urgent
" necessity, or apparent cause, but many ob-
" vious and immediate inconveniences; new
" institutions, and almost instant deviations
" from them; multiplication of offices, and
" increase of salaries. We find them always
" introduced with the flattering schemes of
" increase to the revenue, and diminution
" of expence, which have hardly in any in-

" stance been realized by the event."—After stating the enormous and burthensome expence of the revenue establishments, they continue to observe: " Upon the whole of our inquiry it appears, that the annual expence of collecting our revenues, and commissions charged upon them, have been in a progressive state of augmentation from the year 1766. In the year 1783 they stood at more than double what they were in 1766, and the neat revenues we derived from our territorial acquisitions in Bengal was almost one million sterling less than it was the first year after our accession to the Dewannee [*]."

The directors had good reason to complain of the enormous expence of their establishments, which seemed regularly to grow with the growth of the revenue. In the year 1776, the civil expences of the government of Fort William stood at L.205,399; and in 1783, they had risen to L.927,943. The company's affairs have ever since gone on in the same course, and in place of any surplus arising from India, it appears, from an account contained in an exposition of the company's finances laid be-

[*] Right of collecting the revenues.

fore parliament in 1810, that on a period of nine years, from 1797 to 1805, there is a balance against the government in India of L.5,101,689. About this period a quantity of treasure, to the amount of several millions, was exported by the directors, in the expectation of receiving a valuable return of Indian produce. But the resident government found it necessary to employ the whole in defraying the expence of the wars in which they were involved with the native powers. A large balance was thus incurred to the concern in Europe, to the great embarrassment of the company's finances; and accordingly we again find the two parties, the one renewing its promises, and the other vainly expecting their fulfilment. In the exposition of the company's finances for 1810, it is stated, that in 1805 the directors confidently expected a great reduction of expenditure, in consequence of the peace recently concluded with the Mahratta powers; and that although they were greatly disappointed by the result of the years 1806 and 1807, which still shewed a deficit of L.1,764,000, they trusted to the positive assurances of the governor-general, for a large surplus in the succeeding year; in place of which, however, to their great surprise and mortification, a deficit appeared, according to the estimate of 1808, of L.1,150,000, which was afterwards lessened by L. 200,000.

Adverting to the great increase of Indian debt, the exposé thus proceeds: "Of the many "baneful effects confessedly produced by the "vast increase of the India debt upon all the "interests of the company, one has borne, and "must continue to bear directly and powerfully "on the home finances, namely, the reduction, "and at length the extinction of the surplus "of revenue, from which a million sterling was "to be annually appropriated to the purposes "of investment. This resource has long been "declining, and for a series of years past, in "which European war, always productive of "extraordinary expence to the company, ren- "dered such a resource more necessary, has "entirely ceased. A great part of the interest "on the debt has of late been paid by adding "to the capital of that debt. This change, in "the course of its progress, has had a very un- "favourable influence upon the home concerns "of the company, preventing that improve- "ment of them which would otherwise have "taken place, according to the intention of the

" act of 1793, and at length extinguishing the
" means which formerly enabled the company
" to defray the political charges payable in
" England ; charges for which there will hence-
" forth be no other fund than what the com-
" merce of the company may furnish, until by
" economy and retrenchment a surplus from
" the revenue shall be again restored. During
" the period here spoken of, there has been on
" the whole, as the observation just made im-
" plies, no diminution of the civil and military
" expenditures, to compensate for the heavier
" charge of interest ; but on the contrary,
" whilst the revenues have from different acqui-
" sitions and annexations been greatly enhan-
" ced, the expenditure has kept pace with the
" increase, and has even outrun it ; so that
" although, when in 1793 and 1794, our reve-
" nues were only eight millions per annum,
" we had a surplus of L.1,000,000, now that
" our revenues are fifteen millions per annum,
" we have a deficit even in the second year of
" peace, of L.1,019,097."

After exhibiting a statement of the company's revenue for several years back, the following remarks occur, which are completely descriptive of the company's management ever since the acquisition of the territorial revenues: " What " is most obvious and striking is the in- " crease, not of the charges only, but also of " the debt, as the revenues increased, and " not merely in proportion to the increase " of the revenues; for, whilst from the year " 1793 and 1794, to the year 1805 and 1806, " the amount of the revenues has not been " quite doubled, that of the charges has been " increased as five to two, and that of the debt " nearly quadrupled, besides a very large sum " of debt transferred in the course of that period " to England. The greatest increase under all " these heads has been since the year 1798 " and 1799."

From this management of the company's affairs, the natural results have arisen. The revenues, though increased from 8 to 15 millions, have been swallowed up by the increased expences with which they have been invariably followed; and as the directors formerly calculated that their affairs were in a better train in 1767 with a smaller revenue, than in 1783, when their revenues were doubled, they in like manner reckoned in 1793 on deriving from their Indian territories a surplus revenue of L.1,663,577; and though a much greater revenue has since been collected, in place of affording any surplus for the benefit of the company in Europe, it has generally been found insufficient to maintain the civil and military establishments of the resident government. Since the year 1797 the expenditure has accordingly, with the exception of a single year, exceeded the revenue*.

The Indian debt too, which in 1793 amounted to L.9,142,720, had increased in 1809 to L.30,876,788, while the general statement of the company's affairs, annually submitted to parliament, discloses a continually increasing balance against the concern. In 1784, according to a statement made by the company, the balance in their favour amounted to something more than three millions. By a statement made out in 1811, there appears an unfavourable balance of L.7,138,685; and if to this sum be added the original stock, on which account cash has been paid into the company's treasury to the amount of L.7,780,000, the result shews a deficiency of L.14,918,685†.

* See Appendix, Note [R.]

† The fortifications and other works in India are estimated by the company at 10 millions. But those buildings, whatever they may have originally cost, would, if they were exposed to sale, be found of very little value. The money laid out in this way ought to be placed indeed to the account of expenditure rather than of stock; for it is clear that only a very small part of it will ever be recovered.

It is superfluous to comment on these facts. It is obvious that where the interests of so many individuals are concerned, the difficulty ought to be fairly met, and some remedy devised. If the public are to become bound for the company's debt (and it seems likely that this will be the result) government should have a greater controul over their affairs, and effectual measures should surely be taken for reducing the debt, or at least for preventing its farther and indefinite accumulation. Nor is it easy to see upon what principle so large a dividend as $10\frac{1}{2}$ per cent. should be annually made. In former periods of their history, the company regularly varied the dividend with the state of their affairs; and whenever a dividend is made from the profits of a concern, it ought surely to bear some proportion to those profits. The East India company is the only commercial body which has set at defiance this plain rule of equity; for while every year is adding to their debt, they still continue to keep up their dividend to the high and invariable standard of $10\frac{1}{2}$ per cent.

OF TAXATION.

OF THE TAXES SUCCESSIVELY IMPOSED ON INCOME IN GREAT BRITAIN.

The great waste of capital occasioned by the war which commenced in 1793, began about the year 1797 seriously to affect the money market, by raising the rate of interest, and depressing the value of funded property; and government, being a large borrower, felt in consequence the increasing difficulty of managing its immense loans. To remedy this inconvenience, it was resolved, in place of borrowing the sum necessary for the public service, and of imposing taxes as formerly, for the payment of the interest, to call on the people for a contribution, not of interest but of capital; by which means the sum which it would be necessary to borrow would be considerably reduced. With this view, it was proposed to take one-tenth from every income of L.200 and upwards, and a lower rate from all inferior incomes down to L.60 per annum, below which the tax did not extend. Such was the principle of the measure; and it was to be carried into effect by an addition to the various duties on houses, windows, male servants, carriages, and horses, known under the general name of the Assessed Taxes; the sum paid on account of those taxes being supposed to afford a tolerably fair criterion of income. The rate of assessment rose in proportion to the amount of the tax. Those who formerly paid one pound annually of assessed taxes were now to pay ten shillings additional. Those who paid one pound and under two pounds, were to pay twenty shillings additional. Those who paid two pounds and under three pounds, were to pay double. Above three pounds, the assessment was to be tripled. A distinction was also made between those who paid to the house and window duty, and those who paid in addition for horses, carriages, and male servants, the latter class being liable to pay from L.25 to L.30, a triple rate and a half; from L.30 to L.40, a quadruple rate; from L.40

to L.50, four and a half; and from L.50 and upwards, five times their former rate. Those who were assessed for more than the fair proportion of their income, were entitled to relief on making a declaration to that effect, to be confirmed if required by their oath; some considerable abatements were allowed on account of children; and also where a large house was occupied as the means of a livelihood. But the tax was so far cumpulsory, that the additional rate was levied on the assessed duties for the past year; so that no relief could be procured for the first year at least, by refraining from the use of the taxed article. The expected produce of the tax was estimated at seven millions; but it did not produce above four millions and a half.

In lieu of this measure, intended to operate indirectly on income, a direct tax was substituted in the following year. The rate of contribution was the same as before, namely, L.200 per annum and upwards to pay one-tenth; inferior incomes to pay a smaller proportion; and deductions to be allowed on account of children*. In every society, land, labour, and

---

* On incomes between L.60 and L.400 per annum, a deduction of five per cent was allowed for each child; be-

capital, constitute the three great sources of income; and to these may be added the profit arising from certain professions. The wages of labour would seldom rise so high as to come under the operation of this tax, of which the produce must chiefly arise, therefore, from the profits of stock and of professional labour, and from the rent of land. For the purpose of producing a fair disclosure of the income acquired from these various sources, it became necessary to establish a system of strict regulation.

In all the counties and towns commissioners were appointed, to whom every householder was required, under a penalty, to make a return of his income, either for one year, or calculated on an average of three years back; and to say also, whether any person resided in his house entitled to income. These commissioners were aided by the surveyors of taxes, who were appointed by the crown to see the act strictly enforced, and whose duty it was narrowly to exa-

tween L.400 and L.1000 per annum, four per cent was deducted where there was one child above six years of age, and three per cent. where they were all under that age; between L.1000 and L.5000, three per cent. and two per cent.; and above L.5000 per annum, two per cent. and one per cent. were in like manner to be deducted.

mine all statements of income, for the purpose of checking evasion and fraud. With this view, all returns of income were entered in a book, with the names annexed, and arranged in alphabetical order. The surveyor had access at all times to this list, which he was bound rigidly to scrutinize. At his discretion, he might object, amend, or surcharge. It was his duty, in all doubtful cases, to inquire into the circumstances of individuals, to challenge returns, to object to deductions, and to suggest to the commissioners in what cases to inflict the penalty of double duties, on giving due notice to the individual concerned, who was required, in every case, where the return of his income was unsatisfactory, to make a written disclosure of particulars; which, being verified on oath, settled the matter with the commissioners. But the surveyor, if he was still dissatisfied, might require a written case to be made out for the consideration of another set of commissioners, whose decision was final. In conducting the inquiry, however, a different process might be adopted. The party, or his confidential clerk, might be summoned, and examined, as to his concerns; after which, their depositions being taken down, they might both be required to swear to their truth. They were not bound, indeed, to swear or to answer any question; but, in that case, the commissioners might assess the person according to their discretion; and he could have no relief by appeal, unless he verified his statement on oath, and answered every question put to him.

The income arising from land, whether rent or profit, was subjected to a different and more simple process. An accurate account of the landlord's rent was obtained, by an inspection of the tenant's lease; and the profit of the tenant, if he paid for his farm less than L. 300 per annum, was estimated in England not under one half, and not above three-fourths of his rent; if he paid L. 300 and upwards, at not less than three-fifths, and not more than three-fourths of his rent, a suitable deduction being allowed for the inferior incomes. If his farm had been in his possession for seven years, the profit was then supposed, in consequence of improvements, to bear a greater proportion to the rent; and the commissioners might, in that case, assess the farmer, on actual survey and valuation of his farm. In Scotland, the farmer's profit was made subject to the same rules as commercial income.

Such were the leading provisions of the first direct tax on income established in this country, which lasted about four years, being repealed in 1802, after the peace of Amiens, and having produced about five millions and a half annually.

In 1803, to provide for the expences of the war lately commenced, a direct tax on income was again resorted to, which received the name of the property tax. By the act establishing this tax, the scale of contribution began as formerly at L. 60 per annum, which paid three pence per pound, and gradually rose at the rate of one penny in the pound for every ten pounds of income, to L. 150, which paid one-fifth. Some inconsiderable abatements were allowed for children. The estimate of the farmer's profit was now raised in England, in all cases, to three-fourths, and in Scotland it was fixed at one-half of his rent *. While, every seven years, a new estimate was made of the increased value of the land, and of the additional rent for which it was imagined it might be let in consequence of

* In England the public burdens on the land are much heavier than in Scotland; and these falling on the rent, the farmer's profit must, of course, bear a greater proportion to the surplus produce than in Scotland.

improvements; and the tenant being first assessed as proprietor of this additional rent, one-fifth part of it was, on this account, added to his former tax; while his profit as farmer being afterwards calculated at one-half of the increased rent, he was assessed in an additional fifth on this sum. A proportion of one-fourth was, in 1805, added to the rate of contribution; in 1806, it was raised to 10 per cent.; and various important alterations were at the same time introduced.

Under all former assessments on property, L. 60 per annum was the lowest income which paid any tax. But every income above L.50 per annum, arising from trade, or from the exercise of a profession, was now made liable to a contribution of 10 per cent. a deduction of .5 per cent. being allowed on whatever sum the income fell short of L. 150. The wages of mechanics were exempted, provided they did not in any one week exceed 30s.; a declaration to that effect being required from their masters; or provided they had no property of which the annual rent exceeded L. 5. A distinction was now for the first time made between the sure and lasting revenue of property and the more precarious revenue of trade, or of professional labour, by which every income, however small, arising from property either in land or in money, was made liable to a contribution of one-tenth.

To an equitable tax on income there can be no possible objection, since its object is to take from every individual a just proportion of his means for the service of the state. But the great difficulty lies in the detail of such a measure : 1*st,* In devising an equitable rate for the larger and the smaller incomes, and for such incomes also as, arising from the various sources of property, trade, or profession, are some of them more sure and lasting than others, and require, on that account, to be differently dealt with ; and 2*d,* In providing against the fraudulent concealment of income, without any odious inquisition into the private affairs of individuals.

The injustice of fixing a common rate of contribution for all incomes, however various, is sufficiently obvious; since an income of L. 10,000 per annum might pay, without any great hardship, a proportion which, if exacted from a smaller income, would force a retrenchment, not of comforts merely, but of absolute necessaries. In matters of policy the strict rules of arithmetic do not apply; and to frame a scheme of taxation on any such theory, would be to sanction, under the specious appearance of equality, great practical oppression. The rate of contribution to be equitable ought therefore continually to vary, gradually ascending, until it rise to its maximum among the highest incomes.

The rate of contribution under Mr Pitt's plan was ten shillings per annum for an income of L.60, and this proportion was gradually increased until, at L.200 per annum, it amounted to one-tenth of the income assessed, which was the maximum of contribution. But if the principle be once recognised of suiting the rate of assessment to the income, the same proportion should certainly not be taken from L.200 as from L.10,000 per annum; and it is inconsistent to prepare a scale of assessment for the lower incomes, and, from L.200 and upwards, to confound in one common proportion all incomes, however various.

But the plan of making a heavy addition to the assessed taxes, which Mr Pitt intended as a tax on income, was in reality a tax on expenditure. So long as income was hoarded, it was secure. It was only when it was spent that it incurred the penalty of a tax; so that the largest incomes might still find safety in economy and privation. As a tax on expenditure, this addition to existing duties seems liable to no peculiar objection.

The direct tax on income substituted by Mr Pitt, for this measure, was founded on the same principle of contribution; and, no just medium being fixed between the large and the small incomes, an unequal assessment was in consequence thrown on the latter. In the detail of the measure also, it was found exceedingly difficult to reconcile any inquisition into the private concerns of individuals with the laws and customs of a free government; and, as a large revenue was the main object of the measure, the commissioners were invested with such powers as, if they had been harshly exercised, would have been found extremely oppressive. To disclose the state of a man's private affairs, is in all cases sufficiently vexatious; but in a nation of merchants, such a disclosure may be often highly injurious. The act, however, was administered with lenity. And hence arose another evil, that while those who had no way of concealing their incomes felt the full weight of the tax, a large proportion of income was sheltered under every species of evasion. An unequal burden was in this manner imposed on the community; and it is in this respect that the tax is chiefly objectionable, namely, that however specious in theory, it cannot be carried fairly into practice without too strict and troublesome an inquisition into the private concerns of individuals.

The provision for ascertaining the income of the landed proprietors seems sufficiently fair; but the rule for calculating the farmer's income at from one-half to three-fourths of his rent, must frequently give false results. In the property tax of 1803, this regulation was surely altered for the worse, when in England the proportion was, in all cases, raised to three-fourths, and in Scotland fixed at one-half. But though the rent which a farmer pays, bears, no doubt, some proportion to his profit, this proportion is apt to vary, according to circumstances; and, as there are high and low rents, a tax which takes away a large portion of the farmer's profit, on any theoretical proportion of profit to rent, must frequently lead to great inequality. The profit of the farmer is what remains to him after paying the landlord's rent. The higher his rent the smaller his profit; though, according to this scheme of taxing his profits, the farmer who paid a high rent, and who had, therefore, a smaller income, would be more heavily assessed than his neighbour, with a lower rent, and a better income. Among farmers, besides, there are some who are thriving, and some who are running fast to ruin—some who, having embarked in a course of hazardous cultivation, are laying out their capital, uncertain of a return, while others, having brought the experiment to an issue, may be reaping the fruits of successful improvements, or paying the forfeit of their imprudence;—and yet all these cases, however various, are brought under the same rule, which, while it will no doubt favour some, must of necessity press too heavily on others.

The provision for a new estimate of the farmer's profits, after the first seven years of his lease are expired, has also given occasion to complaint; and in 1810 a representation was made to the chancellor of the exchequer, by the landed proprietors of Scotland, against this mode of assessing the profits of the tenant. They urged, that in the state of agriculture in many parts of Scotland, it was plainly the interest of the tenant to improve the land which he held in lease, that the average rate of rent being always calculated with a view to these improvements, was higher at the commencement of the lease than the actual produce of the land warranted, and that the profit of the tenant being first taxed according to a certain proportion of the rent thus raised, in consequence of expected improvements, and again taxed according to a new estimate, when these improvements actually took place, he was required in this manner to pay twice for the same income. The justice of this complaint was so far admitted, that where the tenant was bound, by the express terms of his lease, to improve at his own charge, and where, on this account, a higher rent was paid than the actual produce of the land warranted, the commissioners for assessing the tax were directed, by an act passed in 1810, to order an actual valuation of the land, and to proportion the assessment of the tenant, not to the rent which he paid to the landlord, but to the rent for which the land could be actually let. Where the lease contained no express provision for improvement, all relief was denied. It was also provided, that where the tenant was allowed by the proprietor an abatement of rent on account of losses, he was entitled to a proportional reduction of his tax, and he was also entitled to deductions on account of accidental losses occasioned by floods or tempests.

It may be remarked of all those regulations for assessing the profit of farmers, that though they may bear hard on the tenant during the currency of his lease, they must ultimately fall on the landlord. It is an established maxim, that in all trades the rate of profit is equal, or tending to an equality. If one trade yields extraordinary profits, it will draw capital from other trades, until the rate of profit is diminished; and, on the other hand, if its profits are already too much reduced, capital will be withdrawn from it, until the balance of profit is restored. In so far, therefore, as the property tax falls with peculiar severity on capital employed in agriculture, it will in the long run operate as a land tax. The farmer, before he takes a new lease, will calculate the property tax as a clear addition to the expences of cultivation. He will on this account claim a suitable deduction of rent; and the peculiar disadvantages which this tax imposes on agriculture, will ultimately fall upon the landlord, in the diminished value of his land.

The property taxes of 1803 and of 1805, were not materially different, in their provisions, from the first tax on income. But when the rate of contribution was raised to one-tenth, various other important alterations were added. In bringing down the scale of contribution from L.60 to L.50, and in fixing so high a proportion as one-tenth for L.150, equality of taxation was certainly sacrificed to a desire of revenue. An assessment of L.15 per annum on an income of L.150, more especially where there is a family to support, must enforce an abstinence from the most necessary comforts, while the same proportion taken from an income of L.15,000 per annum, will be paid by a retrenchment of the most wanton and superfluous expence. These were not the proportions of the first tax on income, which in this respect was more just and lenient, though there was no reason to complain that it pressed too lightly on the smaller incomes. To alter these proportions, therefore, for the purpose of throwing a greater burden on the poor and middling classes, was certainly inconsistent with fair and equal taxation. But the rule for subjecting all incomes derived from property, however small, to a contribution of one tenth, is liable to still greater objections, and it has indeed given rise to many cases of singular hardship; for while the distinction between the revenue derived from property, and the revenue derived from trade, has been urged to no harsh conclusion against the higher incomes, individuals, in the most necessitous circumstances, have in many cases been called on by this regulation, to contribute an equal proportion with the rich, to the service of the state.

The abatements allowed for children by all former acts were now done away; and the other deductions were not considerable. The clause in favour of mechanics is so worded, that it seems only to exempt them, if their wages have never amounted, in any week, to more than 30s., though the exemption should clearly have been granted, on a fair average of their yearly wages; since a mechanic may frequently gain, for successive weeks, more than 30s. and not be worth more, throughout the year, than 20s. Upon this principle, accordingly, the act is administered, no mechanic being subject to the operation of this tax, unless his wages exceed 30s. on an average of a whole year.

The produce of the property tax for the year ending January 1814, amounted to L.14,583,286.

OF THE PLAN PROPOSED BY MR PITT FOR THE REDEMPTION OF THE LAND TAX.

In the year 1797, the land owners of this country were allowed to relieve their estates from the tax with which they were burdened, by paying to government an equivalent in funded property. The terms of the proposed exchange were, that the annual amount of the tax should be valued at 20 years purchase, while the government annuities were to be taken at their market rate of 16 or 17 years purchase; L.100 in the three per cents. being at that time worth L.50, and for every $2\frac{1}{2}$ per cent. of increase in their value, one year's purchase was to be added to the value of the land tax. According to this plan, L.2. 10s. per annum of land tax was valued at 20 years purchase, or at L.50, which being invested in three

OF TAXATION.

per cent. stock at 50, formed a nominal capital of L.100, yielding an annuity of L.3 per annum. The offer on the part of government was therefore to exchange an annuity of L.2. 10s. secured on land, for an annuity of L.3 payable out of its own revenues; and the land tax, amounting to L.2,000,000 per annum, being thus exchanged for 20 per cent. more than its nominal value in funded property, the public would gain by the bargain an additional revenue of L.400,000 per annum.

But it is evident that an annuity of L.3 would never be exchanged for one of L.2. 10s. unless the security of the one were greatly superior to that of the other. Land affords undoubtedly the most eligible species of security; and, on this account, an annuity secured on land is worth more than its nominal amount in stock. All taxes, too, are generally disliked, and a landed proprietor might consent to redeem his property at some expence from the real or imaginary grievance of a public impost. It is only from some such motives that the land owners of this country could have been induced to purchase an exemption from taxation, on the disadvantageous terms offered by government: they must either have exchanged L.3 for L.2

10s. thus losing 20 per cent. on the transaction, for the sake of the superior security afforded by land, or for the supposed advantage of freeing their property from the burden of a tax. The effect of these motives appears, however, to have been overrated, since the stock transferred to government for the redemption of the land tax, amounted, in 1813, only to L.24,378,804. The whole land tax, valued at 20 years purchase, and converted into three per cent. stock, at 17 years purchase, would amount to L.80,000,000; so that, according to this account, about three-fourths of the tax still remain to be redeemed.

At the period when the plan of selling the land tax was proposed, the value of funded property was greatly depressed, chiefly in consequence of the large quantities of this species of nominal capital which it was found necessary to create, in order to provide for the expenditure of the war; and one principal object of the measure was, to restore the value of the public funds. By inducing the landed proprietors to make large purchases of stock, it was supposed that the great demand for the commodity, which would in consequence arise, would be followed by a corresponding advance of price.

OF TAXATION.

The following considerations seem to demonstrate the fallacy of this expectation.

The property known in this country under the name of stock, consists of annuities, payable by government, and secured on the national revenues. The value of all annuities depends on the rate of interest, which is indeed the expression of their value, an annuity of L.5 being worth L.166, L.125, or L.100, according as the rate of interest is at L.3, L.4, or L.5 per cent. The low price of funded property, at the time the land tax was offered for redemption, was the consequence of the great consumption of capital, occasioned by the war, which had raised the rate of interest, and had depressed in proportion the value of all annuities; and there was obviously no way of remedying this evil, but by replacing the capital, which the war had destroyed. The artificial demand for stock, which the proposed sale of the land tax was intended to create, could have no tendency to raise its price; for supposing all the landholders to concur in giving effect to this plan, the sum necessary for so large a purchase of stock must have been previously withdrawn from the money market, the rate of interest must have risen in consequence, and by this operation, therefore, the value of funded property must in the first instance have been still farther depressed. The sudden influx of so many buyers into the market, would no doubt have soon restored its value, or have even raised it higher than before; but the mere shifting of capital from one hand to another could evidently produce no permanent effect on the value either of stock or of any other species of annuity, the value of all annuities being decided by the rate of interest, which depends entirely on the plenty or scarcity of capital; and as the proposed measure tended not to increase, but merely to transfer capital, it is clear that no rise in the value of the public funds could possibly result from such a transaction.

OF TAXES ON CONSUMPTION.

Taxes on consumable articles, though somewhat expensive in the collection, afford unquestionably the most eligible mode of providing for the wants of the state, and while they are light, and imposed chiefly on luxuries, the public revenue may be regarded as the voluntary offering of the people, since those who are aggrieved by the tax may, without any serious hardship, refrain from the use of the taxed article. The tax, while it is inconsiderable, being also gradually confounded with the price, is paid by the consumer, without either complaint or inconvenience.

But when taxes extend from luxuries to articles of necessity or convenience, and when they gradually outgrow the original cost of the article taxed, an exemption from taxation can then only be obtained by the sacrifice of necessary comforts, while the increasing burden can no longer be disguised under a rise of price. For the due collection of the taxes, cumberous establishments are also found necessary; revenue officers are multiplied with large discretionary powers; and in these circumstances it is exceedingly difficult to protect the people against unnecessary vexation.

In Great Britain, taxes on consumption have been long established, and they are now levied on almost every article both of luxury and of necessary comfort, while, in respect of amount, they seem nearly to have reached that point at which no addition of tax will produce a corresponding increase of revenue. The two great establishments by which the taxes on consumable goods are collected in this country are, the Customs and Excise; the one for levying the duties on the importation of foreign goods, and for regulating also the trade and navigation of the country; the other for levying the duties on domestic consumption.

Of the excise, the administration is generally supposed to be sufficiently successful, the trade of smuggling having declined under the increased temptation arising from higher duties; and a revenue of about 27 millions being collected at the diminished rate of about $3\frac{1}{2}$ per cent. The urgent wants of the state have naturally introduced order and economy into the management of its revenues, and, by the retrenchment of unnecessary offices and emoluments, the expences of collection have been gradually reduced. The difference in the expence of collection must not, however, be ascribed solely to improved management, as the rate must necessarily decline with the increase of the revenue. The first and great expence consists in setting in motion the cumberous machinery of taxation; but these necessary arrangements once completed, an additional tax may be collected at a comparatively small additional expence.

Of the management of the customs, Dr Smith has remarked, that, in point of perspicuity, it is much inferior to that of the excise; and at the time this remark was made, the business of this department was undoubtedly involved in much useless and laborious detail.

The customs being in principle an *ad valorem* duty on all articles imported, it is necessary to ascertain, by some simple and invariable standard, the value of what is to be thus taxed. For this purpose, a list being made out of about 900 articles subject to duty, their value has been estimated according to their weight, bulk, or number; while the commodities not thus enumerated, amounting to about 300, are taxed according to their value, as sworn to by the importer. The number of articles thus liable to duty was of itself a source of confusion, and the evil was increased by the carelessness with which new duties were continually accumulated on the old, a per centage being occasionally added to the original tax, while at other times the commodity was estimated by a new standard, either of bulk, weight, number, or value, and charged with an additional tax, without any reference to those formerly imposed. The growing confusion was still farther augmented by the special appropriation of each of these duties, and by the consequent necessity of a separate calculation for each; and this intricacy necessarily gave rise to much inconvenience and delay, and to a certain loss of revenue, in consequence of the abuses which such confusion tended to encourage. To remedy these evils, Mr Pitt, in 1787, united into one all these separate duties, and the business of the customs has been since transacted with much more precision and dispatch. Two subsequent consolidations of the customhouse duties took place in 1803 and 1809.

Notwithstanding this obvious improvement, however, the administration of this branch of the national revenue is by no means freed from its original confusion; and so long as the duties imposed are so numerous, it seems hardly possible to introduce into its management the method and simplicity which prevails in the excise. With a view to a more improved management, Dr Smith proposes the obvious expedient of confining the duties to fewer articles; and such a reformation might be adopted with great advantage, since of about 1200 commodities taxed, it appears, according to a report of a Committee of the House of Commons in 1797, that not more than 160 yielded, at that period, the yearly sum of L.1000 and upwards, and the remaining 1040 did not produce more than from L.85,000 to L.110,000 annually. To each of these, however, some special regulation is annexed, and the laws of the customs are in consequence so numerous, that they fill six large folio volumes.

OF TAXES ON SPIRITUOUS LIQUORS.

Spirituous and fermented liquors form such convenient objects of taxation, that they have in most countries been subjected to heavy duties in every stage of their manufacture.

In this country a tax was first imposed on malt spirits in the reign of Queen Anne. The duties were at that time divided between the low wines of the first, and the spirits of the second distillation. This mode was discontinued in 1784, when the whole duty was charged on the wash, the distiller's stock being credited for every 100 gallons of wash, with 20 gallons of spirits, one to ten over hydrometer proof. The collection of this duty required, of course, a continual and watchful survey; in spite of which, however, opportunities of evasion sometimes occurred, which were eagerly embraced by interested traders. It was alleged, though apparently on no good ground, that those evasions were more frequent in Scotland than in England; and the revenue failing in consequence, it was resolved to place the Scots distillers under peculiar regulations. A calculation being accordingly made of the quantity of spirits which could be annually run off from a still of certain dimensions, an annual tax of 30s. was imposed on each gallon of the still; on the payment of which a licence was granted to distil to any extent for one year. The country was, at the same time, divided into the lowland and highland districts, in the latter of which lower duties were imposed; and the distiller was also allowed a certain quantity of malt free of duty. To counterbalance these advantages, the highland distiller was limited in the quantity of spirits which he could annually distil; and if he exceeded his allowance, he was subjected to the malt duty on the excess, and to an additional duty on the spirits. He was besides restricted, both for the purchase of grain and for the sale of his produce, to his own district.

It soon appeared that a licence duty of 30s. on each gallon of the still was no equivalent for the former tax; since by quickening the process of distillation, such an increased quantity of spirits could be produced for 30s. as to reduce the duties greatly under their former rate*. The licence duty was accordingly increased from time to time; and in 1797, it was raised in the lowland district to L.54 for each gallon of the still; and the highlands were at the same time divided into two districts, in the one of which, nearest the lowlands, the licence duty was fixed at nine pounds, and in the other at six pounds ten shillings †. About this period,

---

* It was stated in evidence before the House of Commons, that by improving the form of the still, the process of evaporation could be so far accelerated as to run off the contents in 15, 12, and even 8 minutes.

† The distillers in the intermediate district had 500 bolls of malt, duty free, and they were allowed to distil 1660 gallons for each gallon of the still. This district was abolished from 10th November 1800, being made subject to the duties and regulations of the lowland district. In the highland district they were allowed 450 bolls, and to distil according to that proportion. For what they distilled in either district above their allowance, a duty was payable of 4s. 4d. per gallon.

in addition to the licence duty, a tax of one shilling per gallon was imposed in Scotland on the spirits; for the due collection of which a strict survey became necessary. Under this system the licence duty was in Scotland raised to L.162, the quantity to be annually distilled being limited to 2025 gallons for each gallon of the still. A farther duty has been imposed of 9d. per gallon on the wash, and one shilling on the gallon of spirits; all which duties will be found to amount, exclusive of the tax on malt used in distillation, to about 7s. 1d. of duty on the gallon of spirits. The duties in England continued in the mean time to be levied on the wash, on which they amount to 1s. 9d. per gallon; and 100 gallons of wash yielding 19 gallons of spirits, the duty on the spirits amounts to 9s. 2½d. per gallon. In seasons of scarcity, distillation from corn has been generally prohibited, and at such times the law has allowed sugar to be substituted in its place; on which a duty has been imposed in England of 1s. 8d. on the wash, amounting to 7s. 4⅓d. per gallon on the spirit; while in Scotland, the licence duty, and the duty on the wash and the spirit, amount to 5s. 3½d. per gallon.

A plan has been lately proposed, and partly

carried into effect, for repealing all those duties, and for taxing spirits according to one uniform system, both in England, Scotland, and Ireland. The distinction of duties which at present subsists, seems indeed quite useless, and is besides contrary to the articles of the union, and to the whole spirit of that treaty; for the union of two kingdoms consists not so much in being ruled by one parliament, as in an entire community of interests, which necessarily implies a system of uniform taxation.

The distinction of duties which prevails in Scotland is still more objectionable, as, in order to enforce it, the respective districts into which the country is divided, are absolutely interdicted from trading with each other in the article of spirits. In the low country, the highland spirit is a prohibited article, which may be seized wherever it is found, and as it is in general request on account of its superior qualities, the great demand is entirely supplied by a contraband trade. There is in truth a tacit conspiracy of the reason and taste of the community against the law which prohibits the use of what is generally preferred, and all the artificial terrors of excise are found insufficient to prevent the surplus produce of the highlands from reaching the natural market of the low country.

Where the produce of the soil is partly employed in the manufacture of spirits, a smaller portion will necessarily remain to the inhabitants in the shape of food; and, as mankind can never multiply beyond the means of their support, the country which maintains extensive distilleries, will, on this account, possess a more limited population. In these circumstances, when distillation is prohibited, a quantity of food will be obtained for present use, which, if no part of the crop had ever been converted into spirits, would have been employed in supporting an increase of people. The effect, therefore, of consuming grain in the distillation of spirits is to repress the population of the country in ordinary years; and when scarcity occurs, and when distillation is in consequence stopped, the whole produce formerly diverted into this channel, may be regarded as a clear addition to the existing supply, in the same manner as if it had been stored up in a granary for the relief of that particular year. And this effect is produced, not by artificially restraining the progress of population, which it would be rash and criminal to attempt, but by the natural course of things;

the legislature only interfering to secure what is provided and laid up in store as it were for a time of need. It is only, however, by freely permitting distillation from grain, in ordinary years, that a fund can thus be provided for a season of want.

OF PUBLIC DEBTS.

The funding system, or the practice of borrowing the money required for the public service, and of imposing taxes for payment of the interest only, seems an improvident device for carrying on war at the expence of posterity; by which means the extent of the evil being for a time disguised, nations are hurried on in a course of prodigal expence, until they are at length oppressed under the burden of intolerable debt. Were a different policy pursued; were every age to defray the expence of its own quarrels, the authors of war would not be defrauded of their due share in its miseries. Wars would then trench more deeply on the comforts of those who undertake them, and hostile states would thus be effectually admonished, by their mutual necessities, of the policy of peace. But when nations contrive to forestal the wealth and industry of future times, and thus to recruit their exhausted strength at the expence of posterity, they are enabled to persist longer in the deadly strife, and to purchase, at a greater expence of blood and treasure, the ruin and distress of such of their fellow creatures as they chuse to oppress and persecute, under the name of enemies.

The facility, however, afforded by the funding system for the raising of a revenue, is more apparent than real; since, under its operation, the growing interest of the public debts must gradually exceed all the other expences of the state. By contracting debt without any provision for its discharge, a nation will soon have to pay a sum for interest, which, if it had been raised in time, would have prevented the accumulation of the principal, and would thus have confined taxation within the limits of actual expenditure. By borrowing, for example, the annual sum of 20 millions, and imposing taxes for the interest only, at the rate of five per cent., the comparatively small sum of one million is all that will be immediately required. This small sum, however, becomes a permanent burden on the community, and every succeeding year, will, under the same system, make a similar addition to its debt. In 20 years, the sum paid for interest will equal the expenditure; and in this manner the system will proceed slowly but surely to undermine the resources of the state.

Revenue is the only legitimate fund of taxation, and no system which encroaches on capital will long preserve the principle of fair and equal contribution. Where the taxes are moderate and judiciously imposed, the pressure is so light that no great effort is made to avoid it, and, in these circumstances, the public revenue generally arises from duties on consumable commodities. But when the demands of a growing debt require an increase of the taxes on consumption, the people fall on various methods of evading the burden; and it is quickly found that increased taxation produces no corresponding increase of revenue. It is then that direct and compulsory taxes are resorted to, which being less liable to evasion, compel economy to surrender its hoards, and by increasing the objects of taxation, open a new and ample source of wealth to the state.

But direct taxation, though it is a resource where indirect taxes fail, may be carried to such an excess as to require an advance, not of revenue, but of capital, in which case the produce of the taxes will gradually decline. Large arrears will remain unpaid, which the tax-gatherer will try to recover by vexation and violence ; and in the conflict between private distress and the public necessities, individuals will be harrassed and ruined, while the produce of all the taxes on consumption will rapidly decrease. To supply the deficiency, the direct taxes will not only be increased, but their collection will be enforced with new rigour, and the system, thus strained to its utmost pitch, will finally give way ; for no system of fair and regular contribution can long be supported by direct violence. In the collection of a revenue which the people are able to pay, compulsion will never be necessary; and where it is frequently used, therefore, it clearly denotes that excess of taxation which trenches on capital, and which finally leads to national bankruptcy ; the process being much easier of stopping the payment of the public creditors, than of extorting by violence a large revenue from an impoverished people.

An act of bankruptcy, though it involves thousands in distress and ruin, strengthens a state, by releasing it from the burden of a heavy debt ; and when a government proceeds a step farther, and resorts to plunder for supplies, it acquires, in the boundless resources of its subjects, the means of exertion to any extent. The rulers of France, after the revolution, pursued this method of providing for the public wants; men, money, provisions, and warlike stores were put in requisition, and by this determined policy they obtained the command of the whole produce of the country; they acquired a fund which no prodigality could exhaust, namely, the labour of twenty-five millions of people, constantly exerted for their service. Although this system oppressed and ruined individuals, and bore hard on the community at large, it could never exhaust the resources of France; as the capital destroyed by public prodigality, was quickly renewed by the economy and industry of individuals.

It was imagined in this country, that the failure of the French finances would form an era in the fortunes of the republic, and that the rulers of France, by resorting to plunder as a resource, would speedily want the means of providing for their lavish expenditure. Plunder, however, is a surer source of revenue than any system of fair and equal contribution; for while the land and labour of a country yields any return, violence may always come in for its share. From this fund, accordingly, namely the labour and property of their subjects, the French rulers drew, by the easiest and the quickest process, whatever was necessary to give vigour to the policy of the state. They overlooked, in the pressing emergencies of the country, the ease and happiness of individuals; and in place of waiting the slow returns of regular taxation, they seized what was required for the public service wherever it could be found. They marched straight forward to their object, and they were surely on this account not the less likely to attain it.

A public bankruptcy is to be avoided, not because it weakens the state, but because it is an act of gross oppression and cruelty to individuals. Most governments, however, have persisted in a continual excess of expenditure over revenue, casting a careless account about futurity, provided they found the means of supplying their immediate wants.

Dr Smith, in treating of the debts of this country, has shewn how much the savings of peace have fallen short of the expenditure of war. But in pursuing the contrast, we shall find all former expence exceeded by that of modern times. During eleven years of peace which succeeded the war of 1763, the public debts were reduced by about 10 millions; and at the beginning of the American war, the principal of the funded and unfunded debt of Britain, amounted to about 129 millions, and the annual interest, which is the real debt, the principal being made up in a great measure of fictitious capital, to L.4,476,821.

During the American war, the money borrowed amounted to about 98 millions, which, being funded, made a nominal capital of 114 millions, bearing an annual interest of L.5,192,614; so that in the year 1786, the funded and unfunded debt of Great Britain, including also the value of the temporary annuities *, amounted to about 260 millions, bearing an annual interest of L.9,479,572 †. The public burdens were in this manner doubled by this rash and unfortunate war.

* Annuities to the amount of about L.700,000 were granted at different periods, so as to expire in the year 1860. Other annuities were also granted for different terms, the whole amounting, in 1786, to L.1,373,550.

† One per cent. interest on L.18,986,300, borrowed at five per cent. and reduced in 1780 to four per cent., being of course deducted.

In the succeeding interval of peace, the revenue of the country, partly by the addition of new taxes, and partly by the improvement of the old, was found, in the year 1786, to yield an annual surplus of one million above the ordinary expenditure. This surplus it was resolved to set apart for the redemption of the debt; and, in the year 1792, an addition was made to it of L. 200,000 per annum. The annual appropriation of these two sums, with the help of some expired annuities, produced, on the 5th January 1801, the yearly sum of L.4,604,508, applicable to the discharge of the annual burden of L.9,479,572, the interest of the debt in the year 1786; from which it will be perceived, that the debt, if no addition had been made to it, would, in the course of a few years, have been discharged, and this even without calculating on any increase in the produce of the permanent taxes. But when it is considered how much of the public revenue arose, previous to the year 1793, from taxes on consumable commodities, and how greatly the use of such commodities has since increased, even under a heavy load of additional taxation, it is obvious that every year of prosperity and peace must have produced a still more marked improvement in all those sources of the national income; and that if the industry of the country had neither been disturbed by war nor taxation, the surplus revenue which would have naturally arisen from the increasing produce of the existing taxes, would have amply sufficed for the redemption of the debt.

But all views of this nature were set aside by the war which commenced in 1793. This war lasted about nine years, being concluded by the peace of Amiens in 1801; and in February 1802, the nominal capital of the funded debt of Great Britain, including 22,348,000 contracted on account of Ireland, amounted, according to accounts laid before the House of Commons, to L. 596,859,611; the unfunded debt to L. 11,065,677; making together the sum of L. 607,925,288. If we add the value of short and long annuities, to the amount of L. 1,558,513, calculated at 15 years purchase, the debt will be increased to L. 631,302,983 *, and the annual charge, which is the real burden, to L. 23,607,582. Adding interest on exchequer bills in circulation on 5th January 1802, equal to L. 750,000, the annual charge will amount to L. 24,357,582. It has been already stated, that

* In this account, the loan to the Emperor is included, amounting to L. 7,502,633.

in 1786, a fund of L.1,000,000 per annum, afterwards raised to L.1,200,000, was established for the redemption of the national debt, which fund was still farther increased by the addition of one per cent. on all money borrowed subsequent to the year 1793. A sinking fund of 1 per cent., according as the rate of interest is at 3, 4, or 5 per cent., will redeem its principal in 47, 41, or 37 years; and within certain periods, the finance system of Great Britain, after the establishment of this 1 per cent. sinking fund, would of course revolve in a perpetual series of loans and redemptions, all future debt being in reality contracted on annuities determinable in a fixed number of years. On the 1st February 1802, these two sinking funds had redeemed stock to the amount of L.59,588,904, and, by the sale of the land tax, a farther sum of L.18,001,148 was transferred to the commissioners for reducing the public debt. From L.631,302,983, therefore, we have to deduct L.77,590,052 redeemed stock, which leaves unredeemed debt to the amount of L.553,712,931. The yearly produce of the sinking fund, and expired annuities, including also the L.1,200,000, annually appropriated to this service by Parliament, amounted, for the year ending 31st January 1802, to about L.5,000,000, which being deducted from the interest and charges of the public debt, leaves an annual burden of L.19,357,582. The interest payable in 1786, amounted to L.9,479,572; so that, in the course of this expensive war, the public burdens were doubled, in spite of every effort to check the progress of debt.

A new war commenced in 1803, which continued for about eleven years, being terminated in 1814, when the funded debt of the country, including L.79,130,250 contracted on account of Ireland, and including also the value of the long and short annuities, amounted to L.993,077,907, the unfunded debt to L.60,968,966, making together a capital of L.1,054,046,873, bearing an annual interest of L.41,418,743. The stock redeemed by the sinking fund, or transferred to government in lieu of the land tax redeemed, amounted, in January 1814, to L.275,568,352, which being deducted from the preceding sum, reduces the capital of the funded and unfunded debt to L.778,478,521, bearing an annual charge of L.28,535,429. In 1803, at the close of the war which commenced in 1793, the unredeemed debt of Great Britain amounted to L.553,712,931, the yearly charge to L19,357,582. The late war has in this manner added about one half to the existing burdens of the country. Great part, however, of what was expended during the two last wars does not appear in the preceding account, as the practice of raising the supplies within the year, i. e. of taxing the people for the principal of the sum wanted, in place of the interest, which was by this time carried to a great extent, rendered it unnecessary to borrow the whole sum required for the public service. This principle was first acted upon by Mr Pitt in 1797, when he raised $4\frac{1}{2}$ millions within the year, by tripling the assessed taxes. A direct tax on income was afterwards substituted for this measure, to which other taxes being added in the customs and excise, besides annual duties, the revenue derived from those various sources amounted, in the year ending 1814, to L.23,500,000. In the course of the two last wars, the produce of those taxes cannot be estimated at less than 200 millions, which must be added to the unredeemed debt of the country, in order to exhibit an accurate view of the national expenditure during this period.

The war taxes, as they are generally termed, consisting of the tax on property, besides various other duties in the customs and excise, of which the produce, not being mortgaged for the payment of the interest due to the national creditors, forms a clear revenue applicable to the public service, were generally understood to be limited, as their title implies, by the duration of the war; and peace being now re-established in Europe, it seems natural to expect that those taxes should be repealed; but this will entirely depend on the state of the public finances, after all the expences of the war are finally brought to account and settled. The necessary funds must be obtained for the support of the civil government, and if they cannot be procured without the war taxes, those taxes must be continued. To decide this question, therefore, we must consider what is likely to be the relative amount of the national expenditure and revenue, after all the establishments of the country are reduced to the scale of peace.

The great proportion of the annual revenue of Britain being mortgaged for the interest of money borrowed and spent in the last and former wars, this debt remains, of course, a permanent burden, until it be discharged; and the current expences of the year must therefore be defrayed out of the revenue which remains after discharging the annual interest due to the national creditors. From the account of the public finances, submitted to Parliament, for the year ending January 1814, it will be found that the revenue of the country for that year amounted to L.62,603,325; the charge of the interest on the unredeemed debt to L.29,013,849; thus leaving a surplus of unencumbered revenue, amounting to L.33,589,476 per annum. This revenue chiefly consists of the sums annually allotted for the redemption of the public debt, amounting to L.12,883,314 *, of the produce of the property tax, amounting to $14\frac{1}{2}$ millions annually, and of the produce of the other war taxes. The act establishing the property tax, limits its duration to the 1st April after the signature of a definitive treaty of peace. If this tax were repealed, therefore, the public revenue would be reduced to L.19,089,476; and if the policy be still persisted in of allowing the

* The sum actually paid in 1813, to the commissioners for the redemption of the public debt, amounted to L.15,006,419; from which, however, L.3,415,967, chargeable against the sinking fund, on account of the loan and exchequer bills of the past year, must be deducted; thus leaving a balance of L.11,590,452, to which the sinking fund on the Imperial and Portuguese loans, and the Irish sinking fund, being added, the amount is L.12,883,314.

sinking fund to accumulate till the whole debt is discharged, L.12,883,314 must be set apart for this purpose, and the annual sum remaining for the expences of the peace establishment will then only amount to L.6,206,162; which will fall far short of the permanent expenditure of the country. If we estimate the expences of the peace establishment at 20 millions per annum, a deficiency will remain in the ordinary revenue of 14 millions, to make up which it will be necessary either to continue the property tax at the rate of 10 per cent., or to apply the produce of the sinking fund to the current expences of the public service. In the one case, the country must continue under all its accumulated burdens, and no relief will be obtained until the yearly produce of the sinking fund, amounting at present to L. 12,883,314, shall have so far increased as to yield a revenue for defraying the ordinary expenditure of the state, besides leaving a surplus for the redemption of the remaining debt. If it were to yield, for example, 24 millions per annum, 14 millions might be spared for the public service, while the remaining 10 millions would be left for redeeming debt. If the produce of the sinking fund were to be at present alienated from its original purpose, the country would indeed be relieved from the burden of the property tax; but no fund would be left for the discharge of its accumulated debt, which would continue, in that case, a perpetual burden on its commerce and industry. It is plain, therefore, that unless the produce of the existing duties greatly increase, no relief from taxation will be obtained in consequence of the recently concluded peace. The prodigal expenditure of the war will indeed cease, and the public debts of the country will not, it is likely, continue to increase. But, if the expences of the peace establishment be estimated at 20 millions, all the taxes must be continued at their present rate, as their whole produce will be required, partly to pay the interest of the debt contracted during the last and former wars, and partly to provide for the ordinary expenditure of the state.

The policy of Britain has hitherto been to take the lead in every war which has distracted the continent of Europe. Under the burden, however, of so heavy a debt, it will naturally become a question how far she is so deeply interested in maintaining the balance of continental power, and how far, in order to ward off distant and uncertain dangers, it is prudent to encounter all the immediate and certain evils of protracted war. The peace of Europe will no doubt be continually interrupted by the jealousy of rival states; but it may be doubted whether the safety of Great Britain is involved in the issue of those contentions; and whether, in that case, it may not be her wisest policy, to profit by the singular advantage of her insular situation, and relinquishing in future all projects of continental war, to devote her whole attention to the more pleasing task of her own internal improvement.

In the observations on Paper Currency, contained in a preceding part of the volume, the depreciation of the notes of the Bank of England, subsequent to the suspension of its cash payments, is inferred from the rise in the market price of bullion above its mint price, and from the depression of the exchange; and the fact is stated to be placed beyond all doubt by the discount which was afterwards established on paper when exchanged for specie; 25s. and 26s. in paper being the market price of a guinea, and the one pound notes of the Bank of England being currently exchanged on the continent, where no law prohibited the transaction, for 13s. 6d. This remarkable depreciation of paper is ascribed to an excess of issue, as no other reason can be imagined adequate to produce the effect; for, if we suppose that the supply of bank notes is not increased in proportion to the demand, how is it possible that their value can decline?

Since the conclusion of a general peace, a fall has taken place in the price of bullion of about L.1 per ounce, and the foreign exchanges have also become more favourable to this country in the same proportion. These facts clearly indicate a rise in the value of bank notes, while it does not appear that their number has been reduced; and hence it has been argued, that the theory which ascribed the former rise in the price of bullion to the depreciation of paper, and the depreciation of paper to an excess of issue, is contradicted by experience; since it appears that bullion has fallen in price, though bank notes have not been reduced in number, which, it is insisted, could never have happened, if the increased issue of paper had formerly occasioned the high price of bullion. The former rise in the price of bullion is now therefore stated to be the consequence of the great foreign expenditure of the country; and the cessation of this expenditure is maintained to be the cause of its decline. It is insisted that the great demand for bullion in this country, for the purpose of being sent abroad, raised its price, and to this local rise of price all the effects which followed are ascribed. But a rise in the price of bullion confined to this country would not have affected the exchange of paper for bullion on the continent, where, according to this hypothesis, no rise of price had taken place. Though paper would not exchange at par for specie in Britain, where the price of specie had risen, it ought still to have exchanged at par for specie on the continent, where the price of specie had not risen. We find, however, that on the continent, the one pound notes of the Bank of England exchanged for 13s. 6d.; which plainly proves that there was really no rise in the price of bullion, and that the apparent rise was solely occasioned by the diminished value of the note. This point, therefore, being clearly established, namely, that the high price of bullion was occasioned by the depreciation of paper, the only question is, as to the cause of this depreciation; and it is clear, that no commodity can either rise or fall in value, except in consequence of an increased demand, or of a diminished supply. The former fall in the value of bank notes was occasioned by an increase in the supply, without any corresponding increase in the demand; and as it does not appear that for some time past the supply has been diminished, the late rise of value must have been occasioned by an increased demand. The causes which may have produced an increased demand, we cannot so exactly ascertain; but it is likely that the late peace may have occasioned a demand for an increased supply of currency. The commerce of this country has for some years past been contracted within a narrow circle by violence and war; it has been suddenly released from its fetters; and may not its sudden expansion have opened new channels for the circulation of bank notes?

Since the continent of Europe has been opened to British commerce, an immense quantity of produce has also been exported; the balance of trade and the real exchange must consequently be entirely in favour of this country; and this decidedly favourable exchange must no doubt have concurred with other causes in the late rise which has taken place in the value of the British currency. It may be remarked, however, that the convertibility of paper into specie, at the will of the holder, is still the only principle by which its value can be permanently secured; for though bank notes were even to rise to par, the public have no certainty that they may not be again issued in excess, and consequently depreciated, so long as the bank have the privilege of refusing specie at discretion.

APPENDIX.

NOTE [A.]

SIR ISAAC NEWTON'S MEMORIAL ON THE STATE OF THE GOLD AND SILVER COIN.

To the Right Honourable the Lords Commissioners of his Majesty's Treasury.

MAY IT PLEASE YOUR LORDSHIPS,

In obedience to your Lordships' order of reference of August 12th, that I should lay before your Lordships a state of the gold and silver coins of this kingdom in weight and fineness, and the value of gold in proportion to silver, with my observations and opinion, and what method may be best for preventing the melting down of the silver coin; I humbly represent, that a pound weight troy of gold, eleven ounces fine, and one ounce allay, is cut into $44\frac{1}{2}$ guineas. And a pound weight of silver, eleven ounces, two penny weight fine, and eighteen penny weight allay, is cut into 62 shillings; and according to this rate, a pound weight of fine gold is worth fifteen pounds weight, six ounces, seventeen penny weight and five grains of fine silver, reckoning a guinea at L. 1. 1s. 6d. in silver money. But silver in bullion exportable is usually worth 2d. or 3d. per ounce more than in coin; and if at a medium such bullion of standard allay be valued at 5s. $4\frac{1}{2}$d. per ounce, a pound weight of fine gold will be worth but 14lbs. 11oz. 12dwt. 9gr. of fine silver in bullion; and at this rate a guinea is worth but so much silver as would make 20s. 8d. When ships are lading for the East Indies, the demand of silver for exportation raises the price to 5s. 6d. or 5s. 8d. per ounce, or above; but I consider not those extraordinary cases.

A Spanish pistole was coined for 32 reaus, or four pieces of eight reaus, usually called pieces of eight, and is of equal allay, and the sixteenth part of the weight thereof. And a doppio moeda of Portugal was coined for ten crusados of silver, and is of equal allay, and the sixteenth part of the weight thereof. Gold is therefore in Spain and Portugal of sixteen times more value than silver of equal weight and allay, according to the standard of those kingdoms. At which rate a guinea is worth 22s. 1d.; but this higher price keeps their gold at home in good plenty, and carries away the Spanish silver into all Europe; so that at home they make their payments in gold, and will not pay in silver without a premium. Upon the coming in of a plate-fleet the premium ceases, or is but small; but as their silver goes away and becomes scarce, the premium increases, and is most commonly about six per cent., which being abated, a guinea becomes worth about 20s. 9d. in Spain and Portugal.

In France, a pound weight of fine gold is reckoned worth fifteen pounds weight of fine silver. In raising or falling their money, their kings edicts have sometimes varied a little from this proportion in excess or defect; but the variations have been so little, that I do not here consider them. By the edict of May 1709, a new pistole was coined for four new Louises, and is of equal allay, and the fifteenth part of the weight thereof, except the errors of their mints; and by the same edict, fine gold is valued at

APPENDIX.

fifteen times its weight of fine silver; and at this rate a guinea is worth 20s. 8½d. I consider not here the confusion made in the monies in France by frequent edicts to send them to the mint, and give the king a tax out of them; I consider only the value of gold and silver in proportion to one another.

The ducats of Holland, and Hungary, and the Empire, were lately current in Holland among the common people, in their markets and ordinary affairs, at five guilders in specie, and five styvers, and commonly changed for so much silver monies in three-guilder pieces and guilder pieces, as guineas are with us for 21s. 6d. sterling; at which rate a guinea is worth 20s. 7½d.

According to the rates of gold to silver in Italy, Germany, Poland, Denmark, and Sweden, a guinea is worth about 20s. and 7d. 6d. 5d. or 4d., for the proportion varies a little within the several governments in those countries. In Sweden, gold is lowest in proportion to silver, and thus hath made that kingdom, which formerly was content with copper money, abound of late with silver, sent thither (I suspect) for naval stores.

In the end of King William's reign, and the first year of the late queen, when foreign coins abounded in England, I caused a great many of them to be assayed in the mint, and found by the assays, that fine gold was to fine silver in Spain, Portugal, France, Holland, Italy, Germany, and the northern kingdoms, in the proportions above mentioned, errors of the mints excepted.

In China and Japan, one pound weight of fine gold is worth but nine or ten pounds weight of fine silver; and in East India it may be worth twelve; and this low price of gold in proportion to silver carries away the silver from all Europe.

So then, by the course of trade and exchange between nation and nation in all Europe, fine gold is to fine silver as $14\frac{4}{5}$, or 15 to one; and a guinea, at the same rate, is worth between 20s. 5d. and 20s. $8\frac{1}{2}$d. except in extraordinary cases, as when a plate-fleet is just arrived in Spain, or ships are lading here for the East Indies, which cases I do not here consider. And it appears by experience, as well as by reason, that silver flows from those places when its value is lowest in proportion to gold, as from Spain to all Europe, and from all Europe to the East Indies, China, and Japan; and that gold is most plentiful in those places in which its value is highest in proportion to silver, as in Spain and England.

It is the demand for exportation which hath raised the price of exportable silver about 2d. or 3d. in the ounce above that of silver in coin, and hath thereby created a temptation to export or melt down the silver coin, rather than give 2d. or 3d. more for foreign silver; and the demand for exportation arises from the higher price of silver in other places than in England in proportion to gold, that is, from the higher price of gold in England than in other places in proportion to silver, and therefore may be diminished by lowering the value of gold in proportion to silver. If gold in England, or silver in East India, could be brought down so low as to bear the same proportion to one another in both places, there would be here no greater demand for silver than for gold to be exported to India. And if gold were lowered only so as to have the same proportion to the silver money in England which it hath to silver in the rest of Europe, there would be no temptation to export silver rather than gold to any other part of Europe. And to compass this last, there seems nothing more requisite than to take off about 10d. or 12d. from the guinea, so that gold may bear the same proportion to the silver money in England which it ought to do by the course of trade and exchange in Europe. But if only 6d. were taken off at present, it would diminish the temptation to export or melt down the silver coin, and by the effects would show hereafter, better than can appear at present, what further reduction would be most convenient for the public.

In the last year of King William, the dollars of Scotland, worth about 4s. $6\frac{1}{2}$d. were put away in the north of England for 5s. and at this price began to flow in upon us. I gave notice thereof to the Lords Commissioners of the Treasury, and they ordered the collectors of taxes to forbear taking them, and thereby put a stop to the mischief.

At the same time the Louis d'ors of France, which were worth but 17s. $0\frac{3}{4}$d. a piece, passed in England at 17s. 6d. I gave notice thereof to the Lords Commissioners of the Treasury, and his late majesty put out a proclamation that they should go but at 17s. and thereupon they came to the mint, and fourteen hundred thousand pounds were coined out of them. And if the advantage of $5\frac{1}{4}$d. in a Louis d'or sufficed at the time to bring into England so great a quantity of French money, and the advantages of three farthings in a Louis d'or to bring it to the mint, the advantage of $9\frac{1}{2}$d. in a guinea, or above, may have been sufficient to bring in the great quantity of gold which hath been coined in these last 15 years, without any foreign silver.

Some years ago the Portugal Moeders were received in the West of England at 28s. a piece; upon notice from the mint that they were worth only about 27s. 7d. the Lords Commissioners of the Treasury ordered their receivers of taxes to take them at no more than 27s. 6d.

APPENDIX.

Afterwards many gentlemen in the west sent up to the Treasury a petition that the receivers might take them again at 28s., and promised to get returns for this money at that rate, alleging that when they went at 28s. their country was full of gold, which they wanted very much. But the Commissioners of the Treasury, considering that at 28s. the nation would lose 5d. a piece, rejected the petition. And if an advantage to the merchant of 5d. in 28s. did pour that money in upon us, much more hath an advantage to the merchant of $9\frac{1}{2}$d. in a guinea, or above, been able to bring into the mint great quantities of gold without any foreign silver, and may be able to do it still, till the cause be removed.

If things be let alone till silver money be a little scarcer, the gold will fall of itself. For people are already backward to give silver for gold, and will in a little time refuse to make payments in silver without a premium, as they do in Spain; and this premium will be an abatement in the value of the gold. And so the question is, whether gold shall be lowered by the government, or let alone till it falls of itself by the want of silver money.

It may be said that there are great quantities of silver in plate, and if the plate were coined there would be no want of silver money: But I reckon that silver is safer from exportation in the form of plate, than in the form of money, because of the greater value of the silver, and fashion together. And therefore I am not for coining the plate till the temptation to export the silver money (which is a profit of 2d. or 3d. an ounce) be diminished; for as often as men are necessitated to send away money for answering debts abroad, there will be a temptation to send away silver rather than gold, because of the profit, which is almost 4 per cent., and for the same reason foreigners will choose to send hither their gold, rather than their silver.

All which is most humbly submitted to your Lordships' wisdom,

Mint Office, September 21, 1717.

(Signed)   ISAAC NEWTON.

NOTE [B.]

Coinage of Mexico from 1733 to 1792 inclusive, extracted from a Work entitled "Mercurio Peruano de Historia Literatura y Noticias publi-"cas," published at Lima 1791 and 1794, vol. x. p. 133.

Year.	Silver.	Gold.	Total.
	Dollars.	Dollars.	Value.
1733	10,000,795 4	151,561 3	10,161,356 6
1734	8,506,553 4	385,275 6	8,891,829 1
1735	7,887,772 0	477,203 4	8,309,975 4
1736	11,016,000 0	748,679 2	11,764,679 2
1737	8,122,132 4	313,947 4	8,436,080 0
1738	9,390,250 0	468,273 4	9,858,523 4
1739	8,680,548 4	310,615 4	8,991,164 0
1740	9,556,040 0	309,900 4	9,865,940 4
1741	8,636,000 0	605,661 1	9,241,661 1
1742	8,177,000 0	624,386 5	8,801,386 5
Average	8,998,209	434,050	9,432,259
1743	8,619,090	704,208 3	9,323,208 3
1744	10,285,000	818,907 0	11,103,907 0
1745	10,327,500	505,760 5	10,833,260 5
1746	11,509,000	428,149 2	11,937,149 2
1747	12,002,000	369,745 6	12,371,745 6
1748	11,628,800	327,411 4	11,956,211 4
1749	11,823,500	313,888 0	12,137,388 0
1750	13,209,000	476,233 6	13,685,233 6
1751	12,631,000	340,234 6	12,971,234 6
1752	13,625,500	266,560 0	13,892,060 0
Average	11,566,030	455,109	12,021,139
1753	11,594,000 0	452,064 0	12,046,064 0
1754	11,594,000 0	309,751 0	11,903,751 0
1755	11,959,150 0	216,746 4	12,175,896 4
1756	12,299,500 0	731,000 0	13,030,500 0
1757	12,529,000 0	554,880 0	13,083,880 0
1758	12,758,500 0	173,317 1	12,931,817 1
1759	13,022,000 0	450,168 4	13,472,168 4
1760	11,968,000 0	465,464 2	12,433,464 2
1761	11,879,711 3	679,505 6	12,559,217 2
1762	10,114,492 4	594,838 4	10,709,331 0
Average	11,971,835	462,773	12,434,608

APPENDIX.

Coinage of Mexico, &c.—*Continued*.

Year.	Silver.	Gold.	Total.
	Dollars.	Dollars.	Value.
1763	11.774,964 3	859,982 4	12,634,947 0
1764	9,792,541 7	553,160 7	10,345,702 6
1765	11,609,496 4	778,428 0	12,387,924 4
1766	11,223,986 7	524,312 0	11,748,298 7
1767	10,455,284 4	599,214 0	11,054,498 4
1768	12,326,499 2	933,352 0	13,259,851 3
1769	11,985,427 2	497,770 0	12,483,197 2
1770	13,980,816 6	606,494 0	14,587,310 6
1771	12,852,166 3	501,266 0	13,353,432 3
1772	17,036,345 3	1,853,440 0	18,889,785 3
Average	12,303,753 0	770,742 0	13,074,494
1773	19,005,007 2	1,232,318	20,237,325 2
1774	12,938,060 1	728,894	13,666,954 1
1775	14,298,094 4	734,100	15,032,194 4
1776	16,518,935 5	796,602	17,315,537 5
1777	20,705,591 7	819,214	21,524,805 7
1778	19,911,460 0	818,298	20,729,758 0
1779	18,759,841 2	675,616	19,435,457 2
1780	17,006,909 0	507,354	17,514,263 0
1781	19,710,334 6	625,508	20,335,842 6
1782	17,180.388 7	400,102	17,580,490 7
Average	17,603,462	733,800	18,337,263 0
1783	23,105,799 1	610,858	23,716,657 1
1784	20,492,432 1	544,942	21,037,374 1
1785	18,002,956 7	572,252	18,575,208 7
1786	16,868,614 5	388,490	17,257,104 5
1787	15,505,324 7	605,016	16,110,340 7
1788	19,540,901 7	605,464	20,146,365 7
1789	20,594,875 6	535,036	21,129,911 6
1790	17,435,644 5	628,044	18,063,688 5
1791	20,140,937 0	980,776	21,121,713 0
1792	23,225,611 6	969,430	24,195,041 6
Average	19,491,309 7	644,040	20,135,340 5

Total Coinage in 60 years, 854,361,070. 2½

NOTE [C.]

Extracts from the evidence of John Fordyce, Esq. Receiver-General of the Land-Tax for Scotland; taken upon oath, the 27th and 28th days of July 1780, before a Committee of the House of Commons, appointed to inquire into the management of the Public Revenues.

" The said examinant deposeth, that he is receiver-general of the land-tax for Scotland, and has been so since the year one thousand seven hundred and sixty six.

" That he does not receive remittances from the collectors at any fixed or stated periods; and that for want of that general commercial intercourse which prevails in England, these remittances are as irregular in the means, as they are in the time of coming to his hands, sometimes coming in bills, and sometimes in money.

" That he believes there is no premium or discount between any part of Scotland and Edinburgh.

" That the mode of this examinant's remittance to London is in bills, which he purchases in Edinburgh, and for which he pays no premium; that he has a fixed correspondent in London, to whom he sends such bills, who pays the money into the exchequer, and to whom he allows a commission for transacting that business.

Mr George Rowley, Collector of Excise for Bedford Collection; examined upon oath the 3d of October 1780.

" This examinant saith, that he has been a collector of excise for upwards of fifteen years; that he is now, and has been for above thirteen years, collector of Bedford collection; that previous thereto, he was, for one year, collector of Grantham collection, and about another year collector for Wales Middle collection.

"That his present collection extends into part of Cambridgeshire, part of Bedfordshire, part of Northamptonshire, and the whole of Huntingdonshire.

"That he finds no difficulty whatever in remitting, and remits about nine-tenths of his whole collection in country bank bills, and other drafts upon London; and thinks he could remit more if necessary, having frequent application from men in trade to take their drafts.

"That the bills were formerly drawn at twenty-eight and thirty days after date; now he is ordered to take none longer than twenty-one days after date.

"That he takes security from all the returners themselves, and one or two sureties, being bound for a sum equal to the value of the bills he takes from them; he pays no premium whatever for the bills, nor ever did in his present collection.

"That the Grantham collection was not to so large an amount as the Bedford one; he found no difficulty whatever in procuring bills, nor in complying with his instructions in remitting within the time limited; that he paid no premium whatever for his bills, and the whole collection was remitted in country drafts, payable at one month after date.

"The collection of Wales Middle is one of the smallest collections: whilst collector there, which is now fifteen or sixteen years ago, he found no difficulty in remitting, the returners being glad to take the money and give bills for the premium then paid, which was seven shillings per cent.; which premium, he is well informed, is now totally abolished, and the remittance punctually made; he remitted the whole collection in country drafts, he believes payable at one month after date, and he thinks he could have procured more bills if necessary."

Richard Paton, Esq. Second General Accountant in the Excise Office, examined upon oath, 1st *September* 1780.

"This examinant saith, that he is second general accountant of the excise.

"That without the limits of the bills of mortality, the collectors of excise all over England, remit the duties collected by them to the commissioners, chiefly in bills, which, in the collection near London, are generally drawn payable at twenty-one days after date; those more remote, at about one month after date; those most remote, from fifty to sixty days after date, and none longer; for the board will not permit the collectors to send bills at longer dates, nor will they suffer them to keep money in their hands.

"That he believes the collectors seldom find any difficulty in procuring bills in the most distant counties, and does not recollect one instance of it, in his branch, since he has been a general accountant.

"That the returners of money had formerly various premiums for their bills, from two shillings and sixpence to twenty shillings per cent.; but the commissioners finding the manufacturers and traders in every collection ready to take the money collected, and to give bills for it, they have by degrees diminished the premium, and about Christmas 1778 totally abolished it."

Mr Richard Richardson, Collector of Excise for Hertford Collection, examined upon oath, 24*th August* 1780.

" This examinant saith, that he is collector for Hertford collection of excise, and that he has been so for near seven years.

" That there are returners of money who meet him at some of the places of collection, and give him a bill or bills for so much of the money as he chuses to let them have, payable twenty-one days after date, which is the term bills have been usually drawn at in this collection since he came into it.

" That the returner of money is some person approved of by him; who gives him a bond, with one or two sureties, to indemnify him against any loss and expence from the bills.

" That no premium whatever is paid by the collector to the returner for the bills; and that if he wanted to return more money than he does by bills, he thinks he should meet with no difficulty in doing it."

Mr Thomas Ball, Collector of Excise for Bath Collection, examined upon oath, 3*d October* 1780.

" This examinant saith, that he has been a collector of excise near seven years; that he is now, and has been for upwards of five years, collector of Bath collection.

" That he receives the duties collected in money, bank notes, and the notes of the banks of Bristol, Warminster, and Bath; and that he remits the money to the commissioners of excise in London, by bills drawn at thirty days after date, which he obtains from the different clothiers, or other gentlemen in the country, and the banks at Bath; about two thirds of the amount from the former, and the remainder from the latter.

" That he has security from all the returners whose bills he takes, in sums from two thousand to four thousand pounds, according to the amount of the bills he takes from them.

" That he finds no difficulty in getting bills, and could, as he believes, obtain them for ten times the amount of his collection.

" That he pays no premium whatever for the bills, nor has he paid any since he has been in his present collection.

" That before he came to the Bath collection, he was, for about eighteen months, collector for Dorset collection, the annual amount of which was upwards of forty thousand pounds; he found no difficulty whatever in remitting the money collected there, but the bills were drawn at forty days after date, and he paid a premium of two shillings and sixpence per cent. to the persons who furnished him with the bills; which premium he has heard is now totally abolished."

NOTE [D.]

That the bank of England was compelled to suspend its cash payments, not in consequence of the demand for specie occasioned by the war expenditure abroad, but in consequence of the demand occasioned by the alarm at home, appears to be satisfactorily established by the following evidence delivered by Mr Giles, governor, and Mr Raikes, deputy-governor, before the Secret Committee of the House of Lords, 4th March 1797.

Lord President in the Chair.

Mr Giles was examined as follows :—

"Has the Bank of England lately experienced an unusual drain of cash ?—Most certainly.

"Are you able to ascertain how far this drain was wholly, or in part, occasioned by demands for cash from different parts of the country ?—It was owing, in great part, to demands from the country; indirectly from the country, but directly from the bankers in London (who are to supply the country), upon us.

" Whether, by the effects of this drain, the balance of cash remaining in your hands has been reduced considerably below the amount at which it has usually been maintained ?—The cash of the bank has of late been considerably reduced. I have known it a great deal lower; but on this occasion the demands have been unparalleledly rapid; they have of late been progressively increasing, but in the last week particularly so; and we had every reason to apprehend that these demands would continue, and even increase.

" Whether such reduction had been continuing in an increased proportion to the balance remaining in your hands up to the date of the minute of council transmitted to you ?—We have generally answered this question in our preceding answer; but we beg leave to add, that the demands have been progressively increasing in the course of the last week, and in the last two days exceeded the demands of the four preceding days.

"Whether by the effect of this reduction, if it were to continue in the same, or in a still further increased proportion, the Bank of England would be deprived of the means of supplying the cash which might be necessary for pressing exigencies of public services?—Undoubtedly; and that led us to make the communication which we did to his Majesty's ministers.

"Whether any such alteration has occurred since the date of the minute of council transmitted to you, as materially to vary your situation in this respect?—No."

17th March 1797.

Mr Giles and Mr Raikes being attending, they were called in and examined.

"Do you think the restriction made by the order in council of the 26th February was necessary?—Certainly.

"Do you consider it as necessary to the interest of the bank?—The rapid drains we had upon the bank, and the continuance of them, made us think it advisable to communicate to his Majesty's ministers the situation of the bank, that they might, in their wisdom, use such means as they might think expedient.

"When was that communication made to the Chancellor of the Exchequer?—We think the first was on Tuesday the 21st February; the drains not only continued but increased, and so rapidly the last day or two, that we communicated it to the Chancellor of the Exchequer on Saturday, and had the honour to meet his Majesty's ministers on the Sunday.

"Were not the drains from Tuesday the 21st of February to the Saturday inclusive, much greater and more ra pid than they had been in the whole of the preceding week?—Certainly; they were unexampled.

" Did you apprehend imminent danger previous to Tuesday the 21st?—We cannot say we did.

" When did you first apprehend imminent danger?—We cannot say we apprehended any imminent danger, but from the fears of the drains continuing. Not wishing to risk the drains continuing, we submitted it to the Chancellor of the Exchequer.

" At what time did you think it necessary to communicate these apprehensions to the Chancellor of the Exchequer?—On Tuesday the 21st.

" Did you continue to communicate these apprehensions in every subsequent day of that week?—Almost every day.

" Had you not reason to apprehend, on Saturday the 25th, that the demands in the ensuing week would progressively increase?—From every communication we had with the public, we had great reason to apprehend it."

The governor and deputy-governor being withdrawn, were again called in and examined.

" When did the bank first conceive apprehensions from the diminution of specie in the bank?—(*Mr Raikes.*) I should think for about a twelvemonth. (*Mr Giles.*) I do not quite concur in that answer. So far I concur in the deputy-governor's answer, that the apprehensions a twelvemonth ago were greater than they were two years ago. I shall concur in the deputy-governor's answer, if you put it to 11th of February 1796."——Withdrew.

Again called in.

" When did you first communicate these apprehensions to the Chancellor of the Exchequer?—(*Mr Giles.*) I made communications long before February 1796.—(*Mr*

Raikes.) I have a private minute, that on the 8th February 1796, in a conversation between the governors of the bank and the Chancellor of the Exchequer, in which they mentioned their uneasiness about the bank's advances on Treasury bills, and in which the drains of cash were specifically mentioned for some time past. A statement was given, by which the Chancellor of the Exchequer might judge of the real state of the cash in the bank.— (*Mr Giles.*) I think the minute I have may be an answer to the question: On the 5th of February 1796, being in conversation with the Chancellor of the Exchequer about bank business, the Chancellor dwelt much on the necessity of further assisting the Emperor, but promised he would not commit himself on that head without communication with the bank directors. At the next Court, which I think was the 11th of February, when that communication was made to them, they came to the following resolution, which I was to carry to the Chancellor of the Exchequer:—' *Resolved*, That it is the opinion of this
' Court, founded upon its experience of the effect of the
' late imperial loan, that if any further loan or advance
' to the Emperor, or any other foreign state, should, in
' the present state of things, take place, it will, in all
' probability, prove fatal to the bank.'

" When did you communicate that resolution to the Chancellor of the Exchequer?—(*Mr Giles.*) I believe on the 12th.

" Did the Chancellor of the Exchequer return any answer?—He answered, that after what he had repeatedly said, he did not see any reason for this paper being delivered to him, which he supposed was penned in a moment of alarm "

APPENDIX. 19

On Sunday, March 18th, Mr Raikes, Mr Darell, and Mr Bosanquet, a director of the bank, were examined.

" In your conferences with the Chancellor of the Exchequer, and discussions with each other, were the rapid demands made upon the bank, beyond the proportion of cash in the bank, considered as the immediate cause of the necessity of the late order in council?—In our opinion, the great drains of cash made upon the bank in the week preceding the 26th of February, were the immediate causes of the order in council, and it was so considered in those conferences and discussions.

" Is it within your observation and knowledge, from your general correspondence and transactions as directors of the bank, that the discredit of the paper issued by the country bankers, and the demand of money from the metropolis to supply that paper, was one principal cause of the drains mentioned in the last answer?—(*Mr Bosanquet.*) I have no scruple to say, Yes."

It may be observed, that both the governor and deputy-governor plainly distinguish between the apprehensions which they entertained on account of the demand for specie occasioned by the war expenditure abroad, and the demand occasioned by the alarm at home. They state that for a year or two years before the bank suspended its payments, they were alarmed by the diminution of its specie; but that they did not apprehend imminent danger before Tuesday the 21st February 1797, when they communicated to Mr Pitt the precise amount of their cash. In the following extract from Mr Pitt's evidence, it will also be observed that he makes the same distinction.

15th March 1797.

Lord President in the Chair.

" Mr Chancellor of the Exchequer being attending, he was called in and examined.

" When did the directors of the bank first communicate to you their apprehensions of danger from a diminution of specie in the bank?—Before I proceed to answer the question, I beg to inform the committee, that I received from the bank confidentially, the particulars I am acquainted with of their precise situation, and must beg to decline stating those particulars unless I receive their permission. With respect to the immediate question, I must beg to distinguish between the apprehensions of danger from the particular drain of specie, which immediately produced the order of the 26th of February, and apprehensions of a more general nature, which were expressed to me at earlier periods. In consequence of the great expenditure for services abroad in the year 1795, and particularly of the loan to the Emperor in that year, strong apprehensions were expressed by the bank that the continuance of such a drain might be attended with dangerous consequences to them. These apprehensions were particularly expressed (I think) in February 1796, in consequence of a new loan to the Emperor being then in contemplation. At different periods in the course of that year it was represented to me that the proportion of cash in the bank was materially reduced, although I was not then informed of the precise particulars. I collected that some fluctuation and some further reduction of cash took place at different periods in the course of the year 1706; but, on the whole, I understood that the state of cash towards the end of that year was not materially different from what it had been at an earlier period, (I think about the middle of the year, but I cannot state that precisely;) and I also understood that the course of foreign exchange, which had become very unfavourable, particularly with Hamburgh in the course of the year 1795, and in part of 1796, towards the end of 1796 became favourable to this country, and has continued so, I believe, till very nearly this time. In the course of the month of January last, I received further representations from the bank of their uneasiness from the further diminution of their cash, but this was then attributed to the great demand from Ireland, and not from foreign countries; and they expressed great apprehension that this drain would be greatly increased by an Irish loan being negociated here, for which, at that time, application had been made. They afterwards expressed more urgent apprehensions of the diminution of their cash in the month of February, particularly in the two weeks immediately preceding the order of council, and most particularly in the last of those weeks. I beg to add, that this drain in the month of February was ascribed, in their opinion, to drains from different parts of this country, in consequence of local alarms.

" Did the directors of the bank, from time to time, continue to state their apprehensions on this subject?—They did, at different times, in the course of the year 1796.

" When did the directors state to you the precise balance of cash in the bank?—The time when they stated to me the precise amount of their cash, and the particulars of their situation, was, if I recollect, on Tuesday the 21st of February.

" Was it upon any representation of yours, or at your

request, that the directors made such communication?—Finding that they were considerably alarmed from the diminution of their cash, I expressed a wish to be as fully informed as they thought consistent with their duty, of the situation of their affairs. I should add, that when they made the communication, they stated that their sense of the urgency of the case made them feel it incumbent on them to make such communication.

" Are the committee to consider the order of council of the 26th of February, as a measure recommended or approved of by the bank?—The circumstances which the bank stated to me, produced a persuasion in my mind of the necessity of the measure for the public service, and I believe from all that passed, that the bank were as sensible of that necessity as I was, and they expressed their readiness to comply with that order if it came to them as the act of government. But I do not consider myself as authorised to state it as originating in their recommendation.

" When you say in your last answer that the circumstances which the bank stated to you produced a persuasion in your mind of the necessity of the measure, do you mean to confine these circumstances to such as were communicated to you on the 21st of February, or to include therein such as were communicated to you subsequent to that day?—I mean to include therein, all such circumstances as came to my knowledge subsequent to that day; my judgment having been formed not merely on a view of their affairs as they stood on the 21st of February, but as they were affected by the further reduction of their cash, arising from the rapid and progressive drain which continued to an unexampled amount, and almost uniformly in an increasing proportion during the remainder of the week.

"In your last answer but one, when you say the bank were as sensible of the necessity as yourself, do you mean to say, "Necessity of the measure for public service?"— In speaking of what I collected to be the opinion of the bank, I meant the necessity for the public service, and did not mean to imply any thing respecting any opinion of theirs, on the necessity in any other view: But I wish to have it understood, that my view of the necessity of the measure, did not rest merely on the necessity of reserving the cash then in the bank, in order that it might be applicable in case of exigency to pressing public services, but also on the conviction that the continuance of the same drain, even for a short time longer, would render the ultimate mischief both to the bank and to the public much more difficult to be repaired, at the same time that it would add greatly to the embarrassment of the public service in the interval."

NOTE [E.]

Return to an Order, dated the 17th of March 1797, of the Secret Committee of the Right Honourable the House of Lords, appointed to inquire into the causes which produced the Order in Council of the 26th of February last; for an Account of the Remittances made, and of Bills drawn and accepted or paid for the Services of the War in the West Indies, the Continent of Europe, the Island of Corsica, and other parts of the World, in the Four last Years; distinguishing the Sums, and Places, and the Services, with the respective dates.

	L.	S.	D.	L.	S.	D.
Bills drawn on the Treasury, as per annexed Account . . .	13,562,844	18	11			
Deduct ditto drawn in four years preceding the 1st January 1793	140,000	0	0			
				13,422,844	18	11
Bills drawn on the Paymasters-General, as per annexed Account	3,028,598	10	1			
Deduct ditto drawn in four years preceding the 1st January 1793	1,045,093	7	1			
				1,983,505	3	0
Remittances made by the Paymasters-General in the last four years	275,427	11	2			
Deduct ditto made by ditto in four years preceding the 1st January 1793	106,573	15	1			
				168,853	16	1
Bills drawn on the Office of Ordnance in the four last years, as per annexed Accounts . . .	619,944	1	4			
Deduct Amount of Bills drawn in the above period for services which it is supposed would have existed in time of peace . . .	146,714	1	2			
				473,230	0	2
Bills drawn on the Navy Office, as per annexed Account . 1,039,568 19 0						
Deduct ditto drawn in four years preceding 1st January 1793 . 232,416 13 11						
	807,152	5	1			

NOTE [E.]—Continued.

	L. S. D.	L. S. D.
Sums paid by Navy Bills for stores of foreign growth or manufacture in the four last years, as per Account, after deducting 30 per cent. . 2,223,053 11 1 Deduct ditto in four years preceding the 1st January 1793, after deducting 30 per cent. 546,060 7 11	1,676,993 3 2	
Specie sent to the Cape of Good Hope in 1796 . . .	5,000 0 0	2,489,145 8 ?
Bills drawn on the Victualling Office in the four last years, as per annexed Account . . 1,311,914 3 9 Deduct ditto in four years preceding the 1st January 1793 . . 134,629 11 6		1,177,284 12 3
Amount of provisions and victualling stores supplied by the Victualling Office in the last four years, as per annexed Account . . 600,586 16 11 Deduct ditto in four years preceding the 1st January 1793 . . 173,364 17 2		427,221 19 9
Bills drawn on and paid by the Commissioners for Transports, as per annexed Account . .	. . . . .	454,663 15 0
Bills drawn on and paid by the Commissioners for sick and wounded seamen for the service of prisoners of war, as per annexed Account	237,510 3 0	
Ditto by ditto for the service of sick and wounded seamen	155,359 16 10	392,869 19 10
Amount of loan and advances to the Emperor	. . . . .	5,570,000 0 0
Amount of Prussian subsidy .	. . . . .	1,223,891 10 6
Amount of Sardinian subsidy .	. . . . .	500,000 0 0

NOTE [E.]—*Continued.*

	L.	s.	D.	L.	S.	D.
Amount of sums paid for foreign and emigrant corps, exclusive of about L. 450,000 expended for different foreign corps during their residence in Great Britain	.	.	.	3,540,252	0	3
Amount of foreign secret service, deducting L. 25,000 per annum	.	.	.	345,079	16	0½
Amount of neutral cargoes	2,284,544	7	9			
Deduct for articles sold, stores delivered into dock-yards, and monies repaid by Mr Claude Scott	942,608	7	2			
				1,341,936	0	7
				33,510,779	0	7½

N. B. Exclusive of the above, are any sums which may have been remitted to Ireland, in consequence of any loans made here for the service of that country.

CHARLES LONG.

Whitehall, Treasury Chambers,
the 13th April 1797.

NOTE [F.]

An Account of the Quantity of Bullion exported in the years 1790, 1791, 1792, 1793, 1794, 1795, and 1796; distinguishing the Countries to which exported.

	1790.		1791.		1792.		1793.		1794.		1795.		1796.	
	Gold.	Silver.	Gold.	Silver.	Gold.	Silver.	Gold.	Silver.	Gold.	Silver.	Gold.	Silver.	Gold.	Silver.
	Oz. dwts.	Oz. dwts	Oz. dwts.	Oz. dwts.	Oz. dwts.	Oz.	Oz.	Oz.	Oz.	Oz. dwts.	Oz. dwts.	Oz. dwts.	Oz. dwts.	Oz. dwts.
Denmark and Norway		400								14,000 0				
Russia		100,000		50,196		12,000				95,866 0		21,300 0		14,400 0
Sweden		15,166						12		96,980 0		48,900 0		
Germany		1,334,312 10		224,500	3,432 0	1,192,663		140,014	7,734 0	2,646,466 0	31,069 13	1,239,882 18	4,119 0	4,706,757 10
Holland				6,819	18,150 0	118,136	89	25,000		62,108 0				
Flanders	12,561 10	613,667 0	6,546 15	586,498	18,174 0	2,909,886	12,600	410,000						
France			55,264 0		3,715 3	27,500								
Portugal						50,000						1,129 0		29,592 0
Madeira													1,271 0	1,000 0
Spain												190,000 0		
Italy	2,209 10	55,172 14		863	109 0	2,091		44,506					300 0	700 0
Isle of Guernsey				90,000								11,208 10	174 12	65,749 4
States of America		151,638 10	19,451 19	95,999 16	37,702 17	119,157	4,809	17,540	7,032 0	21,500 0	1,540 0		4,252 0	10,000 0
British Colonies		3,588,065 10		4,148,279 10	4,000 0	2,595,737		445,077		187,759 10		252,494 0		102,036 0
West Indies		866 0		1,990 0		4,636								
East Indies														
Africa														
	14,771 0	5,858,988	81,262 15	5,135,145 6	85,283 0	7,031,410	17,498	1,082,149	14,766 3	3,127,315 10	32,609 13	1,764,914 8	10,116	16 930,234 14

Inspector General's Office,
Custom-House, London,
March 22, 1797.

THOMAS IRVING,
Inspector-General of the Imports and Exports of
Great Britain, and the British Colonies.

NOTE [G.]

Extract from the examination of Mr Bosanquet, before the Secret Committee of the House of Lords, 20th March 1797.

" Was you a director of the bank in 1783?—I was.

" It appearing by the scale of cash in the bank in 1783 that it was much lower than on the 26th of February last, can you state to the committee what measures were then pursued by the bank?—I cannot answer that question without taking notice of the very different situation the country was in at the two periods of 1783 and the beginning of 1797. In the first period the drain of cash proceeded from the great extension of commerce which followed the peace, and which occasioned so considerable an export of the commodities of this country that the circulation was hardly sufficient to support it. It was evident that if this drain could be supported for a short time, the influx of wealth that must follow from the return of the amount of the exports would amply compensate for the preceding drain, and so it turned out. The bank directors, therefore, without opening the state of their affairs to the then administration, took a bold step of their own authority, and refused to make the advances on the loan of that year; this answered the purpose of making a temporary suspension in the amount of the drain of their specie. The time at which they had the most ground of alarm was not when their cash was at the lowest, but about April or May, when they refused to

APPENDIX.

advance on the loan; and although in October their cash was lower than before, yet they had such reason to expect a turn in their favour by a favourable alteration of the exchanges, that they were under much less apprehensions than they were in the spring. It is notorious that the situation of public affairs at the beginning of the present year was totally different.

"It is to be understood that no measures were taken by the bank at that time to procure cash or bullion?— I do not recollect that any particular mode was adopted to procure cash or bullion, nor do I know how any effectual one could be adopted; for if the exchanges (I do not know what they were at that period) would not enable individuals to bring cash into the country, it could answer no purpose for the bank to attempt to do it, which would only make the exchanges still more unfavourable. On recollection, I do not know whether some attempts were not made to bring gold from Lisbon and Amsterdam at a considerable loss, but think it could not have been to a large amount; certainly, when the object was only to gain time, it might answer to bring it in, although at a loss."

It may be here remarked that the extension of commerce to which Mr Bosanquet ascribes the drain of specie, does not account for the fact. An extension of commerce requires, no doubt, a proportional increase of currency. But by converting bank notes into specie, no increase of currency is procured. When a disposition exists, therefore, to convert bank notes into specie, this would seem to imply that they were in discredit; for paper answers every purpose of specie, and when specie is preferred, therefore, it must be generally on account of its superior security.

NOTE (H.)

Extract from the Report of the Select Committee of the House of Commons on the High Price of Gold Bullion.

" Mr Whitmore, the late governor of the bank, expressly states, ' The bank never force a note in circula-
' tion, and there will not remain a note in circula-
' tion more than the immediate wants of the public re-
' quire; for no banker, I presume, will keep a larger
' stock of bank notes by him than his immediate pay-
' ments require, as he can at all times procure them.'
The reason here assigned is more particularly explained by Mr Whitmore, when he says, ' The bank notes would
' revert to us if there was a redundancy in circulation, as
' no one would pay interest for a bank note that he did
' not want to make use of.' Mr Whitmore further states, ' The criterion by which I judge of the exact pro-
' portion to be maintained between the occasions of the
' public, and the issues of the bank, is by avoiding as
' much as possible to discount what does not appear to be
' legitimate mercantile paper.' And further, when asked, What measure the court of directors has to judge by, whether the quantity of bank notes out in circulation is at any time excessive?—Mr Whitmore states, that their measure of the security or abundance of bank notes is certainly by the greater or less application that is made to them for the discount of good paper.

" Mr Pearse, late deputy governor, and now governor of the bank, stated very distinctly his concurrence in

APPENDIX. 31

opinion with Mr Whitmore upon this particular point. He referred ' to the manner in which bank notes are is-
' sued, resulting from the applications made for discounts
' to supply the necessary want of bank notes, by which
' their issue in amount is so controlled that it can never
' amount to an excess' He considers ' the amount of
' the bank notes in circulation as being controlled by the
' occasions of the public, for internal purposes,' and that
' from the manner in which the issue of bank notes is
' controlled, the public will never call for more than is
' absolutely necessary for their wants.'

" Another director of the bank, Mr Harman, being asked, If he thought that the sum total of discounts applied for, even though the accommodation afforded should be on the security of good bills to safe persons, might be such as to produce some excess in the quantity of the bank issues if fully complied with? he answered, ' I
' think if we discount only for solid persons, and such
' paper as is for real *bona fide* transactions, we cannot
' materially err.' And he afterwards states, that what he should consider as the test of a superabundance would be, ' money being more plentiful in the market.'

" It is material to observe, that both Mr Whitmore and Mr Pearse state that ' the bank does not comply with
' the whole demand upon them for discounts, and that
' they are never induced, by a view to their own profit, to
' push their issues beyond what they deem consistent with
' the public interest.

" Another very important part of the evidence of these gentlemen upon this point, is contained in the following extract:

" Is it your opinion that the same security would exist against any excess in the issues of the bank, if the rate of the discount were reduced from L.5. to L.4. per cent.? —Answer, The security of an excess of issue would be, I conceive, precisely the same.—*Mr Pearse.* I concur in that answer.

" If it were reduced to L.3. per cent.?—*Mr Whitmore.* I conceive there would be no difference if our practice remained the same as now, of not forcing a note into circulation.—*Mr Pearse.* I concur in that answer."

The reader will not fail to remark how much the last answers are at variance with every known and acknowledged principle of trade. It is obvious that the paper of the bank of England answers to those who borrow it the purpose of capital; and yet it is here maintained that, though this capital could be borrowed at three per cent., there would be no greater danger of its being borrowed in excess than if five per cent. were paid for it; so that in this case it appears that the high price has no effect in limiting the demand.

NOTE [I.]

The questions proposed by the Committee of the House of Commons, to the merchants and bankers who were examined respecting the state of the exchange, as connected with the high price of bullion, are exceedingly clear and judicious,—and the answers of the witnesses expose at once the fallacy of their opinions on this subject. The following is an abstract from the evidence of Mr Abraham Goldsmid:

APPENDIX.

12th March 1810.

Francis Horner, Esq. in the Chair.

" You have stated that a guinea, or gold equal to what is contained in a guinea, is worth about 25s. at Paris, that is a difference of L.8. 18s. upon 44 guineas and a half, so that gold equal in weight to what is contained in 44 guineas and a half, would sell at Paris for L.55. 12s. 6d.; do you mean to say that the above quantity of gold would purchase at Paris a bill on London for L.55. 12s. 6d.?— Nearly so.

" What would a pound of gold in London cost, at what you have stated to be the present market price of gold in London, namely, L.4. 12s. per ounce?—L.55. 4s.

" Does it not follow, from what you have now stated, that the pound of gold in London and at Paris is at present nearly of the same value, the difference being only 7s. 6d. per pound?—It does.

" What bill on England could be purchased at Hamburgh, according to the last accounts of the course of exchange, for 100 ounces of English standard gold?—About L.460.

" How much English standard gold for exportation could be purchased in London for L.460?—One hundred ounces.

" Then the price of gold at Hamburgh, and the price of gold in London are nearly equal?—They are.

" Is not the exchange at par between two countries, when a given amount of the currency of the one or the other will purchase an equal amount of bullion, of a given purity, in either?—I always understood it so.

" If 100 hundred ounces of gold, of standard purity,

at Hamburgh would, at the present course of exchange, purchase a bill upon London of L 460., and if L.460. in London would purchase only 95 ounces of gold, of the same purity, would not the exchange of Hamburgh upon London be five per cent. in favour of London ?—If the price at Hamburgh was such, that the produce of 100 ounces of gold sold there would purchase a bill of L.460 upon London, and that bill in London would only purchase 95 ounces of gold, then the exchange would certainly be five per cent. in favour of England.

" In ordinary times, when our gold coin is at its standard, can the exchange be depressed lower, by the state of balance of payments, than what it costs to transport specie or bullion ?—Sometimes one way and sometimes the other, over and above such expence.

" How much over and above such expence do you conceive ?—I have known it differ as much as five per cent. either way.

" Can so great a difference as five per cent. continue for any considerable time ?—I have known from one to five per cent. continue for three or four years.

" How long did it ever continue so high as five per cent. ?—I have known it five per cent., but very seldom, and not for a long time together.

" You have stated that the sum of L.460 would be produced by a hundred ounces of gold, of standard fineness, at Hamburgh, and that the same quantity of gold would be purchased by the same sum in London, at the present price of foreign gold ; then, is not the exchange of Hamburgh upon London now at par ?—No ; because you are paying in London L.4. 12s. for what is intrinsically worth L.3. 17s. 10½d. according to the coinage price."

This witness, it will be observed, states, that, according to the existing rate of exchange, 100 ounces of gold, remitted from Hamburgh to London, would produce L.460—and that L.460 would in London purchase 100 ounces of gold. As it thus appears that a given quantity of bullion, in Hamburgh, might be converted, by means of the exchange, into the same quantity of bullion in London, the witness was asked if the exchange was not therefore at par; and he answers, No; because you are paying in London L.4. 12s. in bank paper for an ounce of bullion, which is only coined into L.3. 17s. 10½d. Now, what has this to do with the question?—We say that the exchange between Hamburgh and London is at par, because an equal quantity of bullion in Hamburgh can be exchanged for an equal quantity of bullion in London; and this is denied, because it requires a greater number of Bank of England notes than before to purchase the same quantity of bullion. But although this fact tends to prove the diminished value of these notes, it has evidently no connection with the state of the exchange between Hamburgh and London.

Similar questions were proposed to other witnesses, and their answers are equally conclusive as to the real state of the exchange. The following is an extract from the evidence of Mr Greffulhe, a great continental merchant:

" Supposing you had a pound weight troy of gold, of the English standard, at Paris, and that you wished by means of that to procure a bill of exchange upon London, what would be the amount of the bill of exchange which you would procure in the present circumstances?—I find that a pound of gold, of the British standard, at the pre-

APPENDIX.

sent market price of 105 francs, and the exchange at 20 livres, would purchase a bill of exchange of L. 59. 8s.

" At the present market price of gold in London, how much standard gold can you purchase for L.59. 8s. ?—At the price of L.4. 12s. I find it will purchase 13 ounces of gold, within a very small fraction.

" Then what is the difference per cent. in the quantity of standard gold which is equivalent to L.59. 8s. of our currency, as at Paris and in London ?—About $8\frac{1}{2}$ per cent.

" Suppose you had a pound weight troy of our standard gold at Hamburgh, and that you wished to part with it for a bill of exchange upon London, what would be the amount of the bill of exchange which, in the present circumstances, you would procure?—At the Hamburgh price of 101, and the exchange at 29, the amount of the bill purchased on London would be L.58. 4s.

" What quantity of our standard gold, at the present price of L.4. 12s., do you purchase for L.58. 4s ?—About 12 ounces and 13 dwts.

" Then what is the difference per cent. between the quantity of standard gold at Hamburgh and in London, which is equivalent to L.58. 4s. sterling ?—About $5\frac{1}{4}$ per cent.

" Suppose you had a pound weight of troy, of our standard gold, at Amsterdam, and wished to part with it for a bill of exchange upon London, what would be the amount sterling of the bill of exchange which you would procure?—At the Amsterdam price of $14\frac{1}{4}$, exchange 31. 6. and bank agio one per cent., the amount of the bill on London would be L.58. 18s.

" At the present price of L.4. 12s. what quantity of our standard gold do you purchase in London for L.58. 18s. sterling ?—Twelve ounces 16 dwts.

"How much is that per cent. ?—Seven per cent.

" What, in your idea, constitutes the par of exchange between any two countries ?—An equality of the respective currencies of the two countries, compared with reference to their fineness and weight.

" Then, does not the difference of the exchange between any two countries, from the established par at any one time, consist in the different quantity of the precious metal which is equivalent at the two places to a given sum in the currency of either ?—I should think not exactly, as the respective market prices of gold and silver may be influenced by momentary circumstances, and not be strictly accordant with the state of exchange."

NOTE [K.]

Extract from Mr Pitt's Speech on submitting to the House of Commons his proposed measure for a free intercourse between Great Britain and Ireland.

" In treating this important question, he would beg leave to recal their attention to what had been, and what was the relative situation of the two countries. They would recollect that, from the revolution to a period within the memory of every man who heard him, indeed until these very few years, the system had been that of debarring Ireland from the enjoyment and use of her own resources; to make the kingdom completely subservient to the interests and opulence of this country, without suffering her to share in the bounties of nature, in the industry of her citizens, or making them contribute to the general interests and strength of the empire. This system of cruel and abominable restraint had however been exploded. It was at once harsh and unjust, and it was as impolitic as it was oppressive; for, however necessary it might be to the partial benefit of districts in Britain, it promoted not the real prosperity and strength of the empire. That which had been the system counteracted the kindness of Providence, and suspended the industry and enterprize of man.—Ireland was put under such restraint, that she was shut out from every species of commerce,—she was restrained from sending the produce of her own soil to foreign markets, and all correspondence with the colonies of Britain was prohibited to her; so that she could not derive their commodities but through the medium of Britain. This was the system which had prevailed, and this was the state of thraldom in which that country had been kept ever since the revolution. Some relaxation of the system, indeed, took place at an early period of the present century. Somewhat more of the restrictive laws were abated in the reign of George II.; but it was not until a time nearer to our own day, and indeed within the last seven years, that the system had been completely reversed."

NOTE [L.]

The following are the principal Articles of the Commercial Treaty concluded between Great Britain and France, 26th September 1786.

ART. I.—It is agreed and concluded between the most serene and most potent king of Great Britain, and the most serene and most potent the most Christian king, that there shall be a reciprocal and entirely perfect liberty of navigation and commerce between the subjects of each party, in all and every the kingdoms, states, provinces, and territories, subject to their majesties in Europe, for all and singular kinds of goods, in those places, upon the conditions, and in such manner and form as is settled and adjusted in the following articles:

Art. II.—For the future security of commerce and friendship between the subjects of their said majesties, and to the end that this good correspondence may be preserved from all interruption and disturbance, it is concluded and agreed, that if, at any time, there should arise any misunderstanding, breach of friendship, or rupture between the crowns of their majesties, which God forbid! (which rupture shall not be deemed to exist until the recalling or sending home of the respective ambassadors and ministers,) the subjects of each of the two parties residing in the dominions of the other, shall have the privilege of remaining and continuing their trade therein, without any manner of disturbance, so long as they behave peaceably, and commit no offence against the laws and ordinances; and in case their conduct should render them suspected, and the respective governments should be obliged to order them to remove, the term of twelve months shall be allowed them for that purpose, in order that they may remove, with their effects and property, whether entrusted to individuals, or to the state. At the same time it is to be understood, that this favour is not to be extended to those who shall act contrary to the established laws.

Art. III.—It is likewise agreed and concluded, that the subjects and inhabitants of the kingdoms, provinces, and dominions of their majesties, shall exercise no acts of hostility or violence against each other, either by sea or by land, or in rivers, streams, ports, or havens, under any colour or pretence whatsoever; so that the subjects of either party shall receive no patent, commission, or instruction for arming and acting at sea as privateers, nor letters of reprisal, as they are called, from any princes or states, enemies to the other party; nor by virtue, or under colour of such patents, commissions, or reprisals, shall they disturb, or infest, or any way prejudice or damage the aforesaid subjects and inhabitants of the king of Great Britain, or of the Most Christian king; neither shall they arm ships in such manner as is above said, or go out to sea therewith. To which end, as often as it is required by either party, strict and express prohibitions shall be renewed and published in all the territories, countries, and dominions of each party wheresoever, that no one shall in any wise use such commissions or letters of reprisal under the severest punishment that can be inflicted on the transgressors, besides being liable to make full restitution and satisfaction to those to whom they have done any damage; neither shall any letters of reprisal be hereafter granted by either of the said high contracting parties, to the prejudice or detriment of the subjects of the other, except only in such case wherein justice is denied or delayed; which denial or delay of justice shall not be regarded as verified, unless the petitions of the person, who desires the said letters of reprisal, be communicated to the minister residing there on the part of the prince against whose subjects they are not to be granted, that within the space of four months, or sooner, if it be possible, he may manifest the contrary, or procure the satisfaction that may be justly due.

Art. IV.—The subjects and inhabitants of the respective dominions of the two sovereigns shall have liberty, freely and securely, without licence or passport, general or special, by land or by sea, or any other way, to enter into the kingdoms, dominions, provinces, countries, islands, cities, villages, towns, walled or unwalled, fortified or unfortified, ports, or territories whatsoever, of either sovereign, situated in Europe, and to return from thence, to remain there, or to pass through the same, and therein to buy and purchase, as they please, all things necessary for their subsistence and use ; and they shall mutually be treated with all kindness and favour. Provided, however, that in all these matters they behave and conduct themselves conformably to the laws and statutes, and live with each other in a friendly and peaceable manner, and promote a reciprocal concord by maintaining a mutual and good understanding.

Art. V.—The subjects of each of their said majesties may have leave and licence to come with their ships, as also with the merchandizes and goods on board the same, the trade and importation whereof are not prohibited by the laws of either kingdom, and to enter into the countries, dominions, cities, ports, places, and rivers of either party, situated in Europe, to resort thereto, and to remain and reside there, without any limitation of time ; also to hire houses, or to lodge with other persons, and to buy all lawful kinds of merchandizes where they think fit, either from the first maker or the seller, or in any other manner, whether in the public market for the sale of merchandizes, or in fairs, or wherever such merchandizes are manufactured or sold. They may likewise deposit and keep in their magazines and warehouses the merchandizes brought from other parts, and afterwards expose the same to sale, without being in any wise obliged, unless willingly and of their own accord, to bring the said merchandizes to the marts and fairs. Neither are they to be burthened with any impositions or duties on account of the said freedom of trade, or for any other cause whatsoever, except those which are to be paid for their ships and merchandizes, conformably to the regulations of the present treaty, or those to which the subjects of the two contracting parties shall themselves be liable. And they shall have free leave to remove themselves, as also their wives, children, and servants, together with their merchandizes, property, goods, or effects, whether bought or imported, wherever they shall think fit, out of either kingdom, by land and by sea, on the rivers and fresh waters, after discharging the usual duties; any law, privilege, grant, immunities, or customs, to the contrary thereof in any wise notwithstanding. In matters of religion, the subjects of the two crowns shall enjoy perfect liberty. They shall not be compelled to attend divine service, whether in the churches or elsewhere; but on the contrary, they shall be permitted, without any molestation, to perform the exercises of their religion privately in their own houses and in their own way. Liberty shall not be refused to bury the subjects of either kingdom who die in the territories of each other, in convenient places to be appointed for that purpose; nor shall the funerals or sepulchres of the deceased be in any wise disturbed. The laws and statutes of each kingdom shall remain in full force and vigour, and shall be duly put in execution, whether they relate to commerce and navigation, or to any other right, those cases only excepted, concerning which it is otherwise determined in the articles of this present treaty.

Art. VI.—The two high contracting parties have thought proper to settle the duties on certain goods and merchandizes, in order to fix invariably the footing on which the trade therein shall be established between the two nations. In consequence of which they have agreed upon the following tariff, viz.

1. The wines of France, imported directly from France into Great Britain, shall, in no case, pay any higher duties than those which the wines of Portugal now pay.

The wines of France, imported directly from France into Ireland, shall pay no higher duties than those which they now pay.

2. The vinegars of France, instead of L.67. 5s. $3\frac{1}{2}\frac{6}{0}$d. sterling per ton, which they now pay, shall not for the future pay, in Great Britain, any higher duties than L.32. 18s. $10\frac{1}{2}\frac{6}{0}$d. sterling per ton.

3. The brandies of France, instead of 9s. $6\frac{1}{2}\frac{2}{0}$d. sterling, shall for the future pay, in Great Britain, only seven shillings sterling per gallon, making four quarts, English measure.

4. Oil of olives, coming directly from France, shall, for the future, pay no higher duties than are now paid for the same from the most favoured nations.

5. Beer shall pay reciprocally a duty of thirty per cent. *ad valorem.*

6. The duties on hardware, cutlery, cabinet ware, and turnery, and also all works, both heavy and light, of iron, steel, copper, and brass, shall be classed; and the highest duty shall not exceed ten per cent. *ad valorem.*

7. All sorts of cottons manufactured in the dominions of the two sovereigns in Europe, and also woollens, whether knit or wove, including hosiery, shall pay, in both countries, an import duty of twelve per cent. *ad valorem ;*

all manufacturers of cotton or wool, mixed with silk excepted, which shall remain prohibited on both sides.

8. Cambrics and lawns shall pay, in both countries, an import duty of five shillings, or six livres Tournois, per demi-piece of seven yards and three quarters, English measure; and linen made of flax or hemp, manufactured in the dominions of the two sovereigns in Europe, shall pay no higher duties, either in Great Britain or France, than linens manufactured in Holland or Flanders, imported into Great Britain, now pay.

And linen made of flax or hemp, manufactured in Ireland or France, shall reciprocally pay no higher duties than linens manufactured in Holland, imported into Ireland, now pay.

9. Sadlery shall reciprocally pay an import duty of fifteen per cent. *ad valorem*.

10. Gauzes of all sorts shall reciprocally pay ten per cent. *ad valorem*.

11. Millinery made up of muslin, lawn, cambric, or gauze of every kind, or of any other article admitted under the present tariff, shall pay reciprocally a duty of twelve per cent. *ad valorem* ; and if any article shall be used therein, which are not specified in the tariff, they shall pay no higher duties than those paid for the same articles by the most favoured nations.

12. Porcelain, earthen ware, and pottery, shall pay reciprocally twelve per cent. *ad valorem*.

13. Plate-glass and glass ware in general shall be admitted on each side, paying a duty of twelve per cent. *ad valorem*.

His Britannic Majesty reserves the right of countervailing, by additional duties on the undermentioned merchandizes, the internal duties actually imposed upon the manufactures, or the import duties which are charged on the raw materials; namely, on all linens or cottons, stained or printed, on beer, glass ware, plate glass, and iron.

And his Most Christian Majesty also reserves the right of doing the same, with regard to the following merchandizes; namely, cottons, iron, and beer.

And for the better securing the due collection of the duties payable *ad valorem*, which are specified in the above tariff, the said contracting parties will concert with each other as well the form of the declarations to be made, as also the proper means of preventing fraud with respect to the real value of the said goods and merchandizes.

But, if it shall hereafter appear, that any mistakes have inadvertently been made in the above tariff, contrary to the principles on which it is founded, the two sovereigns will concert with good faith upon the means of rectifying them.

ART. VII.—The duties above specified are not to be altered but by mutual consent; and the merchandizes not above specified shall pay, in the dominions of the two sovereigns, the import and export duties payable in each of the said dominions by the most favoured European nations, at the time the present treaty bears date; and the ships belonging to the subjects of the said dominions shall also respectively enjoy therein all the privileges and advantages which are granted to those of the most favoured European nations.

ART. XV.—It is agreed, that ships belonging to his Britannic Majesty's subjects, arriving in the dominions of his Most Christian Majesty, from the ports of Great Britain or Ireland, or from any other foreign port, shall not pay freight duty or any other like duty. In the same manner, French ships shall be exempted in the dominions of his Britannic majesty, from the duty of five shillings, and from every other similar duty or charge.

Art. XVI.—It shall not be lawful for any foreign privateers, not being subjects of either crown, who have commissions from any other prince or state, in enmity with either nation, to arm their ships in the ports of either of the said two kingdoms, to sell what they have taken, or in any other manner whatever to exchange the same; neither shall they be allowed even to purchase victuals, except such as shall be necessary for their going to the nearest port of that prince from whom they have obtained commissions.

Art. XX.—It shall be lawful for all the subjects of the king of Great Britain, and of the most Christian king, to sail with their ships, with perfect security and liberty, no distinction being made who are the proprietors of the merchandizes laden thereon, from any port whatever, to the countries which are now, or shall be hereafter at war with the king of Great Britain, or the most Christian king. It shall likewise be lawful for the aforesaid subjects to sail and traffic with their ships and merchandizes, with the same liberty and security, from the countries, ports, and places of those who are enemies of both, or of either party, without any opposition or disturbance whatsoever, and to pass directly not only from the places of the enemy aforementioned to neutral places, but also from one place belonging to an enemy to another place belonging to an enemy, whether they be under the jurisdiction of the same, or of several princes. And as it has been stipulated concerning ships and goods, that every thing shall be deemed free, which shall be found on board the ships belonging to the subjects of the respective kingdoms, although the whole lading, or part thereof, should belong to the enemies of their majesties, contraband goods being always excepted, on the stopping of which such proceedings shall be had as are conformable to the spirit of the following articles; it is likewise agreed, that the same liberty be extended to persons who are on board a free ship, to the end that, although they be enemies to both, or to either party, they may not be taken out of such free ships, unless they are soldiers, actually in the service of the enemies, and on their voyage for the purpose of being employed in a military capacity, in their fleets or armies.

Art. XXI.—This liberty of navigation and commerce shall extend to all kinds of merchandizes, excepting those only which are specified in the following article, and which are described under the name of contraband.

Art. XXII.—Under this name of contraband, or prohibited goods, shall be comprehended arms, cannon, harquebusses, mortars, petards, bombs, grenades, saucisses, carcasses, carriages for cannon, musket-rests, bandoleers, gunpowder, match, saltpetre, ball, pikes, swords, head-pieces, helmets, cutlasses, halberts, javelins, holtsters, belts, horses and harness, and all other like kinds of arms and warlike implements fit for the use of troops.

Art. XXIII.—These merchandizes which follow shall not be reckoned among contraband goods, that is to say, all sorts of cloth, and all other manufactures of wool, flax, silk, cotton, or any other materials, all kinds of wearing apparel, together with the articles of which they are usually made, gold, silver, coined or uncoined, tin, iron, lead, copper, brass, coals, as also wheat and barley, and any other kind of corn and pulse, tobacco, and all kinds of spices. salted and smoaked flesh, salted fish, cheese, and butter, beer, oil, wines, sugar, all sorts of salt, and of provisions which serve for sustenance and food to mankind; also all kinds of cotton, cordage, cables, sails, sailcloth, hemp, tallow, pitch, tar, and rosin, anchors and any part of anchors, ship masts, planks, timber of all kinds of trees, and all other things proper either for building or repairing ships. Nor shall any other goods whatever, which have not been worked into the form of any instrument, or furniture for warlike use, by land or by sea, be reputed contraband, much less such as have been already wrought and made up for any other purpose. All which things shall be deemed goods not contraband, as likewise all others which are not comprehended and particularly described in the preceding article; so that they may be freely carried by the subjects of both kingdoms, even to places belonging to an enemy, excepting only such places as are besieged, blocked up, or invested.

Art. XXIV —To the end that all manner of dissensions and quarrels may be avoided and prevented on both sides, it is agreed, that, in case either of their majesties should be engaged in a war, the ships and vessels belonging to the subjects of the other shall be furnished with sea-letters or passports, expressing the name, property, and bulk of the ship, as also the name and place of abode of the master or commander of the said ship, that it may appear thereby that the ship really and truly belongs to the subjects of one of the princes; which passports shall be made out and granted, according to the form annexed to the present treaty; they shall likewise be renewed every year, if the ship happens to return home within the space of a year. It is also agreed, that such ships when laden are to be provided not only with passports as above mentioned, but also with certificates containing the several particulars of the cargo, the place from whence the ship sailed, and whither she is bound, so that it may be known whether she carries any of the prohibited or contraband goods specified in the 22d article of this treaty; which certificates shall be prepared by the officers of the place from whence the ship set sail, in the accustomed form. And if any one shall think fit to express in the said certificates the person to whom the goods belong, he may freely do so.

Art. XXV.—The ships belonging to the subjects and inhabitants of the respective kingdoms, coming to any of the coasts of either of them, but without being willing to enter into port, or being entered, yet not willing to land their cargoes, or break bulk, shall not be obliged to give an account of their lading, unless they are suspected, upon sure evidence, of carrying prohibited goods, called contraband, to the enemies of either of the two high contracting parties.

Art. XXVI.—In case the ships belonging to the said subjects and inhabitants of the respective dominions of their most serene majesties, either on the coast or on the high seas, shall meet with any men of war belonging to their most serene majesties, or with privateers, the said men of war and privateers, for preventing any inconveniences, are to remain out of cannon shot, and to send their boats to the merchant ship which may be met with, and shall enter her to the number of two or three men only, to whom the master or commander of such ship or vessel shall shew his passport, containing the proof of the property of the ship, made out according to the form annexed to this present treaty; and the ship which shall have exhibited the same shall have liberty to continue her voyage, and it shall be wholly unlawful any way to molest or search her, or to chace or compel her to alter her course.

Art. XXVII.—The merchant ships belonging to the subjects of either of the two high contracting parties, which intend to go to a port at enmity with the other sovereign, concerning whose voyage and the sort of goods on board there may be just cause of suspicion, shall be obliged to exhibit, as well on the high seas as in the ports and havens, not only her passports, but also her certificates, expressing that the goods are not of the kind which are contraband, as specified in the 22d article of this treaty.

Art. XXVIII.—If, on exhibiting the above mentioned certificates, containing a list of the cargo, the other party should discover any goods of that kind which are declared contraband, or prohibited, by the 22d article of this treaty, and which are designed for a port subject to his enemies, it shall be unlawful to break up or open the hatches, chests, casks, bales, or other vessels found on board such ship, or to remove even the smallest parcel of the goods, whether the said ship belongs to the subjects of the king of Great Britain, or of the most Christian king, unless the lading be brought on shore, in the presence of the officers of the court of admiralty, and an inventory made by them of the said goods; nor shall it be lawful to sell, exchànge, or alienate the same in any manner, unless after due and lawful process shall have been had against such prohibited goods, and the judges of the admiralty respectively shall, by sentence pronounced, have confiscated the same ; saving always as well the ship itself, as the other goods found therein, which by this treaty are to be accounted free : neither may they be detained on pretence of their being mixed with prohibited goods, much less shall they be confiscated as lawful prize; and if, when only part of the cargo shall consist of contraband goods, the master of the ship shall agree, consent, and offer to deliver them to the captor who has discovered them, in such case, the captor having received those goods as lawful prize, shall forthwith release the ship, and not hinder her, by any means, from prosecuting her voyage to the place of her destination.

Art. XXIX.—On the contrary it is agreed, that whatever shall be found to be laden by the subjects and inhabitants of either party, on any ship belonging to the enemies of the other, although it be not contraband goods, shall be confiscated in the same manner as if it belonged to the enemy himself; except those goods and merchandizes which were put on board such ship before the declaration of war or the general order for reprisals, or even after such declaration, if it were done within the times following; that is to say, if they were put on board such ship in any port or place within the space of two months after such declaration or order for reprisals, between Archangel, St Petersburgh, and the Scilly Islands, and between the said islands and the city of Gibraltar; of ten weeks in the Mediterranean sea; and of eight months in any other country or place in the world; so that the goods of the subjects of either prince, whether they be contraband or otherwise, which, as aforesaid, were put on board any ship belonging to an enemy before the war, or after the declaration of the same, within the time and limits abovementioned, shall no ways be liable to confiscation, but shall well and truly be restored, without delay, to the proprietors demanding the same; provided nevertheless, that if the said merchandizes be contraband, it shall not be any ways lawful to carry them afterwards to the ports belonging to the enemy.

NOTE [M.]

THE oppressive practices to which the monopolies established in India, under the government of the company, necessarily led, may be easily conceived from the extensive powers possessed by the agent who was entrusted with carrying them into effect. The holder of the opium monopoly agreed to deliver annually to the company a certain quantity of opium, at a given price, on condition of receiving a premium for any surplus, and being liable in a penalty for all deficiencies. It was thus clearly his interest to provide the largest possible quantity, at the cheapest rate; and the cultivators being prohibited from dealing with any other merchant, he could buy their produce at his own price. In these circumstances, his profit consisted in taking the opium at an undervalue; and, under this system, the cultivation of the poppy was forcibly extended, fields green with rice being, on some occasions, ploughed up for its reception.

In a letter from Jonathan Duncan, resident at Benares, and afterwards governor of Bombay, it is stated, that, shortly after the expulsion of Cossim Ali Khan, about the year 1760, " the gentlemen (the company's servants),
" turning their thoughts to the purchase of opium, there
" was so little to be had, that they were content to buy
" the old commodity, that had lain in the merchants
" houses, at no less a rate than 200 rupees; the know-
" ledge of which high price exciting the poppy growers
" to increase the growth of that article, and the compe-
" tition becoming still greater, by the numerous purcha-

"sers, the gentlemen sent their several separate gomas-
"tahs (agents) into the different districts, to make pur-
"chases for them, on advances which they made for that
"purpose, and after the purchase, on the plea that the
"price rose too high, peons (guards) were put on the
"cellars, and the price thereby reduced as low as was
"thought proper."
These practices were, indeed, strictly forbidden; but restraints of this sort were easily overcome by the strong temptations which existed to abuse and tyranny; and some inquiries set on foot in 1788, by the humanity of Lord Cornwallis, exposed various acts of oppression. The cultivator was not only compelled to raise opium, on pain of losing his land, but he was also made answerable for a deficient produce, though occasioned by adverse seasons; and he was liable, in that case, to punishment, unless he could make up the quantity, which he had no way of doing but by paying a higher price for it than he could expect to receive. Various other frauds were practised by the contractor or his agents, such as making advances to the ryots in a light currency, without any allowance, and in using exceptionable weights for the weighing of their produce. [See Appendix to the Minutes of the Trial of Warren Hastings, No. 429, containing answers of the collectors in the opium districts, to the queries of the board of revenue, 1788. Revenue Consultation, 1789.]—In the contract entered into in 1788, new regulations and penalties were devised for checking these abuses, and, in the year 1799, the provision of opium was brought under agency, with the allowance of a commission to the agent, by which plan the revenue derived from it, which amounted, during the last four years of the contract, to sicca rupees 8,19,400, or

L. 95,050, was raised to sicca rupees 59,80,100, or L. 693,700.

Salt, which in 1764 had been declared a free commodity by the court of directors, was again brought under monopoly in 1772, and the power, formerly exercised, of compelling the Molungees, or salt-makers, to deliver to their masters a stated quantity of salt, was at the same time revived. This power of compelling labour by other means than by its just reward, was frequently enforced. The workmen never seem to have received any fair allowance for their labour; and, being unable to live, their subsistence was advanced to them, and allowed gradually to accumulate into a debt, which, as they were wholly unable to discharge, their masters preserved against them as a perpetual instrument of bondage. These pretended debts were sold when the salt-works came under different management; and the workmen were thus transferred from one master to another, and were forced to content themselves with whatever treatment they received. The monopoly of salt was afterwards changed into an agency, the agent being allowed a commission on his sales to the company; but the manufacturers seem to have been still as liable to oppression as before. In 1795, some inquiries were made by the board of trade into the condition of these labourers; and, in a letter addressed to the governor-general, their situation is thus described:—" We " found two principal descriptions of molungees (salt-" makers) in this agency, and in Tumlook; one the " Ticka, who worked upon a system of free compact; " the other the Adjoora, who laboured under a system of " coercion."—Those who were thus coerced received, according to a table of wages exhibited by the board of trade, only about half the wages of those who worked upon a system of free compact. [Appendix to the Second Report of the Select Committee on the Affairs of the East India Company, p. 196.]—And the letter goes on to state, " 1*st*, That the adjoora prices, stated above, " are not proportioned to the ordinary rate of labour in " the country; and that a man cannot earn sufficient by " them to support a family, or even himself, in health or " strength: 2*d*, That the adjoora molungees have not " any compensations or advantages adequate to the low- " ness of their earnings: 3*d*, That the agents must pos- " sess additional powers of considerable authority to be " able to maintain the system."

The following account of the salt-workers in the twenty-four Pergunnahs (provinces), is also contained in the letter of the board of trade:—" The agent, in answer " to our circular letter, informed us, that the produce of " his districts had certainly decreased. This he attri- " buted, in some measure, to the alteration of system, in " relieving the people from the coercion under which they " heretofore manufactured salt; an alteration which can- " not be too highly applauded.—The agent stated the de- " crease to have arisen chiefly in the Barbonny, or those " Collaries that work in the woods. On the alteration of " system, it was found necessary to increase the price " paid to the molungees, but the amount of it was still " extremely inadequate to the actual cost of the salt; the " natural consequence followed, that the agent always " found himself obliged to make advances of additional " sums, for the indispensable disbursements required for " the manufacture, or the people could not procure the " materials wherewith to prosecute their work. These " advances have of late years uniformly been carried to " the dead stock account, as irrecoverable balances due

"by the molungees. Instead of this money having been
"placed to the head of advances, it should have been an
"increase of price, for it was in fact all disbursed for the
"purposes of the manufacture; consequently it could
"only be considered the fair cost of the salt, and should
"have been charged as such. The agent verified his as-
"sertions, by shewing, that the quantity of salt which the
"molungees agreed to manufacture, average about 218
"Maunds Amdanny, of 327 Maunds Sale Weight, of
"82 S$^a.$ W$^t.$ at each Collary, greatly exceeded, with the
"exception of a very few instances, the possibility of
"what could be made. The value of the salt short deli-
"vered of the quantity agreed for, became an outstand-
"ing balance. No excitement was held out to the mo-
"lungees; for if, by excessive exertion, they should
"complete the quantity, the total neat earnings to each
"man would only be six rupees for seven and a half
"months labour, which was about the time he was em-
"ployed in the woods; this was paid him in advance, and
"went to subsist his family during his absence, while he
"himself lived upon the provision furnished to him by
"the company. From this statement of the situation of
"a molungee, it will evidently appear, that he was paid
"a bare subsistence; that he not only could not bring
"any thing home with him on his return from his toils,
"but would most probably be loaded with a heavy debt,
"on account of the salt short delivered of the quantity
"agreed for."

It is satisfactory to learn that these grievances were soon afterwards redressed, the salt manufacturers being all placed on the same footing. An increase of comfort and industry seems to have been the immediate effect of this change. The revenue obtained from the monopoly of salt amounted, on an average of three years previous to 1812, to L. 1,360,180.

NOTE [N.]

THE following evidence delivered before a Committee of the House of Commons in 1781, seems quite conclusive as to the rights and condition of the Zemindars.

George Vansittart, Esq. who had been fifteen years in India, from 1761 to 1776, during which time he was in the council of Calcutta, and also superintended the collections of Midnapore, states, " That on the frontiers of the provinces, particular instances have occurred, where zemindars, pressed for the payment of their balances, have fled the country ; and on the appointment of a collector to demand the rents immediately from the ryots, many of these, as they are in general attached to their zemindars, have followed the zemindar, and made hostile incursions on the remaining inhabitants ; and that the district has, in consequence, so far gone to ruin, that the government has been obliged to enter into a negociation with the old zemindar, and to receive him back on almost his own terms, to prevent the total desolation of the district."

Charles William Boughton Rouse, Esq. who had been employed at Dacca as chief of the provincial council, being asked, " whether, under the Mogul government, a zemindar was considered as a collector of revenue, and a servant of the state, or as a landholder? informed your committee, That he is not quite certain about the first origin of zemindars; but he is very certain, that ever since the subjection of Bengal to the Mogul government, they have been considered as the hereditary landholders of the country."—After mentioning that in Bahar there were many Mahomedan zemindars, and that " some have been sold since (after the company became possessed of the Dewannee) by order of the governor-general and council, for deficiencies of the public revenue, but that the government has always been very tender of coming to that extremity: That the districts of Cherolea and Mudodea were sold in 1776, and the new purchaser confirmed in possession by an instrument of the governor, called a sunnud; but such was the attachment of the inhabitants to their old zemindar, that they revolted against the new purchaser, who was not established in possession but by a military force; and a great deficiency was occasioned in the revenue of those districts;"—he afterwards states, " That the capital zemindars in the Dacca provinces, and other provinces he is acquainted with, are considered as men of rank; that they are very much respected throughout the country; that obedience is paid to their power and influence; and that the attachment of the inhabitants to their zemindar amounts almost to devotion: That in respect to the powers they exercise, the patent of confirmation which is given to every zemindar, under the authority of the Nazim, or Mogul's viceroy, and Dewan, or Mogul's receiver-general, describes their functions and gives them a very considerable jurisdiction; and that it was under the sanction of that patent that the English company exercised civil and criminal jurisdiction in that country, previous to the institution of the supreme court of judicature; and that the criminal court which they held before the acquisition of the Dewannee, was called the zemindary court. That the witness believes this system has prevailed throughout the Mogul empire ever since the reign of Akbar, very near two hundred years ago, who formed a system of regulations which have been much respected ever since.—Being asked, whether the zemindars are looked upon by the people who live under them as their natural hereditary protectors, connected with them in blood and manners, or a set of people acting as mere servants of government, who they think want the interposition of a strong power to prevent their oppressions? the witness answered, That the inhabitants are generally dissatisfied if a servant of government is sent to supersede the power of the zemindar; and he does not think the zemindars in general incline to oppress their husbandmen, but rather to compromise difficulties with them and protect them. That he does not consider zemindars as collectors of the revenue for government, or in any respect as servants of the company, but rather as hereditary proprietors, paying a fixed tribute to government; that they are considered as the natural nobility and gentry of the country; but that the rules of that government give them more power than our constitution can give to persons of equal rank and property here.

" Being asked, whether the son or heir of a zemindar could be refused admission to the succession of the zemindary, by the Mogul or the officers of his government? he said, Whilst he was in Bengal he made much inquiry into this subject, as being of the highest importance to the security of property, the nature of landed tenures in Bengal, and the equitable government of that country; and according to the best information he could ever derive from books, or from conversation with the most intelligent natives, he has the strongest reason to believe, that zemindaries were always considered under the Mogul government, except in times of anarchy and usurpation, to be an hereditary property, which it would have been regarded as an act of tyranny in the sovereign to infringe, unless for default of the possessor in paying the stipulated revenue, or for rebellion, or some atrocious culpability. He has been informed that the heir of a zemindar might have applied to the court of justice, composed of the Cawzee and Muftees, or to the Dewannee (revenue) officers, for a decision upon his title to the succession, if disputed by another claimant; and that even the emperor Aurungzebe was known to purchase zemindary lands from the hereditary zemindars. In a variety of cases which he has known referred to Mahomedan or Hindoo lawyers, the right of a son or heir to succeed to the possession of a zemindary has never been brought into doubt. Moreover, he had seen opinions of Mahomed Reza Cawn, now Naib Subah of Bengal, and of the late Rajah Shitabroy, both of them very able men, and long versed in the affairs of the Indostan government, and the latter brought up at Delhi in the service of Mahomed Shah's ministers, which say most decisively that the son of a zemindar has a right to succeed his father in the possession, even independently of any sunnud (patent) from the government. However, it has been usual to obtain one from the government, in order to confirm the title of the new possessor, and to have it entered in the public records; by which his authority over the lands is more completely established. The patent likewise authorised the zemindar to superintend the internal police of his district, and to bring justice home to the people, who saw it administered by men holding a permanent interest in the prosperity of the country. This was the more necessary when the claimant was heir in a collateral line, or in a more distant degree, to the last possessor. Upon these occasions certain fines were paid to government, and fees to the public officers; this payment is still continued in Bengal, but is rendered very moderate by the regulations of our government; indeed, were it not so, the zemindars in general would not be able to pay it under the enhanced and unsettled rent to which their lands have been subjected by the English government, and in some periods under that of the revolted nabobs, who preceded the English; a system which an attentive consideration of the subject has induced him to think unjust in its principle, pernicious in its consequences, and not productive in the application. He has seen opinions similar to those he has already mentioned, from the Roy Royan, who was the chief superintending officer of the khalsa, or exchequer, of the pundits, or interpreters, of the ancient Hindoo laws, and of the canougoos, who formerly held their appointment from the emperor, and had their deputes in every subordinate district to expound the usages of the country (as the term of canougoo implies), and to authenticate and record all conveyances and transfers of landed property. They say that a zemindary devolves to the son or heir of a zemindar; and although the country belongs to the king, and he may indeed give it to whom he pleases, yet that it is neither conformable to justice nor to the custom of the country, that he should join it to any other than the lawful heir, either male or female."

" Edward Baber, Esq. being examined, informed your committee, That he had resided in Bengal upwards of 17 years; that he left it in January 1780: That he was in the company's employment first, as resident of Midnapore, and afterwards as chief at Muxadabad : That the collections of Cossijurah were under his direction, as resident of Midnapore: That the amount of the revenue actually paid by the rajah of Cossijurah was, he believes, between L.15 and L.20,000 per annum : That he was the principal zemindar of the district : That he was treated by the witness with that respect that was due to a person of his rank and consequence: That he was considered by the natives in general as a man of superior rank: That he was looked up to with respect, and treated with deference: That he was of a high cast of Hindoos, either a bramin, or a cuttery, which is the next cast to a bramin : That he believes the zemindary has been a long time in his family : That he lives in a state of grandeur.

" Then being asked, Whether farmers of lands under the company, are considered in Bengal as mere collectors of revenue would be considered in England? he answered, That in order to afford the committee a satisfactory answer to this question, it will be necessary to give more than a bare negative, and to add an explanation of the tenures in Bengal ; for a parallel can scarcely be drawn between a mere collector of revenue, which arises from taxes on various articles, and a proprietor or farmer of land, where the revenue is paid from the produce of that land. A zemindar, and landholder in Bengal, hath a hereditary right to the district of which he is a kind of feudal lord ; a certain proportion of the produce of his lands, which proportion was fixed by the nabob, who, to carry on the allusion, was the lord paramount, was stipulated to be paid by the zemindars in fixed monthly payments ; this settlement was annual, and the sum so fixed was the revenue of government, all above belonging of course to the zemindar; when he had made his agreement with government, he had then to make his own with the ryots or tenants. Some parts of his lands he might perhaps let to responsible people, and others he would hold in his own hands, and appoint his own collectors, but in both instances the zemindar had a judicial authority, and to his court and cutchery appeals were made, and complaints were lodged, if either the farmers, or his own collectors, oppressed the tenants by exactions, or if there were litigated accounts; on this judicial authority was built the foundation of that power which was to enable him to enforce his collections; and consequently it met with every reasonable support from that government, which was to look to those collections for its revenue. This is a very summary and general account of the mode of settlement in the nabob's government."—Report of the Committee, p. 41—44.

Captain Gabriel Harper, who had resided in Bengal, Bahar, and Orissa, from the year 1761 to 1774, was examined by the committee; and being asked, " whether, during his residence with the vizier, he ever knew of a zemindar being dispossessed of his zemindary by him? he said, That he can only recollect one instance; that it was for arrears of rent, and that it happened to a man who had been frequently in arrear, and frequently pardoned, and who was notorious not only for ill payment of the revenue, but for his conduct towards those who were under his government. Being asked, what was his mode of proceeding on that dismission? said, That the zemindar was summoned to attend at Fizabad, the vizier's court; that being unable to pay his arrears, or find security for the payment, he was dispossessed of his zemindary, and imprisoned; where he remained some time, but was afterwards released at the intercession of some of the Gentoo officers about the court.

"Being asked, what he meant by imprisonment? said, A guard set over his person, in a place near the cutchery, appointed for the confinement of Gentoo prisoners, where his own servants attended him in the same manner as if he had been in his own house: That he was suffered sometimes to sit under a tree, and to sleep under a tent occasionally pitched for him: That in the province of Oude, persons of different religions or casts are never confined in the same place; for they are very careful not to offend the customs and religions of one sect or the other, and it would give great offence.

"Being asked, whether it was usual in Soujah Dowlah, or Bulwant Sing, to raise the rents, or let the zemindaries to the highest bidder? he said, Never. That he believed they would rather have lowered the rents, if an abatement was necessary, to a man who had been punctual in his former payments; and in times of public misfortune, such as the want of rain, that upon proper representation being made, he knows that part of the balance has been remitted. Being asked, if the zemindaries were considered as hereditary in the families of the zemindar? he said, No; it depended upon the will of the prince, but that he made a point of continuing it in the family, provided there was no particular objection to the next in succession. Being asked, if he knew what proportion the revenue paid by the zemindars bore to their income? he said, he could not describe the proportion, but that the zemindars had always sufficient to maintain themselves and their families with dignity and respect, correspondent to their situation."—Report, p. 54, 55, 56.

The risk of error, from not distinguishing between the form and the real nature of those tenures, is apparent from the preceding evidence. The witness states that the zemindaries were not hereditary, which is in direct contradiction to the evidence already adduced. But when he comes to explain, that though a new grant depended upon the will of the prince, it was never refused to the heir, provided there was no legal objection to his succession, we have the precise form of certain feudal tenures, in which the property at each succession must be formally surrendered to the superior for a new title. But no one ever dreamed of reasoning from this empty form against the hereditary transmission of feudal property.

The proprietory rights of the zemindars are plainly recognised in the following extract of a letter, from the governor-general and council to the directors, dated Fort William, Bengal, 3d November 1772.

" We have allowed a degree of weight (he observes) to the arguments of the zemindars and talookdars in favour of their plea of right, which, by adopting the first mode of settlement, would doubtless be exposed to risk; for as the authority given to the farmers would reduce the present incumbents to the level of mere pensioners, and greatly weaken their claims as proprietors, so, in the course of a few long leases, their rights and titles might, from the designs of the farmers to establish themselves in their estates, the death of the old inheritors, and the succession of minors, be involved in such obscurity, doubt, and controversy, as to deprive them totally of their inheritance. To expose the zemindars and talookdars to this risk, is neither consistent with our notions of equity nor with your orders, which direct, 'that we do not by any sudden change, alter the constitution, nor deprive the zemindars, &c. of their ancient privileges and immunities.'

"Another argument, drawn from the conduct naturally to be expected from the zemindars and talookdars, weighs strongly with us, and proves an objection to adopting the first mode. From a long continuance of the lands in their families, it is to be concluded they have rivetted an authority in the district, acquired an ascendency over the minds of the ryots, and ingratiated their affections. From causes like these, if entire deprivation were to take place, there could not be expected less material effects than all the evils of a divided authority, prejudice to the revenue, and desertion and desolation to the lands: Whereas, from continuing the lands under the management of those who have a natural and perpetual interest in their prosperity, provided their value is not of too great an amount, solid advantages may be expected to accrue. Every consideration then sways us, where it can be done with the prospect of the advantage before-mentioned, to adopt the second mode in settling with the inferior zemindars and talookdars; first, an equivalent revenue may be thereby obtained, with security for its punctual payment; secondly, the converting them into farmers establishes the government's right of putting their lands on that footing whenever they shall think proper, the awe of which must constantly operate to insure their good behaviour and good management; thirdly, the clause of scrutiny to which they are subjected will also have the same tendency, at the same time that it may be strictly put in force where there is cause to suspect concealment, or a prospect presents of increase to the revenue."

NOTE [O.]

The principle on which the land tax was assessed by the British in India, and its effects upon the country, are explained in the following letter:

Extracts of a Letter from Mr Becher, Resident at the Durbar, to the President of the Select Committee, dated 24th March 1769.

"It must give pain to an Englishman to have reason to think that, since the accession of the company to the Dewannee, the condition of the people of this country has been worse than it was before; and yet I am afraid the fact is undoubted, and I believe has proceeded from the following causes: The mode of providing the company's investment; the exportation of specie instead of importing large sums annually; the strictness that has been observed in the collections; the endeavours of all concerned to gain credit by an increase of revenue during the time of their being in station, without sufficiently attending to what future consequences might be expected from such a measure; the errors that subsist in the manner of making the collections, particularly by the employment of aumils, (collectors or revenue farmers): These appear to me the principal causes why this fine country, which flourished under the most despotic and arbitrary governments, is verging towards its ruin, while the English have really so great a share in the administration."

He afterwards observes,

"When the English received the grant of the Dewannee, their first consideration seems to have been their raising as large sums from the country as could be collected to answer the pressing demands from home, and to defray the large expences here. The zemindars not being able or willing to pay the sums required, aumils have been sent into most of the districts. The aumils on their appointment agree with the ministers to pay a fixed sum for the districts they are to go to; and the man that has offered most has generally been preferred. What a destructive system is this for the poor inhabitants? The aumils have no connexion or natural interest in the welfare of the country where they make the collections; nor have they any certainty of holding their places beyond the year; the best recommendation they can have is to pay up their kistbundies (monthly payments) punctually, to which purpose they fail not to rack the country where they make the collections, wherever they find they cannot otherwise pay their kists, and secure a handsome sum for themselves. Uncertain in their office, and without opportunity of acquiring money after their dismission, can it be doubted that the future welfare of the country is not an object with them? nor is it to be expected in human nature. These aumils also have no check on them during the time of their employment; they appoint those that act under them; so that during the time of the year's collection their power is absolute. There is no fixed hustabood (valuation of the lands from actual survey) by which they are to collect, nor any likelihood of complaint, till the poor ryot is really drove to necessity by having more demanded of him than he can possibly pay. Much these poor wretches will bear rather than quit their habitations to come here to complain; especially when it is considered that it must always be attended with loss of time, risk of obtaining redress, and a certainty of being very ill used, should the aumil's influence be sufficient to prevent the poor man's obtaining justice, or even access to those able to grant it to him. On this destructive plan, and with a continual demand for more revenue, have the collections been made ever since the English have been in possession of the Dewannee."

Mr Francis, in his observations respecting the best system to be adopted in regard to the letting or disposing of the lands in Bengal, gives the same account of the state of the country.

" *Fort William, 22d Jan.* 1776.

" 1. The company, I believe, had conceived an early but erroneous opinion, that by the constitution of the Mogul empire, the governing power was proprietor of the soil; consequently, that in the management of their territorial acquisitions, they ought not to content themselves with a fixed tribute as government, since they had a right to engross the entire produce as landlord. On this principle, which, if true, would not in prudence have warranted the practice deduced from it, it has never yet been thought necessary to limit the annual demand on the country to any fixed sum once for all. The general tendency of the company's instructions, and of course the professed object of every settlement here since our acquisition of the Dewannee, has been to raise the greatest possible revenue from the country. The leading members of each different administration, in conformity to the views and expectations of their superiors, seem to have rested their chief merit with the company on their success in the pursuit of this object, but to have limited their views to the probable period of their respective continuance in office. A temporary system provides for immediate exigencies only. It was not considered, nor was it a consideration likely to be regarded by a fluctuating government, that swelling the rent-roll, if not directed by a perfect knowledge of the resources, and a due attention to the circumstances of the country, must be followed by a general strain in the collections. That such a strain must be attended by a future diminution of the revenue, was too obvious not to be foreseen; but the effect succeeded the cause much sooner than was expected. Every government endeavoured to make good its promise to the company; but having engaged for more than they could perform, they distressed and racked the people without accomplishing their purpose. The truth is, that a nominal increase in the jumma (tax) has usually, if not constantly, been attended by a real decrease in the collections. By exacting from the landholder a greater return than it is possible for him to pay, he is furnished with pretences for paying less than he ought; or supposing the nominal revenue to be realised for a few years, yet if it exceeds that proportion of the produce which government should demand from the land, the excess can only be made good by invading the sources of future revenue. I am convinced it will be found, that for some years past, the government of this country has been living upon its capital; that is, they have annually taken a portion of the existing wealth, which ought to have been reserved for future production.

" 2. Whether it be owing to excessive impositions, or to any unequal distribution, or to an injudicious mode of collection, or to the united operation of these causes, it is notorious that the country is impoverished, and in a great degree depopulated ; yet with every auxiliary expedient that could be devised, or with every exertion of rigour that could be enforced by government, there is not a single year in which the actual collections have not fallen considerably short of the settlement. In those districts where they have been tolerably kept up, we may observe a constant ostentation of extraordinary merit on the part of the collectors, to which they could have no pretence, if the service they are employed in were not really attended with extraordinary difficulties. In every other country the collection of a land-tax is one of the simplest and easiest operations of government.

" 3. From the constant failure in the estimated produce of the lands, it is apparent that there must be some gross fallacy in the system hitherto pursued ; since it is not even calculated to answer a temporary purpose. The permanent welfare of the people, the moderate but lasting advantages which the governing power might continue to derive from that source, and the future security of the acquisition itself, though often inculcated by the court of directors, do not seem, at least for some years past, to have been the direct object of the policy of this government ; nor was it possible they should be so, when instant profit, without regard to immediate or distant consequences, was the general principle of action. If any conclusion may be drawn from facts to principles, the company's servants must be supposed to have considered Bengal as an estate to which the company had no good title, which they had no hopes of possessing long, and which it was their interest to exhaust and make the most of while they had it in their power. I speak of public measures only. On what other principle can we understand the committee of circuit to have proceeded?—From the year 1768 to 1771, the letters from Bengal were filled with the most urgent and alarming representations of the decay of trade and circulation, the depopulation produced by the famine, and the general decline of the country; yet in the year 1772 the committee made a settlement for the Dewannee lands, which promised a higher revenue upon the whole than they had ever paid in any period of the government. The balances have increased in a much higher proportion than the promised improvement. Personal censure is not my object. I mean to expose false principles, both of policy and economy, in order to discover and establish true ones."

* * * * * *

" 9. The moderation of the tribute imposed by all the Mahomedan conquerors, and the simplicity of their method of collecting it, accounts for the surprising facility with which they retained possession of their conquests. The form of their government was despotic; but in fact it was not oppressive to the mass of the conquered people. In general they introduced no change but in the army, and in the name of the sovereign. With respect to the collection of the revenues, the system of the present government is upon a principle directly the reverse of what it ought to be, and, I believe, such as never was adopted by another government. Instead of leaving the management to the natural proprietors of the lands, and demanding from *them* a fixed portion of the produce, we take the management upon ourselves, and pay *them* a tribute; government stands in the place of a zemindar, and allows him a pension.

" 10. Before these provinces are reduced too low to bear the operation of any vigorous measure, it will deserve to be considered, whether a great acquired dominion can be retained on any other principle, particularly if situated at an immense distance from the seat of empire? And although it may be doubted, whether, in the present circumstances of the country, the government of it can be completely established even by the power of parliament; on this simple principle it cannot be useless to keep the model in view, and endeavour to approach to it, as near as we are able, in forming a new settlement for the present, until a definitive arrangement shall be determined at home, or until some person equal to the trust, shall be invested with power to restore the ancient constitution of the country, or to give it a new one.

" 11. It cannot be disputed, that Bengal was in a much more flourishing state during the last century than it ever has been under the English establishment. In forming considerations, therefore, for a future settlement, if the prosperity of the country be the medium through which we wish to make the possession of it beneficial, we should endeavour to trace the ancient policy of its government, and the methods formerly used in collecting the revenues; to discover whether the same principles have been adhered to, or how, or at what time alterations have taken place; and whether such alterations have been disadvantageous or beneficial to the country."

* * * * * *

" 26. It must be evident, from the preceding state of facts, that, when the Dewannee was ceded to the company, the country was already in a very reduced condition. A quick succession of wars and revolutions, a foreign influence prevailing both in matters of government and commerce, the drain of large sums of money carried away by individuals, or by the company for the supply of their other settlements, had undoubtedly contributed to impoverish Bengal. The ancient establishments were overthrown, great numbers of the zemindars were dispossessed and reduced to beggary, and the greater part of the wealthy families, and people of reputation and ability in business, cut off or brought to ruin. In such a state of poverty and decay, the wisest internal establishments and most lenient measures seemed necessary to prevent the approaching ruin of the country, especially as all its commercial resources were in future likely to be cut off. Instead of imports of treasure from Europe, a tribute was actually required from hence. Large sums in specie were sent out. The wealth formerly enjoyed by the natives, and diffused by an equal and constant circulation through the country, was engrossed by foreigners, who either exported it directly, or by supplying the other European factories, made it unnecessary even for them to import bullion for providing their investments.

" 27. The acquisition of the Dewannee was attended with another ruinous consequence to the country. In order that the East India company might avail themselves of their increased revenues, it was necessary their investment should be enlarged at once from 20 or 30 to 60 and 70 lacks of rupees annually. This could not be suddenly done without a monopoly of the manufactures, nor a monopoly supported but by numerous servants and agents armed with authority, which caused great oppression of the manufacturers, and has been felt, with other causes, both in the quality and price of every article, to the present time. By this monopoly, the Indian merchants were excluded from sharing in the produce of Bengal, and driven to establish manufactures at home, of articles which they formerly received from hence; consequently Bengal was deprived of its returns both from the Indian and European markets, and its resources cut off on every side.

" 28. In this declining state of the country, it is self-evident, that even the moderate revenue which was before collected with ease, and left ample sources for the maintenance of the landholders, must become a rack-rent and a grievous oppression to the tenants, and could not be realised without additional taxes, schemes, and expedients, and the use of rigorous methods. Yet it was equally apparent that the use of such means could not fail to depopulate the country, diminish the quantity of lands in cultivation, and annually accumulate the burden on the remaining tenants, and on such lands as might be continued in tillage, till at length, all personal wealth being drained out of the pockets of the people, a rapid and sensible decline, the forerunner of a general stop or bankruptcy, would be felt in every part. An apprehension of these consequences, however obvious, does not appear to have influenced the measures of any administration since the collection of the revenues was obtained for the company. Their servants, who made the acquisition, were themselves dazzled by its importance, and thought they could not represent it in too advantageous terms. The succeeding administration foresaw the loss of their own credit if they suffered the object to waste under their care. The last and most unjustifiable measure of all was that which proposed a plan to increase the revenue while the country was perishing, and which the projectors of it must have left to be executed by the present administration.

" 29. When the company took possession of the Dewannee, their servants were unacquainted with the constitution of the country, the mode of collecting the rents, or what had been the amount of the former revenue. In making the first settlement they seem to have had no rule in view, but providing for the demands of government at any rate, and collecting as great a surplus as possible. At the same time, or very soon after, the necessities of the company at home produced constant orders to increase the investment almost to the amount of the revenue of the Dewannee lands, and much beyond the produce of the manufactures.

" 30. That period of delirium, during which it was asserted by some, and believed by many, that the resources of Bengal were inexhaustible, will long be remembered in England. It is not wonderful that the representatives of the company should endeavour to act up to the promises of their predecessors, and to the prejudices of their employers, and to aim at increase of revenue, which they saw was the only merit considered at home. Besides that, it is in the nature of short-lived fluctuating administrations to provide for the demands of the day, without regard to the difficulties they entail on their successors."

* * * * * *

" 32. The mode of collecting the rents from 1766 to 1769, is of itself a strong presumptive proof of the general reduction of the country. As the greater part of the zemindars were ruined and dispossessed of the management of their lands, and there were few people of rank and family left, or of those who had formerly held high employments, such as there were looked for large profits, which the country could not afford them and pay the rents also. People of lower rank were therefore of necessity employed as aumils, or collectors on the part of government; these people executed a contract for a sti-

APPENDIX.

pulated sum for the district to which they were appointed, and in effect may be considered as farmers of the revenue. They then proceeded from the sudder, or seat of government, to the districts, to settle with the zemindars and tenants for the revenue they had engaged to pay. If the rents already established afforded a sufficient produce, they had the less occasion to lay on aboab (fixed taxes) or muthote (occasional taxes); if not they were compelled to have recourse to these expedients. As the country became poorer, and the lands less cultivated, taxes of course were multiplied to make good the agreement with government, until the ryots, finding the demands made upon them annually accumulating, sought various expedients for procuring or extorting abatements in the awsil, or original rent. A timid people have no defence against oppression but fraud. It is now the usage in several districts for the ryot to extort abatements at the beginning of the year, and the farmer to levy a muthote in lieu of it when the harvest is upon the ground.

" 33. During the first years of the Dewannee, while upon the whole there was produce to answer the accumulated demands of government, the revenue, though not entire, came in by some means or other. As one place failed, assets were found in another. Contractors, on the search for employment, hunted out every casual improvement of the lands, for which, if the incumbent was unwilling to pay an increase to government, they were ready to take the trouble from him. In many instances, the state of the lands has been misrepresented, for the mere purpose of employment and possession, and increases offered on paper for lands where in fact there were no assets to pay them; yet the natives did not suffer so universally in the beginning of our government as they have done since, because many of them enjoyed offices, the emoluments of which they spent in the districts, and thereby gave bread to others. The revenues were also supported from external sources, such as loans from the shroffs to the zemindars, and the aboab fougedary, or fines in the criminal courts, which have been since abolished. The above loans, contracted to pay the demands of government, were swept into the treasury, and have never been repaid. This fact shews, that even while the rents were paid, it was not entirely from the produce of the lands.

" 34. I have heard that Mahommed Reza Cawn was sensible of the decline of the country, and of the fatal consequence of keeping up the revenues on this oppressive system; and that he frequently recommended in his discourses with the members of administration, that a more moderate rent should be fixed, and the country relieved. I find that Mr Becher, when resident at the Durbar, was sensible of the true causes of the decline of the country, and represented them in his letters to the select committee. He proposed a more liberal plan for the provision of the investment, recommended the employing of the zemindars, and made it his constant argument that something should be left for the natives. But the resources of the country being thought at that time much greater than they have since proved, and a strong prejudice operating against Mahomed Reza Cawn and his officers, who were suspected of concealing the true value of the lands, and perhaps might be guilty of some embezzlements, a general opinion prevailed, that a greater revenue might be collected by employing company's servants in the detail; that the decline was owing solely to the oppression of Mahomed Reza Cawn and his officers, and not to the true causes, a rack-rent and general failure in the resources of the country, which forced the ministers to make use of every expedient to answer the expectations of the company. This decline being universally perceived in the years 1768 and 1769, though the causes were not generally understood or admitted, occasioned the appointment of the supervisors. The declared purpose of it was to inform the administration of the actual condition of the provinces, their trade, mode of collecting their rents, the administration of justice, and other capital objects. From these materials it was proposed to form a general plan for the future government of the country. Supposing this to have been the object of the measure, and that proper persons could have been found to carry it into execution, the advantages that might have been obtained from it are obvious. It was chiefly committed to young men, with powers, whether granted or assumed, much greater than were necessary for the purpose of obtaining information. Every view of this kind, however, was laid aside when the council of revenue went up to the city immediately after the conclusion of the famine; and although that dreadful calamity, in addition to the other distresses of the country, had swept away near one-third of the inhabitants, and the poverty of the natives was manifest in every part except Calcutta, the profest object of that board was to procure an increase of the revenue, by discovering the latent advantages still enjoyed by the zemindars, and reducing the allowances to the native officers; that is, by taking away so much more of the bread of people already reduced to palpable misery. The information derived from the researches of the supervisors was applied to this purpose only. In some respects their accounts contributed to promote it, as the supervisors in general aimed at procuring accurate hustaboods, (valuations of the whole rents), which of course included the profits of the zemindars, farmers, talookdars, &c. A knowledge of the produce was in general followed by an effort to sweep the whole of it into the treasury, with little or no consideration of the particular state of each district, or whether the trade and imports of it were likely to furnish permanent resources for such remittances.

" 35. Mr Middleton's letter quoted in the appendix, the proceedings of the board of revenue at Moorshedabad, and the settlement of 1178, (1771) the only one made by that board, proved beyond dispute, that they acted on the principles I have ascribed to them. An increase was made of near eleven lacks * of rupees in the Dewannee lands, although a balance had remained of eighteen lacks † on the former settlement, and the country was but just emerged from the miseries of the famine. This settlement however was collected with a degree of rigour and exactness, which called loudly, but in vain, for mercy and relaxation in the subsequent assessments.

" 36. The profest object of the committee of circuit, whose settlement succeeded in 1179, (1772) was still increase of revenue. It is a singular fact, and well worth observation, that it was the misery of the country, and the general dis-

* " Net Revenue for the Bengal year 1177,—Rs. 1,55,52,472 5 9
    Do.   for   Do.   1178,—   1,66,38,147 12 14
  Increase for 1178,---Rs. 10,85,675 7 5.

† Sicca Rupees, 18,38,61 4 2 3.
  Vide Letter from the Council of Revenue, 7th October 1771.

Signed { J. Alexander.
         J. Lawrell.
         J. Graham.
         W. Lambert."

tress of all ranks of people, which enabled them to establish an increased and increasing revenue for five years; I mean upon paper. The state of the country was then such, and there were so many people in desperate circumstances, and out of all employment, ready to sign any engagements for mere present bread, that it is no wonder when the rents were put up to public auction, if nominal increases were obtained, and the lands bid up beyond their real value, for the sole purpose of keeping or obtaining the possession of them. Had this settlement been collected with all the seve ity which the custom of the country and the agreements of the farmers allowed, of necessity would have driven the farmers to have fallen upon the ryots with such rigour and distress, that a general bankruptcy and universal depopulation of the districts must have been the immediate consequence.

"37. I presume the remissions and balances from the provinces since April 1772, do not amount to less than a crore of rupees; and it may be said that balances not exacted, or a moderate rent demanded in the first instance, are eventually an equal relief to the landholders. But in effect the difference is very great both to the country and to government. It would have been happy for the country and no loss to government, if the settlement had not been made for a greater sum than has been actually collected; (though I do not say that even this is not more than the country can support.) The landholder, whether zemindar or farmer, would then have foreseen the probability of making good his engagements and keeping his farm. To excite industry there must be a prospect of success. But if a balance must at any rate be incurred, it becomes indifferent to the landholder to what amount he is indebted to government; or rather it is his interest to incur a large balance than a small one. He collects as much as he can from the ryot, and pays as little as he can to government. At the worst he can but lose his farm, in which he has no permanent interest, and which, when he has had it a year or two, is no longer worth keeping. In the mean time the high rent he stands engaged for furnishes him with pretences for oppressing the ryots, and for protesting against any interposition of government in their favour. The desertion of the ryots, the loss of cultivation, and general depopulation of the country, flow directly from this source. On the other hand, the immediate consequences to government, from taxes without produce, are obvious: New burdens laid on the subject, an additional expence of collection, but no additional receipts in the treasury, and probably a real established expence proportioned to an estimated revenue.

" 38. From the preceding state of facts, collected from the records, it appears, that the company have levied higher rents from this country, whilst labouring under the greatest disadvantages, than it ever paid to the emperors in its most flourishing condition, when the principal part of the revenues were spent within the provinces, and the remainder went no farther than Delhi."

NOTE [P.]

This evil is forcibly set forth in the fifth report of the select committee, printed in the year 1812, where it is stated, that in the district of Burdwan alone, the number of civil suits pending before the judge amounted to 30,000; and where it was shewn by computation, that the determination of a cause could not be expected in the ordinary course of the plaintiff's life.

The collector of Burdwan, in a letter to the board of revenue, [See Appendix to Report of Select Committee, No. 8.] observes, that " the rajah of the Burdwan
" begs leave to submit it to your consideration, whether or
" no it can be possible for him to discharge his engage-
" ments to government with that punctuality which the
" regulations require, unless he be armed with powers,
" as prompt to enforce payment from his renters as go-
" vernment had been pleased to authorise the use of, in re-
" gard to its claims or heirs ; and he seems to think it
" must have proceeded from an oversight, rather than
" from any just and avowed principle, that there should
" have been adopted two modes of juridical process under
" the same government ; the one summary and efficient,
" and the satisfaction of its own claims ; the other tardy
" and uncertain in regard to the satisfaction of the claims
" due to its own subjects ; more especially in a case like
" the present, where ability to discharge the one demand
" necessarily depends on the other demand being pre-
" viously realized." The collector of Midnapore, in a letter, dated 1802, also observes, " All the zemindars with
" whom I have ever had any communication, in this and
" in other districts, have but one sentiment respecting the
" rules at present in force for the collection of the public
" revenue. They all say, that such a harsh and oppres-
" sive system was never before resorted to in this coun-
" try : that the custom of imprisoning landholders for
" arrears of revenue, was, in comparison, mild and bene-
" volent to them : that though it was no doubt the inten-
" tion of government to confer an important benefit on
" them, by abolishing this custom, it has been found, by
" melancholy experience, that the system of sales and

"attachments, which has been substituted for it, has, in the course of a very few years, reduced most of the great zemindars in Bengal to distress and beggary, and produced a greater change in the landed property of Bengal than has ever happened, in the same space of time, in any age or country, by the mere effect of internal regulations." In another part of the same report, the collector, after commenting on a regulation then recently introduced, observes, " Before this period (1799) complaints of the inefficacy of the regulations were very general among the zemindars, or proprietors of large estates; and it required little discernment to see, that they had not the same powers over their tenants which government exercised over them. It was notorious, that many of them had arrears of rents due to them, which they were utterly unable to recover; while government were selling their lands for arrears or assessments." The collector adds, " Farmers and intermediate tenants were till lately able to withhold their rents with impunity, and to set the authority of their landlords at defiance. Landholders had no direct controul over them. They could not proceed against them, except through the courts of justice; and the ends of substantial justice were defeated, by delays and costs of suit."

NOTE [Q.]

In extending the decennial settlement to the conquered countries, the company's servants have occasion to investigate the nature of the various tenures, under which the landed property was held in different parts of the country. In the course of those researches the clearest

rights of property were brought to light, and it invariably happened, that, when those rights were respected, cultivation flourished.—" It is not to be discovered," says one of the collectors *, " that, during the revolutions of many
" ages, from the reign of the first princes, until the down-
" fal of the Hindoo authority, any questions ever existed in
" any stage of the Hindoo history, as to the rights of the
" people to the lands of the country, excepting villages or
" lands totally waste, and that had escheated to govern-
" ment. On the contrary, they appear to have been
" transmitted to them from the most remote era down to
" the present time, without interruption; these rights
" are supported by usages, which could never have pre-
" vailed but for their universal acknowledgment; and in
" the repositories of their history and their laws, we find
" the right of the people to property in lands repeatedly
" acknowledged and preserved. It has been the custom
" to consider the Hindoo governments of old, despotic,
" and regulated solely by the arbitrary will of the reign-
" ing prince :—theoretically received, they were so; but
" in practice they had little of this character; the ordi-
" nances of their religion had generally the force and
" effect of laws; and in their operation, they were benefi-
" cent and just."

After expressing the same decided opinion respecting the rights of the landed proprietors, the principal collector of Tanjore observes †, " It is fortunate that, at a
" moment when we are consulting on the means of estab-
" lishing the property and welfare of the numerous peo-

* Report of the Collector of Southern Pottegur Peshcush, dated December 29, 1800.

† Fifth Report Select Committee on India Affairs, Appendix, p. 826.

"ple of these provinces, we find the lands of the country in the hands of men who feel and understand the full rights and advantages of possession; who have enjoyed them, in a degree more or less secure, before the British navy was known in India; and who, in consequence of them, have rendered populous and fertile the extensive provinces of Tanjore and Trichinopoly."

Mr Place, to whom the management of the jaghire, that surrounds the presidency of Madras, was committed, when describing a certain species of tenant, observes, that by granting them the lands " to them and their heirs for ever, as long as they continued in obedience to the Circar, and paid all just dues, he was enabled to convert the most stubborn soil and thickest jingle into fertile villages."

The same sentiments were expressed by Colonel Munroe, who had the charge of several districts. He saw clearly, that the high assessment on the land checked agriculture and population; and on this account, he strongly recommended to government a remission of the tribute. His views were admitted to be just; but the public necessities were pleaded as an apology for a tax, the effect of which it appears is to keep back the cultivation of the country. —" It is the high assessment on the land," the members of the board of revenue observe, " which Colonel Munroe justly considers the chief check to population. Were it not for the pressure of this heavy rent, population, he thinks, ought to increase even faster than in America; because the climate is more favourable, and there are vast tracts of good land unoccupied, which may be ploughed at once, without the labour or expence of clearing away forests, as there is above three millions of acres of this kind in the ceded districts. He

"is of opinion that a great increase of population, and
" consequently of land revenue, might be expected in the
" course of twenty-five years, from the operation of the
" remission. But a remission to a few zemindars, he
" apprehends, would not remedy the evil, nor remove the
" weight which at present depresses population.

" Under the system proposed, Colonel Munroe con-
" ceives, that cultivation and population would increase so
" much, that, in the course of twenty-five years, lands
" formerly cultivated, amounting to star pagodas
" 5,55,962, would be relieved and occupied, together
" with a considerable portion of waste, never before cul-
" tivated. The extension of cultivation, however, would
" not make the farms larger, and thereby facilitate collec-
" tion. The enlargement of farms or estates is at pre-
" sent prevented by the want of property; hereafter it
" would be prevented by its division.

" This is the outline of Colonel Munroe's plan, which
" is not less applicable to all the districts as yet unsettled,
" than to the ceded districts; and, if the exigencies of
" government allowed of such a sacrifice as a remission
" of the present standard rents, to the extent of 25 per
" cent., or even of 15 per cent., we should consider the
" measure highly advisable, and calculated to produce
" great ulterior advantages. Indeed, it would be absurd
" to dispute, that the less we take from the cultivator of
" the produce of his labour, the more flourishing will be
" his condition."

" But, if the exigencies of government do not permit
" them to make so great a sacrifice; if they cannot at
" once confer the boon of private property, they must be
" content to establish a private interest in the soil, as ef-

" fectually as they can under the farming system. If
" they cannot afford to give up a share of the landlord's
" rent, they must be indulgent landlords."—[See Report
Select Committee, Appendix.]

NOTE [R.]

An Account of the total Annual Amount of the Revenues and Charges of the several Presidencies in India, as estimated in 1793, and by the actual accounts from the year 1792-3, to the year 1808-9, with the estimate of the same for the year 1809-10, as laid before Parliament.

	Total gross Revenues.	Total Charges and Interest.	Surplus Revenue.	Surplus Charge.
Court's Estimate, Feb. 1793,	L.6,963,625	L.5,800,048	L.1,163,577	L. ....
—— 1792-3	8,225,628	7,007,050	1,218,578	....
—— 1793-4	8,276,770	6,633,951	1,642,819	....
—— 1794-5	8,026,193	6,629,888	1,396,305	....
—— 1795-6	7,866,094	6,993,151	872,943	....
—— 1796-7	8,016,171	7,609,228	406,943	....
—— 1797-8	8,059,880	8,178,626	....	118,746
—— 1798-9	8,652,033	9,260,031	....	607,993
—— 1799-1800 ...	9,736,672	10,126,753	....	390,081
—— 1800-1	10,485,059	11,624,510	....	1,139,451
—— 1801-2	12,163,589	12,651,265	....	487,676
—— 1802-3	13,464,537	12,523,728	940,809	....
—— 1803-4	13,271,385	14,699,461	....	1,428,076
—— 1804-5	14,949,395	16,487,346	....	1,537,951
—— 1805-6	15,403,409	17,672,017	....	2,268,608
—— 1806-7	14,535,739	17,688,061	....	3,152,322
—— 1807-8	15,669,905	15,979,027	....	309,122
—— 1808-9	15,525,055	15,551,097	....	26,042
Estimate 1809-10	15,655,985	15,657,671	....	1,686

INDEX.

AGRICULTURE, the price of its produce not lessened by improvements in the implements of, p.38. Such improvements only benefit the landlord, 40. Not more productive to the community than manufactures, 134. Alternate progress of manufactures and, 138. Was the sole pursuit of the Romans, 182.

America, silver used in the main payments of, 8. Its capital and industry chiefly engaged in agriculture, 140. Rude produce of, exchanged for the manufactures of Britain, ibid. The assistance it has derived from the capital and industry of Europe the cause of its rapid growth, 143. Invasion of, by a British force, and causes of the failure of this enterprize, 192.

American mines, fall in the value of silver on the discovery of, 22. Their produce greatly increased within the last 80 years, 84.

Archduke Charles of Austria, view of his campaign in 1796 in Germany, 197, *note*.

Armies, superiority of regular over undisciplined troops, 173. A regular army the only sure defence of an invaded country, 175. The success of an army in war greatly depends on the means of supplying the necessary waste of men, 178. Want of this supply the cause of Hannibal's failure in his invasion of Italy, 185,—and of the failure of the allies in their invasion of France in 1792, 193. Successes of the French revolutionary armies greatly owing to the ample means afforded for their renovation, 194.—See *National Defence*.

INDEX.

B.

Balance of trade, how it may affect the foreign exchanges, 115.
Bank of England, silver currency issued by, of which the nominal value exceeded the real value, 27. Depreciation of its paper in 1813, 82. No other currency used in London than the notes of, 96. Exposed to a great drain of specie in 1792, 99. Mistaken policy of, on that occasion, ibid. Discredit of its notes in 1797, 101. Order in Council for the suspension of its cash payments, 102. Amount of its notes in circulation in 1782 and 1783, 96. And in 1797, 107, 108. Its advances to government in 1797, injurious to its credit, 108. Suspension of its cash payments occasioned rather by domestic alarm than by foreign expenditure, 110. No proper security against an excessive issue of its notes during a suspension of cash payments, 112. Amount of its notes in circulation from 1792 to 1812, 115. Interposition of Parliament to maintain the value of its notes, 120. Its notes made a legal tender by Parliament, 121. Suspension of its cash payments in 1797, a necessary measure, 129. Might safely resume payments in cash in two years, 130.
Bankers, facilities afforded by, to the cash transactions of distant places, 92. The economy with which the London bankers use bank notes and specie, 96.—See *Paper Currency.*
Banks, number of, in Britain, 91. Establishment of, favourable to the dispatch of business, 92. Dangers they are exposed to from the failure of confidence, 98.
Bankruptcies, causes of the great number of, in 1810, 111. National bankruptcy, though it ruins individuals, strengthens a state, 299.
Benevolence, all general plans of, impolitic, 65. That of private individuals not objectionable, 72.
Bonaparte, invasion of Italy by, in 1796, 198, *note.*
Brazils, produce of the mines of, greatly decreased for the last 60 years, 85.
Britain, Great, amount of its foreign expenditure from 1793 to 1797, 106. Exchanges its manufactures for the provisions and rude produce of Europe and America, 140. See *Bank of England, Paper Currency, Metallic Currency, Taxation, Public Debts, &c.*
Bullion, the price of, together with the state of foreign exchanges, the best rule for regulating a paper currency not convertible into cash, 112. Rise in the market price of, caused by an excessive issue of bank paper, 115. A rise in

INDEX.

its price indicates a depreciation of bank paper, 118. 123.
Report of a committee of the House of Commons on the
high price of, 122. High price of, in 1810, ascribed by the
merchants and bankers, to the unfavourable balance of
trade, 126.

Burnet, Bishop, justly condemns the English system of poor
laws, 69.

C.

Capital attracted by trades which afford great profits, 33.
Every increase of, tends to raise the wages of labour, 53, 57.
Extent of, regulated by the consumption for which it provides, 75. Increases with revenue, ibid. Increase of, reduces profit, 76. No limit to its increase, 77. No evil arising
from its increase, ibid. Ratio in which profit diminishes as
capital increases, 78.

Charity, that bestowed by individuals not productive of the
evil consequences attending public charities, 72.

China, market of, always overstocked with common labourers,
54.

Coin, indicates the progress of improvement in a country, 4.
Attempts to alter the value of the coin used in great payments, always produce a rise of prices, 14. Causes which
may occasion a variation in the value of, 21. Temptations
to convert it into bullion, 22. 25. A charge on the workmanship of, some security for its preservation, 23. See *Metallic
Currency*.

Commerce. See *Manufactures and Trade*.

Commercial Treaties, rendered necessary by the restraints which
the policy of Europe formerly imposed on trade, 161. Ruinous prohibitions to which the trade of Ireland was formerly
subjected, 162. Propositions made in 1785 for removing
those restraints, 163. Opposed by the British merchants,
but carried into effect in 1800, 164. Commercial part of the
Irish union considered, 165. Treaty concluded between
France and Britain in 1786, 167. Enlightened speech of
Mr Pitt on the subject, 170.

Commodities, on the price of those which afford a rent, 33.
Such as are produced by labour and capital, cannot long be
higher or lower than what will pay wages and profit, ibid.
This principle not applicable to the produce of land, ibid.
High price of land produce arises from its comparative
scarcity, 34. Price the great regulator of consumption, 35.
Price of commodities which yield a rent wholly independent
of their original cost, 36. This principle misconceived by
a writer in the Edinburgh Review, 38.

INDEX.

Copper coin, often answers all the purposes of currency in poor countries, 3. It did so in the early ages of the Roman Republic, ibid. Four denominations of, formerly in Scotland, ibid. Formerly none in England, ibid. The general use of, marks a rude state of society, 4. Regulated on a wrong principle in Britain, 28. Amount of the issue of, in Britain, in 1798, ibid. Should not be made a legal tender for more than sixpence, 129. See *Metallic Currency*.

Corn, the price of, wholly independent of its original cost, 36. Price of, always affords a rent, 37. Improvements in agricultural implements do not lessen its price, 38. Neither would a bounty on its production, ibid. Rent a bounty on the production of, 39. Late great rise in its price partly caused by a fall in the value of the currency with which it is purchased, 81, 153. Paper and money price of, in the year 1813 compared, 82.

———, on the laws for regulating its exportation and importation, 147. Review of the various laws which have been enacted in Britain for this purpose, 148. Their practical effect, 149. Plans proposed in 1813, 150. Must have caused a considerable rise in the price of corn, ibid. Inconsistency of the arguments urged in their favour, ibid. Causes of the rise in the price of corn in the course of the last century, 152. Bounties on the exportation of corn, naturally tend to raise its price, 154. Every violent interference with the corn market must check the natural progress of improvement, 155. Bounties and restraints on commerce afford no argument for extending the system to agriculture, 157. All laws for preventing importation mischievous, 159.

Currency.—See *Metallic Currency* and *Paper Currency*.

Customs and Excise, the two great establishments by which taxes on consumption are collected in Britain, 286. Management of the customs defective, 287.

D.

Debts, public, the funding system, or practice of borrowing money for the public service, an improvident device for carrying on war at the expence of posterity, 296. Under its operation the growing interest of the public debts must gradually exceed all the other expences of the state, 297. Compulsion in the collection of the revenue clearly denotes that excess of taxation, which trenches on capital, and finally leads to national bankruptcy, 299. An act of national bankruptcy, though it involves thousands in ruin, strengthens a state, ibid. Example of this in the case of France after the revolution, 300. The public debts of Great Britain doubled by the American war, 302. Great progress of the

INDEX.

sinking fund, in reducing the national debt, 303. 305,—checked by the war begun in 1793, 304. Amount of the public debt in 1802, ibid,—and in 1814, 306. The war ended in 1814, added one half to the existing burdens of the country, ibid. Amount of the national expenditure since 1797, 307. How far the re-establishment of peace is likely to reduce the public debt, and the taxes of Great Britain, 308.

De Foe, Daniel, justly condemns the use of public work-houses, 64.

E.

East India, silver used throughout, in the great payments of, 8. Copper not a subsidiary currency in, 17. Specie regularly exported to, from Europe, 103. Quantities of specie exported in the years 1790, 1791, 1792, 104. State of property and manners in, under the Mogul government, 225. See *East India Company*.

East India Company, Dr Smith's view of their affairs in many respects imperfect, 208. Of the constitution and transactions of the Company in Europe, ibid. Amendments in the original constitution of the Company, 209. Amount of their capital, ibid. Mr Fox's plan for the reformation of their affairs, 210. Measure proposed by Mr Pitt for the same purpose, 212. All plans for the government of India by European controul impracticable, 213. Renewal of their charter in 1793, 214. Their territorial revenues generally inadequate to defray the expences of the resident government, 216. Renewal of their charter in 1813, 217. Account of their dividends at different periods, 218, *note*. Of the transactions of the Company in India, ibid. Effects of their acquisition of political power on the commerce of the country, 219. Cossim Ali Khan deposed by their servants, ibid. Monopoly exercised by their servants in the internal commerce of the country, 220. Decline of the commerce and manufactures of the country in consequence, 222, 224. Fatal consequences of the trade carried on by their agents, described by Mr Hastings, 223, *note*. State of property and manners under the Mogul government, 225. Amount of the land-tax under the Emperor Akbar, 233. Tyrannical government of Cossim Ali Khan, 234. The Company's servants claim the right, as sovereigns, to the whole produce of the soil, and displace the landholders who hesitate to make good their assessments, 235, 242. All questions regarding public revenue left to the decision of its collectors, 236. Deficiencies in the revenues of Bengal, occasioned by a famine, re-assessed on the survivors, 237. Decline of the country in consequence

INDEX.

of these severe measures, 238. Important reforms introduced into the domestic policy of the country, under the government of Lord Cornwallis, 247,—afforded no relief to the landholders, 249. How far the Company in Europe have derived advantage from the contributions levied by the resident government, 253.

Emigration from the Highlands of Scotland, caused by the decline of the feudal system, 144. Injustice of restraining emigration in these circumstances, 145.

England, formerly no copper coin in, 3. Both gold and silver have been alternately banished from the currency of, 22. Alternate progress of the trade and agriculture of, 138. See *Britain*.

Europe, copper a subsidiary currency in all parts of, 6. Silver still used in great payments, in most countries of, 8.

Exchange, the state of, together with the price of bullion, the best rule for regulating the issue of a paper currency not convertible into cash, 112. Unfavourable state of, in Britain, caused by an excess of bank paper, 115. May be affected by an unfavourable balance of trade, 117. Connection of the, with the present state of British currency, 122. State of, between different countries, a sure test of the value of their respective currencies, 123. Par of, between Hamburgh and London, 124. The expence of transporting specie from one country to another, the limit of an unfavourable exchange, 125. The rate of, may appear to vary though it is really at par, ibid. Fall of, in 1810, erroneously imputed by the merchants of London to an unfavourable balance of trade, 126. The foreign exchanges appear more unfavourable to Britain, when remittances are made in paper, than when they are made in specie, ibid. 127. This difference accounted for by the depreciation of paper, 128.

Expenditure increases with revenue, 75. Foreign expenditure provided for, either in specie or goods, 103. Great expenditure of Britain in Germany in 1793, ibid. 104—and in 1763, 105. Amount of the foreign expenditure of Britain, from 1793 to 1797, 106.

F.

Feudal system, state of manners under, 143. Has declined throughout Europe with the progress of trade and manufactures, 144. Decline of, in the Highlands of Scotland, the cause of emigration, ibid.

Food, an increase of, without an increase of capital, is not a

INDEX.

fund for the support of mere labour, 58. High price of, a certain proof of a deficient supply, 59. A deficient supply of, must be remedied by a diminished consumption, 60. Wages of labour do not rise with the price of, 59. 159.

Fox, Mr, his plan for the reformation of the affairs of the East India Company, 210.

France, commercial treaty concluded with Britain and, in 1786, 167. Invasion of, in 1792, 193.

French Economists, their notions of the pre-eminence of agriculture erroneous, 134.

Funds, public. See *Debts, Public*.

G.

Germany, wars in, in 1796, 197, *note*.

Gold coin takes the place of silver in the main payments of highly improved countries, 4. This not the case in the currencies which circulate in the continent of Europe, 6. In Britain exclusively used in the main payments, 8. When introduced into the Roman currency, 16. Amount of the new coinage in 1774, 84. Probable amount of that presently in circulation in Britain, ibid. Produce of the mines in Mexico since 1762, 85.

Gold and Silver, observations on the price of, since 1773, 80. Fall in the value of, occasioned principally by the increase of bank notes, 81. Increased produce of the Mexican mines has also caused a decline in the value of, 83. Amount of the coinage of gold and silver in Mexico, from 1762 to 1805, 85.

Greece, ancient, warlike manners of, connected with the state of property, 145. Invasion of, by the Persians, 180. Wars between the ancient states of, 181.

H.

Hamburgh, how the par of exchange is computed between, and London, 124. The premium for bills on Hamburgh should never exceed the expence of remitting specie thither, ibid. State of the exchange with, in 1810, 127.

Hannibal, invasion of Italy by, 185—failed for want of the means of supplying the waste of troops, ibid.

Hastings, Mr, his description of the evils arising from the private trading of the East India Company's agents, 223, *note*.

INDEX.

Highlands of Scotland, decline of the feudal system in, the cause of emigration, 144.
Holland, invasion of, by Louis XIV., 189.

I.

Ireland, its commerce formerly subjected to ruinous prohibitions, 162. Propositions for removing these restraints in 1785, ibid.—opposed by the British merchants, 163—but finally carried into effect in 1800, 164. Interruption to her intercourse with Britain arising from the different modes of taxation in the two countries, 165. Benefits which would arise from extending the same system of taxation to both, 166. Plan proposed for effecting this object, 167.
Italy, invasion of, by Hannibal, 185. Campaign in, under Bonaparte, in 1796, 198, *note*.

K.

King, Lord, his proposal for remedying the defects of the British currency proceeded on a misconception, 24.

L.

Labourers, their wages rise and fall with the demand, 42. 59. Every increase of capital improves their condition, 53. Ingenious artists better rewarded than common labourers, ibid. The Chinese market overstocked with, 54. Their wages not regulated by the price of corn, 59. 159. Their poverty, arising from want of food, or of work, cannot be relieved by legislative enactments, 61. Pernicious effects of the English poor laws in debasing the minds of, 68. See *Wages of Labour*.
Liverpool, Lord, ascribes the exclusion of silver from the main payments of Britain to a wrong cause, 13. Inconsistent proposal of, relative to the expence of making gold coins, 24. Calculations of the amount of silver coin in circulation in Britain by, 27.

M.

Malt spirits first taxed in this country in the reign of Queen Ann, 289.

INDEX

Malthus, Mr, abstract of his leading doctrines on population and labour, 42. Fallacy of his reasoning on the wages of labour, 49. Error of, regarding the price of corn, 55. Over-rates the importance of agriculture at the expence of trade, 57. Fallacy of this principle illustrated by the case of Poland, 58. His objections to private charity erroneous, 72.

Manners, the state of, in every country, depend greatly on the equivalent given for the surplus produce of the soil, 143. State of, under the feudal system, ibid.

Manufactures, improvements in, benefit society, 40. Nature of profits arising from secrets in, mistaken by Dr Smith, ibid. Equally productive with agriculture, 134. The price of, in an improving country, gradually reduced by the use of machinery, 136. Take the lead in improving countries alternately with agriculture, 138. 153. Have received no real encouragement from the laws enacted in their favour, 156.

Marlborough, Duke of, view of the wars of, 190. His celebrated march from Flanders to the Danube, 200, *note*.

Metallic Currency, on the principles of, 1. Different metals used as coin in different periods of improvement, ibid. The more precious metals used in great transactions, 2. Farthings, although generally disused, sometimes required in London in the retail of beer, ibid. In poor countries copper often answers all the purposes of currency, 3. This was the case in the early ages of the Roman republic, ibid. Different functions of the different metals used in, 4. Copper a subsidiary currency in all the countries of Europe, 6. Silver a subsidiary currency in Britain, 7. 19. Great change which took place in the British currency during the reign of William III., 7. Gold used exclusively in the main payments of Britain, and partially in the retail trade, 8. Silver in consequence assumes the character of a subsidiary currency, 9. State of the silver coin referred to Sir Isaac Newton, 11. Measures taken in consequence, 12. At what period of improvement silver becomes a subsidiary currency, 13. Coin used for great payments can only pass at its intrinsic worth, 14. Intrinsic worth not necessary to a subsidiary currency, ibid. 18. 26. The peculiar property of a subsidiary currency overlooked by Dr Smith, 20. Causes which may occasion variations in the value of coin, 21. All new silver coins, at present, soon vanish from circulation, ibid. Value of the new silver coinage issued in the reign of William III., 27. The probable value of silver at present in circulation, ibid. New copper coinage issued in 1798, regulated on a wrong principle, 28. Loss to the community in consequence, 29. For what particular sums subsidiary currencies should be made a legal tender, ibid. Consequences arising from an over-issue of a subsidiary currency by private traders in London, in 1798, 31.

Mexico, produce of the mines of, since 1762, 85.

Money, steadiness in the value of, essential to trade, 21. See *Paper Currency and Metallic Currency.*

Monopoly of the internal trade of India by the servants of the East India Company, 220. Its injurious effects, 224.

N.

National Defence. Discipline, numbers, and military skill decide the events of war, 173. System of defence for a country attacked by a regular army, and defended by undisciplined troops, 174. Remark of the Roman general Sertorius on the value of time in the operations of war, 177. System of warfare between two regular armies in a country defended by fortified towns, 178. Those principles illustrated by a reference to history, 180. Invasion of Greece by the Persians, ibid. Contests of the Greeks with each other, 181. Invasion of Persia by Alexander, ibid. Rise of the Roman power, 182. Invasion of Italy by Pyrrhus, 184. By Hannibal, 185. Fall of the military power of Rome, 186. Causes which served to prolong its power, 187, *note.* Contests of the middle ages, 188. Invasion of Holland by Louis XIV., 189. Wars of King William, ibid. Of Marlborough, 190. 200, *note.* Of Frederick the Great, 191. American war, 192. Invasion of France in 1792, 193. View of the modern system of tactics, 195. Campaign of 1796 in Germany by the Archduke Charles, 197, *note.* In Italy by Bonaparte, 198, ibid. Want of science in the civil wars in England under Charles I., 199. ibid. Account of the campaign of 1805, 202. ibid. In ancient warfare, armies in distant parts followed no common principle of action, 203. Divided policy of European courts one cause of the rapid successes of the French armies since the revolution, 204. Decline of the French military power caused by the destruction of the army which invaded Russia in 1812, 205.

Newton, Sir Isaac, his report on the state of the silver coin in Britain in the reign of William III., 11,

O.

Opulence, National, on the progress of, 137. Commerce between the inhabitants of the country and those of the town, ibid. The trade between distant countries in no respect different, ibid. Alternate progress of trade and agriculture, 138. 153. Dr Smith's theory of the progress of Europe considered, 141. His hypothesis respecting the prior

INDEX.

improvement of the town inaccurate, 142. Cause of the rapid growth of America, 143. State of property and manners in all countries greatly depends on the equivalent given for the surplus produce of the soil, ibid. Feudal system, 144. The progress of trade and manufactures has caused its decay, ibid. Emigration, ibid. Warlike manners of Greece and Rome connected with the state of property, 145.

P.

Paper Currency, its value depends on its convertibility into cash, 87. May vary in value, by reason of discredit or of excess, 88. Secured against depreciation, while convertible into specie, 89. Has almost entirely superseded specie in the currency of Great Britain, 91. Its progress in Britain, ibid. System of money-dealing connected with, and facilities thence arising for the management of distant payments, 92. Economy with which the London bankers use bank notes and specie, 96. Advantageous as a medium of exchange, although not so safe for this purpose as specie, 97. Dangers to which it is exposed, 98. Effects of the mercantile alarm which prevailed in Britain during the year 1792, 99. Parliament interposes to relieve the merchants, 100. Interruption of credit in 1797, 101. Suspension of cash payments at the Bank of England, 102. Causes of the discredit of paper in 1793 and 1797, 105. Suspension of cash payments at the bank, occasioned more by domestic alarm than by foreign expenditure, 110. Failure of confidence in 1810, caused by the general stagnation of trade, 111. State of the paper currency in Britain, subsequent to the suspension of cash payments by the Bank of England, 112. The price of bullion and the state of the exchange, the best rule for regulating the issue of a paper currency not convertible into specie, ibid. Privileges bestowed by parliament on Bank of England paper, 120. Connection of its value with the market price of bullion, and the state of the exchange, 122. Evidence given by the British merchants on the subject, 126. Propriety of suspending cash payments in 1797, 129. Cash payments might be resumed by the bank in two years, 130.

Persia, invasion of, by Alexander the Great, 181.

Pitt, Mr, his commercial propositions in favour of Ireland, 163. Treaty concluded by, with France, 1786, 168. Enlightened speech of, in parliament, on the subject, 170. Plan of, for regulating the affairs of the East India Company, 212. View of his plan for the redemption of the land tax in Britain, 280. Improvements introduced by, into the administration of the customs, 288.

INDEX.

Poland, abounds in food, but wants capital to support manufactures, 58.
Poor Laws, the English system of, justly condemned, 60, 66. Has been carried far beyond the original plan, ibid. Plans proposed in 1795 for its correction, 67. Pernicious effects of, on the moral character of the labourer, 68. Radical error of, 70. Plan proposed for correcting the abuses of, 71.
Population, abstract of the doctrines of Mr Malthus respecting, 42. Checked in Poland for want of capital, 59. Effects of the maintenance of extensive distilleries on, 294.
Price, the great regulator of consumption, 35.
Productive and unproductive labour, Dr Smith's distinction between, simple and obvious, 131. Perplexed by the ingenuity of subsequent reasoners, ibid. That which is subservient to production, not to be confounded with what actually produces, 132. Dr Smith's distinction implied in the arguments urged against it by a writer in the Edinburgh Review, 133. The pre-eminence of agriculture, as maintained by the French economists, founded on a wrong principle, 134.
Profit diminishes as capital increases, 76. Ratio in which this diminution takes place, 78.

R.

Rent, a surplus above wages and profit, which arises from the price of the commodities which yield it, 34. Is the consequence of high price, 35. 134. Price of corn always affords a rent, 37. Really a bounty on the production of corn, 39.
Revenue, an increase of, causes an increase of expenditure, 75. Saving of, increases capital, 76.
Review, Edinburgh, proposal of a writer in, relative to the British coin, 24. Error of, respecting a bounty on the production of corn, 38. Argument of, to shew the evils arising from an increase of capital, 77. Theory of, respecting productive and unproductive labour considered, 133.
Rome, in the early ages of, copper coin effected all the necessary payments, 3. The introduction of luxury and wealth rendered it necessary to employ silver coin, ibid. When silver and gold was introduced into, 16. Warlike manners of, connected with the state of property, 145. 182. Popular institutions of, 183. Decline of its military power, 186.

INDEX.

S.

Scotland, formerly four denominations of copper coin in, below a halfpenny, 3. The poor chiefly maintained by voluntary charity in, 65. Objections to the method of taxing spirits in, 292.

Silver coin, lowest denomination of, in England, in the reign of William the Conqueror, 3. Supplants that of copper in the main payments as wealth increases, 4. Used in Britain only in the smaller payments, 7. Still used in main payments in most parts of Europe, America, and throughout India, 8. Present state of, in the British silver currency, offers great facilities for forgery and fraud, 25. Plan proposed for preventing this evil, 26. Probable value of, presently circulating in Britain, 27. Should not be made a legal tender for more than a guinea, 29. Quantity produced in Mexico since 1762, 85. See *Metallic Currency*.

Smith, Dr, overlooks the peculiar property of a subsidiary currency, and in consequence falls into some serious mistakes, 20. Mistakes the nature of profits arising from secrets in manufactures, 40. His doctrine, that the price of labour is regulated by that of provisions, erroneous, 59. His distinction between productive and unproductive labour well founded, 131. His theory of the progress of Europe considered, 141. His hypothesis respecting the prior improvement of the town, inaccurate, 142. Plan of, for a more improved management of the customs, 288.

Spain, quantity of dollars remitted to, from Mexico, since 1790, 85.

Specie almost entirely superseded by paper in the currency of Britain, 91. A safer instrument of exchange than paper, 97. Laws enacted for preventing a premium being taken in exchanging it for paper, 121. See *Metallic Currency and Paper Currency*.

Subsidiary currency, the nature and functions of, 4. Intrinsic worth not necessary to its circulation, 14. 18. 26. The peculiar property of, overlooked by Dr Smith, 20. Should only be made a legal tender for a particular sum, 29. Evils arising from an excessive issue of, 31. See *Metallic Currency*.

T.

Taxation. View of the taxes successively imposed on income in Great Britain, 263. Tax of 10 per cent. imposed on income in 1797 raised by an addition to the assessed taxes, 264. Direct tax on income substituted in lieu of this measure in the following year, 265. Extensive powers granted to the commissioners and surveyors for levying this tax, 266. Method of assessing the income arising from land, 268. Income tax of 1803, 269. Injustice of fixing a common rate of contribution for all incomes, 271. 273. The heavy addition to the assessed taxes, intended as a tax on income, was in reality a tax on expenditure, 272. Practical objections to a direct tax on income, 273. Objections to the rule for calculating the income of farmers, 274. Plan proposed by Mr Pitt for the redemption of the land tax, 280. Taxes on consumable articles the most eligible mode of providing for the wants of a state, 284. 298. While they are inconsiderable, being confounded with the price, they are paid without complaint or inconvenience, 285. 298. In Great Britain they have nearly reached that point at which no addition will produce a corresponding increase of revenue, ibid. Customs and excise, the two great establishments by which taxes on consumption are collected in Britain, 286. Management of the customs in point of perspicuity, inferior to that of the excise, 287. Obvious expedient proposed by Dr Smith, with a view to a more improved management of, ibid. View of the various taxes imposed on spirituous liquors in Britain and Ireland, 289.

Taxes on farm servants, horses, or agricultural implements, in reality land taxes, 37. See *Taxation*.

Tea, at present pays a duty of 100 per cent.

Trade, great stagnation of, in 1810, 111. The trade between distant countries no way different from their internal trade, 137. Alternate advance of trade and agriculture in the progress of every improving country, 138. 153. A community will flourish most when trade is left perfectly free, 156. Has received no real encouragement from the laws enacted in its favour, ibid.

V.

Vineyards, some of them pay a higher rent than corn land, 40.

W.

Wages of labour, regulated by the supply and the demand, 42. 59. Abstract of the doctrines of Mr Malthus respecting population and labour, ibid. Error of Mr Malthus, 49. An increase of capital tends to increase wages, 53. 78. Bear no relation to the price of food, 59. 159. The impolicy of legislative interference in the regulation of wages, 61. Plans for improving the condition of the labourer considered, 63. English system of poor laws considered, 66. Their pernicious effects on the character of the labourer, 68. Plans

INDEX.

for their abolition considered, 69. Radical error of the system, 70. Private benevolence not productive of the evils attending public charities, 72. Mr Malthus's doctrines on this subject erroneous, ibid.

War, the events of, decided by discipline, numbers, and science, 173. Advantages of regular over undisciplined troops in, 174. Nothing more valuable than time in, 177. Remark of the Roman general Sertorius on this subject, ibid. Effects of discipline and skill againt numbers in the wars of the Greeks and Persians, 180. 182,—in those of Frederick the Great, 191,—and in the American war, 192. Where armies are equal in number and discipline the contest will be decided by science, 181,—exemplified in the wars of the Greek states, ibid,—in those of the states of Christendom against the Turks, 188,—and in the wars of Marlborough, 190. 200, *note.* View of the modern system of tactics, 195. See *National Defence.*

Wealth of a country accurately measured by the state of its coin, 4.

Wheat. See *Corn.*

Work, a general scarcity of, only remedied by an increase of the funds for the support of industry, 63. Employment of the poor in workhouses does not increase these funds, 64.

Workhouses, the employment of the poor in, impolitic, ibid.